Block Scheduling Handbook with Team Teaching Strategies

World History
The Human Journey

HOLT, RINEHART AND WINSTON

A Harcourt Education Company

Austin • Orlando • Chicago • New York • Toronto • London • San Diego

ISBN 0-03-065733-4

5 6 7 8 9   054   05

Contents

Block Scheduling Handbook with Team Teaching Strategies

Each chapter and unit of *Holt World History: The Human Journey* has a corresponding lesson plan to meet the needs of block scheduling programs. These lesson plans provide motivational activities, a wide range of teaching strategies geared to different learning styles and levels, and suggestions for lesson extensions, review, assessment, and reteaching in a block scheduling environment.

Additionally, each chapter has a team teaching strategy that enables historical subjects to be examined through a literary concept. These strategies focus on the links between history and literature, thus providing students with the oppertunity to gain new insight into past events. Students will also be able to work on projects that demonstrate their understanding of both disciplines and that provide a method of alternative assessment.

Emergence of Agriculture

Have students examine the map on page 9. Ask students to identify the major areas in which farmers lived. What were the crops that the earliest farmers grew? What did later farmers grow?

Lesson 1

(For use with Sections 1 and 2, pp. 6–17)

OBJECTIVES

1. Describe how anthropologists, archaeologists, historians, and geographers use limited evidence to study prehistory.

2. Identify major achievements of Neanderthal and Cro-Magnon peoples.

3. Explain the important changes caused by the Neolithic agricultural revolution.

4. Identify the three main characteristics shared by civilizations.

5. Explain what other two characteristics may be shared by civilizations.

6. Describe the other characteristics and achievements that marked the first river valley civilizations

BELLRINGER

As students enter the classroom, ask them to look at the picture of the archaeologists on page 6. Explain to them that anthropologists, archaeologists, historians, and geographers study the objects of earlier civilizations. Ask students what types of tools they think archaeologists might use and what kinds of difficulties they might encounter. *(Students might list digging tools and guess that archaeologists might encounter difficulties based on the geographic and environmental conditions of sites under study.)* Tell students that in Section 1 they will learn how anthropologists, archaeologists, historians, and geographers have contributed to our understanding of the human record.

TEACH OBJECTIVE 1

Level 1: Ask a volunteer to read aloud the first two paragraphs under "Exploring Prehistory" on page 6. Then ask students to explain what anthropologists and archaeologists do. *(Anthropologists study the remains of the skeletons of hominids. Archaeologists dig into ancient settlements and study the artifacts they find.)* Have another volunteer read the next paragraph before asking students to describe how scientists date remains and artifacts. *(They use advanced technology but must also make educated guesses because artifacts give limited evidence.)*
[English Language Learners]

Level 2: Write the following terms on the chalkboard: *hominids, artifacts, culture, Lucy,* and *Mary Leakey.* Ask students to define or identify each term and record their answers on the board. *(hominids: human and early human-like creatures; artifacts: objects made and used by early hominids such as tools, clothing, works of art, weapons, and toys; culture: the set of beliefs, knowledge, and patterns of living that a group of people develops; Lucy: female hominid who may have lived 3 million years ago; Mary Leakey: an anthropologist who found the remains of a skeleton dating back about 3.7 million years)*
[English Language Learners]

Level 3: Tell students to review the text under the heading "Exploring Prehistory." Write the following terms on the chalkboard: *archaeologist* and *anthropologist.* Ask students to define each term and to explain what is used by each to gather their information. Then, have students create a graphic organizer to display their definitions and samples of what the archaeologist and anthropologist use to gather their information.
[English Language Learners]

TEACH OBJECTIVE 2

Level 1: Create a chart on the chalkboard with the following column headings: *Neanderthal* and *Cro-Magnon.* Have students fill in the chart with characteristics of both peoples. Make sure students include time periods, rituals, and ways of life. (*Neanderthal: located in Europe and Southwest Asia, lived about 35,000 to 130,000 years ago during Old Stone Age, wore animal skins as clothing, used fire, buried the dead, buried meat and tools with the dead showing they believed in some form of life after death; Cro-Magnon: located in Europe, lived about 35,000 years ago, effective hunters, use of spear-throwers, created artwork*)

Levels 2 and 3: Tell students that a significant part of trying to understand the lives of prehistoric people is understanding the environment in which they probably lived. Using the information under "The Ice Age" on pages 7–8, point out the extreme challenges presented by the environment for many thousands of years. Help students further explore what scientists have learned about prehistoric peoples by having them complete a Venn diagram comparing and contrasting the Neanderthal and Cro-Magnon peoples. (*Neanderthals: wore animals skins, used fire, buried their dead; Cro-Magnons: effective hunters, artists; Neanderthals and Cro-Magnons: Homo sapiens*)
[**English Language Learners**]

TEACH OBJECTIVE 3

Level 1: Write the following terms on the board: *Mesolithic Age, Neolithic Age, nomads, agriculture, domestication,* and *hunter-gatherers.* Ask students to define each term. Record responses on the chalkboard. (*Mesolithic Age: Middle Stone Age, 10,000 to 5,500 years ago, use of tools such as bow, arrow, fishhooks, fish spears, and harpoons made from bones and antlers widespread; Neolithic Age: New Stone Age, 4,000 years ago, people shaped stone tools by polishing or grinding, tools made from stone and wood, domestication, agriculture; nomads: people who wandered from place to place in search of food; agriculture: the raising of crops for food; domestication: the taming of animals such as cattle, goats, sheep, and pigs; hunter-gatherers: men hunted animals, women cared for children and gathered plants and fruit for food*)
[**English Language Learners**]

Level 2: Have students create a chart using "Middle Stone Age" and "New Stone Age" as headings. Underneath each heading, students should write the characteristics of each time period, focusing especially upon the cultural advancements.
[**English Language Learners**]

Level 3: Have students create illustrated time lines with known facts about life during the Paleolithic, Mesolithic, and Neolithic time periods. They should include several appropriate illustrations to help clarify advancements in the lives of early humans during each time period. Have several volunteers share their time lines. Point out the Neolithic agricultural revolution was one of the most significant turning points in human history. Ask students to explain why the rise of agriculture was so important to human development. (*It allowed people to establish permanent settlements and produce a surplus of food, paving the way for the development of civilizations.*)

TEACH OBJECTIVE 4

Level 1: Have students list the three main characteristics shared by civilizations. (*surplus food, government, division of labor*) Ask students to write a short paragraph explaining why each characteristic is necessary. (*Answers will vary. Surplus food allows the population to grow. Government regulates people's behavior and helps to ensure order and security. A division of labor allows people to specialize in different jobs.*)
[**English Language Learners**]

Level 2: Have students review the three main characteristics shared by civilization. Record responses on the chalkboard. (*surplus food, government, division of labor*) Then ask students to determine how the United States conforms to these characteristics. Have students provide specific examples of each characteristic.
[**English Language Learners**]

Level 3: Have students review the three main characteristics shared by civilizations. (*surplus food, government, division of labor*) Pretend that an individual of the Nile River Valley refuses to accept the importance of these characteristics in a civilization. This person does not want to contribute to society and begs to be left alone. Compose a convincing argument that reveals the problems with such an attitude and the difficulties this reluctant person will face.

TEACH OBJECTIVE 5

Levels 1 and 2: Ask students what other two accomplishments are characteristic of civilizations. *(a calendar and some form or writing)* Have students draw a two-column chart, with one of these characteristics at the top of each column. Then, ask students to list the reasons why each characteristic is important in a civilization. *(Students might mention that a calendar was important to river valley civilizations because it told people when the yearly floods would occur. A system of writing allowed people to communicate and pass on ideas more easily.)* [**English Language Learners**]

Level 3: Review with students what other two accomplishments are characteristic of civilizations. *(a calendar and some form or writing)* Then discuss what difficulties a society would face if they did not have these two accomplishments. How might they compensate for the lack of each? Is it possible to do so?

TEACH OBJECTIVE 6

All Levels: Have students use their textbooks to make a list of facts about the Neolithic agricultural revolution and the economic, social, and geographic factors that led to the growth of the first civilizations in one column of a two-column chart. In the other column, tell them to write any logical conclusion they can draw regarding the significance of each fact in the first column. *(Example: fact—people began making tools and weapons out of bronze; significance—they could work more efficiently with stronger tools, produce surplus food, and make division of labor possible.)*

Level 1: Have students identify the other two characteristics of a society. Discuss the reasons why these are important and the difficulties

that people faced as a result. [**English Language Learners**]

Level 2: Have students review the information under the heading "Other Characteristics." Then discuss the following question: How did the needs of early civilizations lead to the development of calendars and systems of writing? *(calendar was necessary for agriculture, writing was necessary for increased communication)*

Level 3: Organize students into four or five groups to take on the role of a museum planning committee that is planning an exhibit called "The Dawn of Civilization." Their job is to come up with a list of the types of artifacts they would like to display. Their exhibit should identify and explain the following:

• advances in farming and metalworking

• the rise of governments

• division of labor

• the development of calendars and alphabets.

(Students' lists will vary, but should include items such as tools and written documents that demonstrate the achievements of early civilizations.) [**Cooperative Learning**]

REVIEW AND ASSESS

Have students complete **Section Reviews 1 and 2**. Have students complete **Daily Quizzes 1.1 and 1.2**. As Alternative Assessment, you may want to use the civilization graphic organizer or the museum exercise in Section 2.

RETEACH

Have students complete **Main Idea Activities for English Language Learners and Special-Needs Students 1.1 and 1.2**. Then ask them to write a main idea question and answer for each subsection. [**English Language Learners**]

CHALLENGE AND EXTEND

Alphabet letters may have evolved from pictures. A picture of a tree began to look like the letter T, which became the first letter of the word *tree.* Have students invent several original letters and create a chart to show how each evolved.

Visualizing Mythology

GOAL

In this activity, students will learn how the culture and history of a group of people is reflected in its mythology. Students will study myths, relating each to its culture of origin.

PLANNING

- **Purpose** This activity incorporates teacher-directed lessons and individual and group assignments. It could be used as a culminating activity to a study of ancient civilizations.

- **Suggested Time** Plan to spend three lesson blocks and two homework assignments on this activity. Provide time for students to share and discuss their myths and displays.

- **Teaching Team** At least one social studies teacher and one language arts teacher should take part in teaching this activity.

- **Group Size** This activity can be adapted for either individuals or groups.

- **Materials and Resources**

1. Student photocopies of "Flood" on pages 992–996 in *Man, Myth, and Magic,* Volume 4 (Edited by Richard Cavendish, published by Marshall Cavendish, New York, 1985)

2. Video *Mesopotamia: Return to Eden from Time Life's Lost Civilizations Series* (Time-Life Video and TV, Alexandria, Virginia, 1995)

3. Student photocopies of Rubric 3: Artwork and Rubric 29: Presentations from Portfolio and Performance Assessment for Social Studies

4. Variety of myths such as those available in *World Literature* (Holt, Rinehart, Winston, Inc.) or in library resources

IMPLEMENTATION

1. Give students an overview of the activity by explaining that they will read a variety of myths and identify cultural elements found in those myths. Tell them that mythology serves a variety of purposes for the people who create it: to preserve history of a culture; to teach cultural values and belief systems; to explain the inexplicable; to entertain. For us, mythology is a valuable tool for studying cultures.

2. View *Mesopotamia: Return to Eden* (48 minutes), which traces Middle Eastern history from modern times back to Gilgamesh. As they watch, the students should be able to see that people are influenced by the environment in which they find themselves. Discuss specific examples of influences on Hebrew culture. Explain to students that flood stories, such as the Gilgamesh epic discussed in the end of this video, are found in the mythology of many world civilizations.

3. Read the "Flood" article from *Man, Myth, and Magic.* List elements common to all flood stories. Then read the excerpt from the *Epic of Gilgamesh* in the *World Literature* textbook. Have students work with a partner to find examples of cultural elements found in the epic. As they read, have students consider the following questions: What technology was utilized by the culture? What are the social values of the culture? What are the religious beliefs of the culture? Upon what is the economy of this civilization based? How is this civilization governed? What social classes exist and what is their order of importance in this society?

4. Assign students myths from various cultures discussed in Chapter 1 (students may work as individuals, with partners, or in groups). Have the class decide on the format for sharing all the myths (examples: theme park, museum, Web sites, etc.). Students assigned to each myth create individual displays (such as rides, shops, exhibits, or Web pages) which include details of the myth (plot, characters, theme) and connections between the myth and its culture of origin. When sharing their display with the class, the students

should include a brief summary of the myth and cite specific passages illustrated in their display and explain how their display fits into the overall class project.

ASSESSMENT

1. To assess students' presentations, use Rubric 3: Artwork and Rubric 29: *Presentations in Portfolio and Performance Assessment for Social Studies.*

2. Additional grades can be based on students' participation in class discussion or written responses citing cultural elements in the textbook, the video, or the *Epic of Gilgamesh.*

The Nile Map

Have students examine the map on page 21. Ask them to identify the body of water into which the Nile flows. How might the ability to travel both north and south along the Nile have helped early Egyptian civilizations?

Lesson 1

(For use with Sections 1 and 2, pp. 20–29)

OBJECTIVES

1. Explore how geography affected the development of ancient Egypt.

2. Identify the events and discoveries that marked the development of Egyptian civilization.

3. Explain how Egyptian kingdoms developed and why they collapsed.

4. Describe Egyptian achievements in the arts and architecture.

5. Examine how the Egyptians expressed their religious beliefs.

6. Explain how farming and trade were carried on in Egypt.

BELLRINGER

Ask students to write down the reasons why they believe civilizations often develop along rivers. *(Students might mention the need for a plentiful water supply, transportation, and fertile soil.)* Have volunteers share their responses with the class. Tell students that in Section 1 they will learn about the civilization that developed along the Nile.

TEACH OBJECTIVE 1

Level 1: Ask students to imagine that they are members of an agricultural community and are searching for a new home. Ask them what kind of geographical features they would look for. *(rich soil; a sunny, frost-free climate; deposits of minerals; the Nile River; deserts; and seas)*

Discuss how each geographic factor contributed to the success of the Egyptian civilization. **[English Language Learners, Cooperative Learning]**

Levels 2 and 3: Ask students to review the section, "The Land: Its Geography and Importance." Have students create a chart listing four key characteristics of the natural environment of Egypt, citing examples of how each characteristic affected the culture of Egypt. Then have them create a similar chart reflecting how the natural environment of their town or region has affected the local culture.

TEACH OBJECTIVE 2

All Levels: Ask students to imagine they are illustrators for a book on ancient Egypt. Their task is to produce drawings or models for the book that will describe, without using words, one accomplishment, or achievement, of early Egyptian society. After students have completed their illustrations, compile them into a class book. **[English Language Learners]**

TEACH OBJECTIVE 3

All Levels: Draw a time line beginning with the date 2650 B.C. and ending with 200 B.C. and have the periods of the Old Kingdom (2650 to 2180 B.C.), Middle Kingdom (2040 to 1650 B.C.), and New Kingdom (1570 to 1100 B.C.) marked on it. Have students illustrate the time line with important events in Egypt's history during each time period. *(Possible answers: Old Kingdom—pyramids, science, art, civil war; Middle Kingdom—Hyksos rule Egypt, falls into disorder; New Kingdom—empire, strict government, army, conquering of new territories)*

TEACH OBJECTIVE 4

All Levels: On the board draw a chart with the following column headings: *Then, Now;* and these row headings: *Architecture, The Arts, Science, Mathematics, Medicine.* Have students fill in the columns with achievements of

ancient Egypt and comparable modern-day achievements.
[**English Language Learners, Cooperative Learning**]

TEACH OBJECTIVE 5

Levels 1 and 2: Tell students that the Egyptians did not believe that their life cycle ended with death. The Egyptians thought the body needed to be preserved to make life after death possible. Ask students what other objects or people the Egyptians may have wanted with them in the afterlife and why.
English Language Learners, Cooperative Learning]

Level 3: Have each student write a paragraph that describes ancient Egyptian religious beliefs and how these beliefs influenced Egyptian burial practices.

TEACH OBJECTIVE 6

Level 1: Inform students that most people in ancient Egypt were farmers. The pharaohs directed and profited from the farmers' labor. Remind students that farmers grew more crops than they could use in order to have items to trade with other civilizations. Have students look at the map on page 24. Ask them how Egypt might have conducted trade with people in Europe and western and central Africa *(built ships that could have carried them across the Mediterranean, sail ships down the Red Sea, cross the desert)*
[**English Language Learners, Cooperative Learning**]

Levels 2 and 3: Have students write a first-person account from the point-of-view of a farmer. Students should explain the types of crops they grow, their relationship with the pharaohs, and the ways in which they trade their crops.

REVIEW AND ASSESS

Have students complete **Section Reviews 1 and 2**. Have students complete **Daily Quizzes 2.1 and 2.2**.

RETEACH

Have students complete **Main Idea Activities 2.1 and 2.2**. Ask students to write a question and answer that covers the main idea for each subsection in the section.
[**English Language Learners**]

CHALLENGE AND EXTEND

Have students work in groups to build a pyramid. They may use a problem-solving process to create a pyramid modeled after one that exists in Egypt or create a new pyramid with whatever type of materials they choose.
[**Block Scheduling, Cooperative Learning**]

Lesson 2

(For use with Sections 3 and 4, pp. 30–40)

OBJECTIVES

1. Explore how geography affected the development of the Sumerian civilization.

2. Identify the achievements of the Sumerian people.

3. Describe what life was like in Sumerian society.

4. Explain why outsiders attacked the Sumerians.

5. Examine the characteristics of Babylonian society.

6. Investigate what invaders conquered Babylon and why they failed to control it.

7. Describe the achievements of the Persians.

BELLRINGER

Remind students that Egypt was geographically isolated. Ask them why that was important to the success of Egyptian civilization. *(Students should point out that it lessened the threat of outside invasions.)* Have them predict the difficulties a civilization that was not geographically isolated might have faced. *(Students might note that outsiders could attack more frequently.)* Tell students that in Section 3 they will learn about the effect geography had on Sumerian civilization.

TEACH OBJECTIVE 1

All Levels: Have students compare the map of ancient Egypt (page 24) with the map of the Fertile Crescent (page 30). Ask them what similarities they found in the geography of the two civilizations. (*Both civilizations have some natural protections, such as mountains, seas, and desert.*) Then have students make up questions about the geographic distribution of the peoples in these regions. Use the questions for class discussion. [**English Language Learners**]

All Levels: Tell students that, like the Egyptians, the Sumerians created a successful civilization. Ask students to use their knowledge of early civilizations to predict Sumerian achievements. As a class, have students create a set of 26 cuneiform-style wedge shapes to represent all the letters of the alphabet. Draw these shapes on the chalkboard so that students can copy them. Have each student write a word or phrase in the new alphabet that relates to an aspect of Sumerian society. Have students exchange papers and translate each other's work.

TEACH OBJECTIVE 3

Level 1: Distribute sheets of drawing paper to students. Tell students to draw a map of a Sumerian city-state. Explain that the maps should include symbols for places such as homes, schools, government buildings, markets, ziggurats, and farms. Students should include a map key to explain the models. [**English Language Learners**]

Levels 2 and 3: Have students create a social hierarchy that reflects Sumerian society. Students should draw a large triangle and fill the various spaces with the appropriate titles of Sumerian society.

TEACH OBJECTIVE 4

Levels 1 and 2: Have students compose a list of possible reasons why the Akkadians, led by Sargon, might have conquered the Sumerians. Why would other civilizations continue to conquer the area? [**English Language Learners, Cooperative Learning**]

Level 3: Tell students to imagine that they are Sumerians preparing for an attack by outside invaders. Have students use a problem-solving process to determine why outside invaders attack and to develop a method for defending their city-state. Ask them to develop a plan for governing the area that would unite all the city-states and prevent outside invaders from conquering them. Have students share their plans with the class.

TEACH OBJECTIVE 5

All Levels: Ask students to write a short paragraph describing the Code of Hammurabi. Have students state whether or not they believe the code was just, and have them support their position. [**English Language Learners, Cooperative Learning**]

TEACH OBJECTIVE 6

All Levels: Have students write their definition of the word *empire*. Then ask students what systems and skills are necessary to run an empire. Then tell students to make a chart with the headings *Pros* and *Cons*. Have students list the following empires along the left side of the chart: *Akkadians, Babylonians, Hittites, Assyrians, Chaldeans, Persians.* Tell students to fill in their charts as they read the section.

TEACH OBJECTIVE 7

All Levels: Have students compare and contrast the Persians with two other civilizations. Make sure students cover the following areas: government, religion, and the society's decline.

REVIEW AND ASSESS

Have students complete **Review Sections 3 and 4**. Have students complete **Daily Quiz 2.3 and 2.4.**

RETEACH

Have students complete **Main Idea Activities 2.3 and 2.4.** Then pair students to answer the **Reading Check** questions in **Sections 3 and 4.** [**English Language Learners, Cooperative Learning**]

CHALLENGE AND EXTEND

Divide students into six groups and assign each group an empire. Tell students that they are to use sources such as computer software, biographies, and artifacts to produce a contemporary magazine about their empire.

Lesson 3

(For use with Sections 5 and 6, pp. 41–49)

OBJECTIVES

1. Examine how trade influenced Phoenician culture.

2. Describe how a money economy developed in Lydia.

3. Explain how the migrating Hebrews found a homeland.

4. Explore how religious views affected Hebrew culture.

BELLRINGER

Ask students what caused culture to spread between ancient civilizations. *(Travel to other areas for trade.)* Tell students that in Section 5 they will learn about Phoenician trade and the cultural diffusion that resulted.

TEACH OBJECTIVE 1

All Levels: Have students work in pairs to conduct a business transaction replacing written words with visuals. Then ask how the development of an alphabet influenced the spread of Phoenician culture.
[English Language Learners, Cooperative Learning]

TEACH OBJECTIVE 2

All Levels: Ask students to write a short discussion of how salespeople conduct business today. How do these methods compare with those used by Phoenicians and Lydians?
[English Language Learners]

TEACH OBJECTIVE 3

All Levels: Have students create a graphic representation showing how the migrating Hebrews found a homeland.
[English Language Learners]

TEACH OBJECTIVE 4

Levels 1 and 2: Review the Ten Commandments on page 45 with students. Ask them to write a response to each commandment, explaining why such a rule would help to preserve the Hebrew community.

Level 3: Review with students the meaning of the word *ethics.* Have students brainstorm actions that are ethical and actions that are not ethical. Ask students how ethical they feel the laws of the Egyptians, Babylonians, Hittites, Assyrians, and Persians were. Ask students to evaluate how ethical these civilizations' laws seem in comparison to those of the Hebrews.

REVIEW AND ASSESS

Have students complete **Review Sections 5 and 6.** Have students complete **Daily Quiz 2.5 and 2.6.**

RETEACH

Have students complete **Main Idea Activities 2.5 and 2.6.** Then ask each student to create an annotated time line of Hebrew history.

CHALLENGE AND EXTEND

Have students create a map like the one on page 41. First, have them shade the Jordan Valley and the regions where the Canaanites and Philistines lived. Tell students to use lines and arrows to show the movement of the Hebrews from the days of Abraham up through the 500s B.C., and to label locations with dates.

Reporting Live from Ancient Egypt

GOAL

In this activity, students will utilize their knowledge of ancient civilizations to create newspaper articles. Students will produce a newspaper as a class and present their articles to each other.

PLANNING

- **Purpose** This activity may be used in combination with teacher-directed lessons, as an enrichment activity, or as a performance-based assessment of content mastery.

- **Suggested Time** Plan to spend two lesson blocks and one homework assignment on this activity.

- **Teaching Team** At least one social studies teacher and one language arts teacher should take part in teaching this activity.

- **Group Size** Students must be divided into nine groups.

- **Materials and Resources** Provide students with copies of "An Early Agricultural Village" on page 6 of *Readings in World History* and Rubrics 14 and/or 23. Have students use their textbooks to help them find information about the ancient civilizations.

IMPLEMENTATION

1. Give students an overview of the activity by explaining that they will first read "An Early Agricultural Village" on page 6 of *Readings in World History*. Discuss the main features of the Jarmo culture. Discuss the following questions: What was the diet of the people of Jarmo? Why does Braidwood find it interesting that portable pottery did not appear until late in the life of Jarmo? Why does the existence of obsidian tools indicate that the people of Jarmo were involved in trade? Why did these obsidian tools "point to a newer age"?

Also analyze the style and point-of-view of the piece.

2. Have students create a chart with the following column headings: *Geographic Location, Government, Economics, Religion, Cultural Achievements, Scientific Achievements,* and *Mathematical Achievements.* Have students create the following row headings: *Egyptians, Sumerians, Babylonians, Assyrians, Chaldeans, Persians, Phoenicians, Lydians,* and *Hebrews.* Students should fill in the chart with the information for each group under the proper heading.

3. Ask students to keep "An Early Agricultural Village" in mind as they complete the next step of the activity. Using the chart they have created, organize the class into groups to write feature stories for a local newspaper and to create accompanying artwork for their feature story. Have each group of students write feature stories that focus on the significance of their assigned aspect of their civilization. For example, one group might be assigned the task of writing a feature story on the cultural achievements of the Lydians. In assigning topics from the chart, make sure that as many different civilizations and topics about the civilizations are covered as possible. Groups may approach their topic creatively; for example, they may choose to present their information through a series of editorials or an advice column.

4. Once groups have completed a draft of their article, ask them to exchange articles with another group for peer editing. Ask students to keep the following things in mind as they revise the articles: spelling, punctuation, grammar, style, flow, and clarity. Also ask each group to list three general areas that could be improved upon as well as three comments indicating the strengths of the article.

5. Conclude by compiling student writing and artwork into a class newspaper. Allow

students to present their particular articles and answer questions posed by classmates.

ASSESSMENT

1. To assess students' speeches, use Rubrics 14 and/or 23.

2. Additional grades can be based on students' participation in the concluding presentation.

Drawing Conclusions from Maps

Have students examine the map on page 53. Ask them to identify the major waterways in the Indus River valley. (*Indus River, Jhelum River, Chenab River, Ravi River, Sutlej River*) How might the location of Harappa and Mohenjo Daro have affected their relationship? Why? (*Both Mohenjo Daro and Harappa are located along the same river system. This allowed the inhabitants to travel easily to and from the other city, which allowed trade and cultural exchange.*)

Lesson 1

(*For use with Sections 1 and 2, pp. 52–59*)

OBJECTIVES

1. Examine the role geography and climate played in the settlement of the Indian sub-continent.

2. Investigate how people in the first Indus River valley civilization lived.

3. Explain how life in northern India changed with the coming of the Indo-Aryans.

4. Identify the major contributions of the Indo-Aryans to ancient Indian society.

BELLRINGER

Ask students to describe how physical geography affected settlement of the United States. (*Students might mention the waterways and mountain ranges of the United States.*) Then have them describe how climate affects their lives today. Tell students that in Section 1 they will learn how geography and climate impacted the settlement of the Indian subcontinent.

TEACH OBJECTIVE 1

Level 1: Ask students to summarize India's climate. Remind the class that the first civilizations arose in four great river valleys; point out that one of these four valleys was the Indus

River valley and help students locate the region on a map. Ask students why they think this civilization arose in the Indus Valley rather than in the Ganges Valley. (*Students should note that the Ganges Valley receives the heaviest rainfall during the monsoon.*)
[**English Language Learners**]

Levels 2 and 3: Give students an outline map of India. Have them locate and label the major landforms and rivers of India, as well as the two famous Harappan cities. Then have them explain what geographic factors might have helped or been hurt by early civilizations in India.

TEACH OBJECTIVE 2

Levels 3: Have students make a chart that lists 10 to 15 facts about the Harappan civilization using the information on pages 53–55. Have them organize their charts into four columns labeled *government, religion, technology,* and *economy*. Call on each student to share one fact from his or her chart. Ask students what causes, other than an earthquake or flood, might explain the unburied skeletons and abandoned homes at Mohenjo Daro and Harrapa. (*Students might suggest a plague, a drought, a deadly heat wave, and so on.*)

All Levels: Have students look at the chart they created about Harappan achievements. Have students draw at least one other type of graphic organizer that could convey this information effectively. (*Students might draw cluster diagrams, branching or webbing organizers, horizontal or vertical lists, circular [pie] charts, concentric circles in a "bulls-eye" formation, and so on.*)
[**English Language Learners**]

TEACH OBJECTIVE 3

Levels 1 and 2: Have students read Section 2 and then list some of the ways that life in northern India changed with the arrival of the Indo-Aryans, including major political, economic, and cultural developments. (*Students should*

mention the Vedas, Indo-Aryan religion, the formation of states, and the spread of Sanskrit.)
[**English Language Learners**]

Level 3: Tell students that throughout history
urban societies have often come into conflict
with their nomadic neighbors. Although the
Harappan civilization was well-protected by
the natural barrier presented by the northern
mountains, the Khyber Pass through the Hindu
Kush mountains provided a means for the
Indo-Aryans to invade India after about 1750
B.C. Ask students why they think the Indo-
Aryans invaded India. If students guess that the
Indo-Aryans were interested in the cities, tell
them that they ignored the cities, leaving them
to decay.

TEACH OBJECTIVE 4

All Levels: Tell students that most of what we
know about the Indo-Aryans comes from the
Vedas. The Vedas are literature of the Indo-
Aryan religion that have been memorized and
passed on for centuries. After the development
of writing, scholars wrote them in the Indo-
Aryan language. Draw a three-column chart on
the board. Title it *Characteristics of Indo-Aryan
Society*, and label its three columns *Government*, *Social Life*, and *Economy*. Have students
copy this chart and categorize the information
as they read Section 2.
[**English Language Learners**]

REVIEW AND ASSESS

Have students complete the **Section Reviews 1
and 2**. Have students complete **Daily Quizzes
3.1 and 3.2**. As Alternative Assessment, you
may want to use the map or chart exercises in
this section's lessons.

RETEACH

Have students complete **Main Idea Activities
3.1 and 3.2**. Ask them to write a paragraph
describing the developments of Indo-Aryan
society using standard grammar, spelling, sentence structure, and punctuation.
[**English Language Learners**]

CHALLENGE AND EXTEND

Ask students to use computer software to locate
an excerpt from the Vedas in English transla-
tion. Encourage them to make a dramatic reading from the Vedas.

Lesson 2

(For use with Sections 3, 4 and 5, pp. 60–71)

OBJECTIVES

1. Describe the importance of religion in
   ancient Indian society.

2. Identify the principle elements of
   Hinduism.

3. Identify the basic beliefs of Buddhism.

4. Explain how the Mauryan rulers increased
   their power.

5. Examine the reasons for the decline of
   Gupta rule.

6. Describe how women's rights were limited
   in ancient Indian society.

7. Identify the most important achievements
   of the Gupta period.

BELLRINGER

Ask students to think about social divisions in
American society today. Ask them how structured they believe American social classes are
and if it is possible for a person to move to a
higher social class. Tell students that in Section
3 they will learn about the structure of social
classes in ancient India.

TEACH OBJECTIVE 1

Levels 1 and 2: Have students name and
summarize the important texts of Hinduism
and Buddhism as identified in "The
Upanishads and the Epics." Ask them to identify how the epics helped spread religious
understanding among India's ordinary people.
[**English Language Learners**]

Level 3: Have students study the information
in the sections titled, "A Changing Society" and
"Hinduism." Ask students to describe how the

Indian caste system and Hinduism were related. (*According to Hinduism, people who fulfill their dharma gain good karma and are born into a higher social group in the next life. People who do not live moral lives will be born as members of lower groups.*)

TEACH OBJECTIVE 2

Level 1: Remind students of the connection between Hinduism and the Indian caste system. Tell them to create a graphic organizer that clearly shows how the classes were categorized and ranked in early India. (*Students' organizers should include the following points: Upper class or Brahmins: priests, scholars, rulers, warriors; middle class: merchants, traders, farmers; lower class, peasants bound to the land; pariahs: untouchables*) Point out to students that these classes eventually divided into thousands of smaller groups called *jati*.
[English Language Learners]

Levels 2 and 3: Have students practice imparting their knowledge of Hinduism to a friend who knows nothing about Eastern religions. Ask students to write a statement explaining Hindu beliefs. Ask them to include the Hindu view of how to live your life, the names of important gods, and the many religious practices.

TEACH OBJECTIVE 3

All Levels: Have students create a Venn diagram comparing Hinduism and Buddhism. The diagram should include elements that are unique to each religion as well as elements they have in common. (*Hinduism: belief in dharma and karma, belief that the sensory world is an illusion; Buddhism: belief in the way to enlightenment, ethical guidelines—Four Noble Truths and Eightfold Path; both: belief in reincarnation, belief that progress of soul depends on life led, belief in nirvana.*)
[English Language Learners]

TEACH OBJECTIVES 4 AND 5

Level 1: Have students create a chart that categorizes Mauryan and Gupta rulers and their

actions/beliefs.
[English Language Learners]

Levels 2 and 3: Have students create a time line that shows the approximate length of time each ruler controlled India. Tell them to include Chandragupta, Maurya, Asoka, and Chandra Gupta II. Ask students to give the major accomplishments of each of these leaders. (*Chandragupta Maurya: made Patalipura into a beautiful city, united northern India; Asoka: enlarged the empire to include all but the southern tip of India; Chandra Gupta II: founded the Gupta empire, society and the arts prospered, Hinduism became the dominant religion*)
[English Language Learners]

TEACH OBJECTIVE 6

All Levels: Ask students to imagine that they are women in ancient India. Have each student write a letter to a friend explaining what life is like in Indian society.
[English Language Learners]

TEACH OBJECTIVE 7

Level 1: Have students draw a four-column chart in their notes with the columns labeled *Art and Architecture, Education, Mathematics and Astronomy,* and *Medicine.* Have them fill in their charts with cultural achievements during the Gupta period. (*Students' charts should include the* Panchatantra, *stupas, Nalanda, algebra and Arabic numeral, astronomy, and inoculation.*)
[English Language Learners]

Levels 2 and 3: Have students compare and contrast the education they receive in American schools with that experienced by students in ancient India. (*Education differs because in the United States, all children are entitled to receive a public education, and public schools offer formal education in many subjects. It is similar in that wealthy children in the United States may have access to better educational opportunities than children of poverty.*)
[Cooperative Learning]

REVIEW AND ASSESS

Have students complete the **Review Sections 3, 4, and 5**. Have students complete **Daily Quizzes 3.3, 3.4, and 3.5**. As Alternative Assessment, you may want to use the letter or chart exercises in this section's lesson.

RETEACH

Have students complete **Main Idea Activities 3.3, 3.4, and 3.5**. Have students write three Indian cultural achievements and describe why each was important.
[English Language Learners]

CHALLENGE AND EXTEND

Have students imagine that they are policy advisors in an ancient Indian kingdom. Have students use a decision-making process to plan attractions that promote an understanding and appreciation of Indian culture during the Gupta Empire. Have them compile a list of policies they would recommend to their ruler to help establish a strong, stable government.
[Cooperative Learning]

Vacation to Ancient India

GOAL

In this activity, students will learn more about ancient Indian life and culture, including Buddhist and Hindu views on social class and the roles of women.

PLANNING

- **Purpose** This activity may be used in combination with teacher-directed lessons, as an enrichment activity, or as a performance-based assessment of content mastery.

- **Suggested Time** Plan to spend two lesson blocks and one homework assignment on this activity.

- **Teaching Team** At least one social studies teacher and one language arts teacher should take part in teaching this activity.

- **Group Size** This activity works best by organizing students into groups of two or three. You may wish to assign the activity as an extra credit option for individual students.

- **Materials and Resources** Provide students with copies of "Buddhism and Equality" and "The Place of Women in Hindu Society" on pages 17 and 22 of *Readings in World History*. Also provide Rubric 40. Have students use their textbooks to help them find information about Hindu and Buddhist culture and beliefs.

IMPLEMENTATION

1. Give students an overview of the activity by explaining that they will first read "Buddhism and Equality" and "The Place of Women in Hindu Society" on pages 17 and 22 of *Readings in World History*. As students read, ask them to take notes on the readings, recording both positive and negative aspects of the beliefs being described. Discuss the following questions upon the completion of "Buddhism and Equality": How did Buddha answer Assalayana's claim that only the Brahmans "are the true sons of Brama"? On what two factors did Assalayana base the Brahmans' claim to be the highest class? Explain Buddha's views on how to judge people. Discuss the following questions upon the completion of "The Place of Women in Hindu Society": According to the Sacred Law, what was the highest dharma, or morality, of all four Hindu classes? According to the Sacred Law, what were suitable tasks for a Hindu woman? How is this excerpt contradictory in the way it views Hindu women?

2. Have students compare the beliefs expressed in the readings with those that dominate American culture. For example, do the majority of Americans live by values similar to those of Buddha? Do American and ancient Hindu men view women similarly or differently?

3. Expand the discussion by having students create a Venn Diagram, labeling one side "Hinduism" and the other "Buddhism." Ask students to supply elements that are unique to each as well as elements they have in common.

4. Then organize the class into groups to create an informational guidebook about "Indian Life and Culture." Have each group choose one of the following aspects of Indian society to illustrate and describe in the guidebook: Economy and Women's Position in Society, Literature, Art and Architecture, Education, Mathematics and Astronomy, and Medicine. Encourage students to be as descriptive as possible using information from the textbook when needed. Students should also be as creative as possible.

5. Compose the finished pieces into a guidebook and give each student a copy.

ASSESSMENT

1. To assess students' speeches, use Rubrics 14 and/or 23.

2. Additional grades can be based on students' participation in the discussions preceding the actual project.

Reviewing Map Basics

Have students examine the map on page 77. Ask them to identify the subject of the map. Around what geographic feature were most of the cities built and why? What does the activity of rice farming, shown on the map, demonstrate about the geographic distribution of agriculture in early east Asia?

Lesson 1

(For use with Sections 1 and 2, pp. 76–83)

OBJECTIVES

1. Explore the role that rivers played in Chinese life.

2. Investigate how geography influenced the development of Chinese culture.

3. Examine how the Chinese explained their early history.

4. Describe how the Shang government and economy were organized.

5. Identify the religious beliefs held by the Shang.

6. Explain why the Shang Dynasty collapsed.

BELLRINGER

Have students think about how interaction with other societies influences the development of a society's culture. Ask students what a society's culture might be like if the people had no contact with foreigners. Tell students that in Section 1 they will learn about the geographic isolation of China and how it influenced Chinese culture.

TEACH OBJECTIVE 1

All Levels: Draw a three-column chart on the chalkboard. Label the columns with the following river names: Huang, Chang, and Xi. Ask students to explain how the Chinese used each river and fill in the chart as students give their answers. *(Huang: fertile farming; Chang and Xi: commercial waterways.)* Ask class members

what other geographic features of China played a part in shaping its development and how they were important. *(Isolating influence of mountains, deserts, vastness.)*
[**English Language Learners**]

TEACH OBJECTIVE 2

All Levels: Tell students that early Chinese called the region in which they lived "All Under Heaven." Ask the class what clues this name provides about how the Chinese regarded their culture. *(Students should suggest feelings of cultural superiority, a link with the divine, a blessed land and people.)* Ask students what other name the Chinese had for their land that indicates they felt culturally superior. *(the Middle Kingdom)* Then discuss what caused these feelings of superiority. *(China's geographic isolation and lack of contact with foreigners)*

TEACH OBJECTIVE 3

All Levels: Explain that in cultures without writing, history depends on stories passed from one generation to the next. Have students write a short legend about Xia's rule. Form small groups and have one member tell his or her legend to another. That student should repeat it to a third, and so on, until it has passed through the group. Have the last person in each group tell the legend to the class. Ask the class to assess the value of legends as historical sources. Then discuss what the accuracy of China's legends suggests about the importance people put on their past.
[**Cooperative Learning**]

TEACH OBJECTIVE 4

All Levels: Ask students to identify two ways that the Shang dynasty maintained its power. *(Force of arms, such as war chariots and bronze weapons; public works systems, such as irrigation and flood control)* Ask them to deduce the role that technology played in sustaining the dynasty.
[**English Language Learners**]

TEACH OBJECTIVE 5

Level 1: Call on volunteers to name some of the religious beliefs held by the Shang. *(Combination of animism and ancestor worship, Shangdi, and the interpretation of oracle bones)* Ask students how Shang rulers used the religious beliefs of the early Chinese to legitimize their rule. *(They claimed that their decisions were the will of Shangdi.)*
[English Language Learners]

Levels 2 and 3: Have students summarize the religious beliefs of the Shang period. How did Shang leaders use religious beliefs to build support for their rule? *(Claimed that their decisions were the will of Shangdi.)*

TEACH OBJECTIVE 6

Level 1: Ask students why the Shang dynasty collapsed. Have students explain who conquered the Shang dynasty and how they justified their conquest.
[English Language Learners]

Levels 2 and 3: Have students identify the causes and effects involved in the collapse of the Shang Dynasty. Why would the conquering peoples justify their conquest the way they did? Why might nearby tribes help to overthrow the Shang Dynasty?

REVIEW AND ASSESS

Have students complete **Review Sections 1 and 2**. Have students complete **Daily Quizzes 4.1 and 4.2**.

RETEACH

Have students complete **Main Idea Activities 4.1 and 4.2**. Then ask students to use correct social studies terminology to write a question that covers the main idea for each subsection in the section.
[English Language Learners]

CHALLENGE AND EXTEND

Have students research and report on bronze casting and a writing system, two important technological breakthroughs that took place in Shang China. Have them create visuals such as charts and graphs to illustrate their reports.

Lesson 2

(For use with Sections 3 and 4, pp. 84–92)

OBJECTIVES

1. Explain why the Zhou fell from power.
2. Describe how the Qin dynasty used power to maintain its authority.
3. Identify the achievements of the Han emperors.
4. Examine why the Chinese valued the concept of balance.
5. Explore what the Chinese philosopher Confucius taught.
6. Analyze how Daoism and Confucianism worked together in Chinese society.
7. Investigate how beliefs such as Legalism and Buddhism influenced Chinese history.

BELLRINGER

Have students think about the qualities of a good leader. Ask them to list some of the ways leaders can legitimize their authority. *(Students might answer that they can be honest, be fair to all, and practice moderation.)* Tell students that in this section they will learn about the leaders of ancient Chinese dynasties.

TEACH OBJECTIVE 1

All Levels: Have students list four reasons why the Zhou dynasty collapsed. Which governments have fallen from power most recently? What has replaced them? In this way, relate Zhou discussion to current events.

TEACH OBJECTIVE 2

All Levels: Tell students to imagine they are newspaper editors during the Qin dynasty and to write an editorial about the emperor. Editorials should either charge that the emperor has lost the Mandate of Heaven or defend him as having it. Remind students that

editorials explain to readers the reasons for the writer's point of view. (*Has lost mandate: Qin's harsh rule, popular unrest; has mandate: dynasty's accomplishments, maintains strong power*) Have students read their editorials to the class. Then hold a discussion on whether the Qin had the Mandate of Heaven.
[**English Language Learners**]

TEACH OBJECTIVE 3

Level 1: Have students list the achievements of the Han emperors. Then ask students to decide whether they would have preferred to live under Zhou, Qin, or Han rule.
[**English Language Learners**]

Levels 2 and 3: Have small groups conduct short interviews with Hsiao Yen, focusing on some aspect of his rule, such as conquest of the Xiongnu. One student takes the role of the interviewer and another of Hsiao Yen. The third student plays an imperial assistant such as a general. Have groups present their interviews to the class.
[**Cooperative Learning**]

TEACH OBJECTIVE 4

Level 1: Ask students why the Chinese valued the concept of balance. Draw a two-column chart with one column labeled *yin* and the other labeled *yang*. Have students list the characteristics of each in the chart.
[**English Language Learners**]

Levels 2 and 3: Have students define the principles of *yin* and *yang*. Ask students to reflect on their own personalities and determine if they have more qualities related to *yin* or *yang*. Take a survey of responses. Be sure to ask students if any believe they are balanced.

TEACH OBJECTIVE 5

All Levels: Write the following passage from the Analects on the chalkboard: "*To see what is right and not to do it is want of courage.*" Tell students that the passage is a teaching of Confucius. Ask the class what they think the

saying means and what effect following it would have had on the government of China. Discuss whether these are words to live by today.
[**English Language Learners**]

TEACH OBJECTIVE 6

All Levels: Present the class with the following situation: A weak, inefficient, and corrupt ruler is governing their country; crime and disorder are rampant and a revolt is likely. Have students write the solutions a Confucian and a Daoist might offer in this situation.
[**English Language Learners**]

TEACH OBJECTIVE 7

Levels 1 and 2: Explain that a maxim is a saying that sets out a truth or rule of conduct. Then have pairs of students write a maxim for Buddhism with the purpose of attracting Chinese converts to the faith. Have pairs read their maxims to the class. Ask the class to discuss whether each maxim accurately represents Buddhism.
[**Cooperative Learning**]

Level 3: Organize groups of three students with each taking one role: a Daoist, a legalist, or a Confucian. Have them debate, in their roles, one of the following questions: (1) What should be the main goal in life? (2) Are people basically bad or good? (3) What is the best kind of government? After the discussion, ask them to describe their positions. Then have the class predict the consequences of following each philosophy.
[**Cooperative Learning**]

REVIEW AND ASSESS

Have students complete the **Review Sections 3 and 4**. Have students complete **Daily Quizzes 4.3 and 4.4**.

RETEACH

Have students complete **Main Idea Activities 4.3 and 4.4**. Then have students write one question and answer for each Chinese philosophy.
[**English Language Learners**]

CHALLENGE AND EXTEND

Have students use a problem-solving process to devise a plan of government for their community based on a Chinese philosophical tradition.

Lesson 3

(For use with Section 5, pp. 93–95)

OBJECTIVES

1. Explain why the family was a central institution in Chinese society.

2. Describe how farmers lived in ancient China.

3. Identify the artistic and scientific achievements of the Chinese.

BELLRINGER

Ask students to think about the concept of family in the United States today. Have students them describe various family units. Tell students that in Section 5 they will learn about the ancient Chinese concept of family.

TEACH OBJECTIVE 1

All Levels: With the class, develop a list that describes a typical family in ancient China. Then ask them to cite ways in which this family illustrates the philosophy of Confucianism. *(importance of family, respect for elders, members' acceptance and fulfillment of their roles)*
[**English Language Learners**]

All Levels: Organize the class into small groups to discuss how rural life in ancient China compares to rural life in the United States today.

(similarities: most people farmed, paid taxes, contended with nature; differences: most Chinese lived in rural areas, Chinese farmers lived in villages, often worked field in common, had to perform public services)
[**Cooperative Learning**]

TEACH OBJECTIVE 3

Level 1: Have students draw a chart listing Chinese achievements in the arts and sciences.
[**English Language Learners**]

Levels 2 and 3: Have students name and describe Chinese accomplishments in the arts. Specifically, what did the Chinese contribute to technology?

REVIEW AND ASSESS

Have students complete the Section 5 Review questions. Have students complete **Daily Quiz 4.5.**

RETEACH

Have students complete **Main Idea Activity 4.5.** Ask students to list the main ideas of each heading.
[**English Language Learners**]

CHALLENGE AND EXTEND

Have students complete **Main Idea Activity** ave students find out about research ancient Chinese achievements in science and technology.

Confucianism or Daoism?

GOAL

In this activity, students will reinforce their knowledge of Confucianism and Daoism. Students will either apply their knowledge to create fiction or explore their own experiences through the lens of philosophy.

PLANNING

- **Purpose** This activity may be used in combination with teacher-directed lessons, as an enrichment activity, or as a performance-based assessment of content mastery.

- **Suggested Time** Plan to spend two lesson blocks and one homework assignment on this activity.

- **Teaching Team** At least one social studies teacher and one language arts teacher should take part in teaching this activity.

- **Group Size** This activity works best by organizing students into groups of two or three.

- **Materials and Resources** Provide students with copies of "The Wisdom of Confucius" and "The *Dao De Ching* of Laozi" on pages 23–28 in *Readings in World History*. Also provide students with a copy of Rubric 37.

IMPLEMENTATION

1. Give students an overview of the activity by explaining that they will first read "The Wisdom of Confucius" and "The *Dao De Ching* of Laozi" on pages 23–28 in Readings in World History. Upon the completion of "The Wisdom of Confucius," discuss the following questions: According to Confucius what paves the way for civic obedience? Why does Confucius call loving and reverencing others without first loving and reverencing one's parents a perversity?

Why do you think Confucius believes a son who is guilty of the three evils cannot be considered filial? Upon completion of "The *Dao De Ching* of Laozi," discuss the following questions: Which verse in the excerpt is illustrated by the statement: "You can only know peace by having war"? What do you think the "nothing" referred to in Verse XI is? "The *Dao De Ching* of Laozi" has been characterized as mystical. What do you think this means? Give two examples from the excerpt to support your statement.

2. Divide students into groups. Referring to the text and these two readings, have each group compose a detailed list of Confucian and Daoist beliefs.

3. Ask each member of the class to write a short story in which the main character is a loyal Confucian who obeys all teachings. Have students create a plot diagram and character sketches before they begin writing their stories. Remind students that a good story must have an interesting conflict. Once students have written a draft, ask them to exchange papers for peer editing. Students should pay close attention to spelling, grammar, punctuation, style, flow, and clarity. Then ask students to choose one statement from "The *Dao De Ching* of Laozi" and write a personal essay about an experience he or she has had that in some way relates to the statement. Make sure that students reflect on whether the people involved in their particular situation behaved according to or in opposition of the principles of Daoism.

4. Ask students to choose one of their pieces to read aloud to the class. Allow students to react to one another's work. Perhaps after each student has read his or her piece, three different students could offer positive comments about the writing.

ASSESSMENT

1. To assess students' speeches, use Rubric 37 or a customizable format on the One-Stop Planner.

2. Additional grades can be based on students' participation in group activities.

The Mediterranean Region

Have students examine the map on page 107. Ask them to identify physical features that are common to several of the countries. *(Example: mountains and islands)* Have students note unusual characteristics of the physical geography and the size of these countries.

Lesson 1

(For use with Sections 1 and 2, pp. 104–118)

OBJECTIVES

1. Analyze the role that geography played in early Greek history.

2. Explain the influence that Minoan and Mycenaean civilizations had on Greek civilization.

3. Describe the development of the Greek city-states.

4. Explain the importance of Homer's works.

5. Identify major religious beliefs and practices of the ancient Greeks.

6. Describe changes that occurred in the governments of the Greek city-states.

BELLRINGER

Brainstorm with students reasons why people relocate to other areas. List as many suggestions as possible on the chalkboard. Ask students what factors would be important to them when choosing a new location.

TEACH OBJECTIVE 1

Level 1: Before students read "The Sea and the Land," have them examine the maps on pages 107 and 108. Ask students what geographical features they notice on the Balkan Peninsula. *(Students should mention the numerous mountain ranges, the lack of long rivers, the long irregular coastline, and many islands.)* Guide a discussion of the advantages and disadvantages these features posed for people living in the region.
[**English Language Learners**]

Levels 2 and 3: Ask the students to think specifically about how the Mediterranean, Aegean, and Ionian seas influenced the professions and city locations of the early Greeks. *(Many Greeks became fishers, sailors, and traders and major cities were located on the coast.)* Once this is established, ask the students to form in their groups and discuss how the easy access to Egypt, Asia Minor, and Africa might have affected Greek culture. Have each group find specific examples in previous sections of the cultural and intellectual benefits the Greeks gained from their interaction with other countries. Present findings to the class. *(The Minoans adopted an alphabet based on the Phoenician system. Greek art was influenced by the Egyptians, i.e., Sphinx in Delphi, etc.)*
[**English Language Learners, Cooperative Learning**]

TEACH OBJECTIVE 2

Level 1: Draw a compare-and-contrast chart on the chalkboard. Guide students in filling in the chart. Then have students pose and answer questions about the influence of the Minoans and Mycenaeans on Greek civilization.
[**English Language Learners, Cooperative Learning**]

TEACH OBJECTIVE 3

Level 1: After students read the paragraphs under "The City-States of Greece," create a chart with four columns on the chalkboard. Label each column with these key features of the city-state: small size, small populations, setting on a hill, and public meeting place. Have students copy the chart and list details about each key feature as it relates to the development of city-states. Then have students write details about each feature as it applies to their city or town.
[**English Language Learners, Cooperative Learning**]

Levels 2 and 3: As noted on page 108, the concept of polis includes these three factors: geographical territory of the city-state; the

community that it represented; and the political and economic independence that it produced. Ask students to think of other instances of countries that have similar communities. Have students write about the connection to their own community and how it may differ or resemble these Greek city-states.
[English Language Learners]

TEACH OBJECTIVE 4

All Levels: Ask students why the poems of Homer were important to the ancient Greeks. (Told about the Trojan War; form of entertainment; told about Greek history and heroes, values and culture.) Then ask what modern scholars might learn about ancient Greeks from these epics. (They would learn about the history and culture of the Greeks in the Homeric Age.)
[English Language Learners, Cooperative Learning]

TEACH OBJECTIVE 5

Level 1: Assign several groups of students the task of reading one myth about a particular god or goddess (Zeus, Athena, Dionysus, Apollo, etc.). Have each group define each god's characteristics. Have each group present their findings to the class.
[English Language Learners, Cooperative Learning]

Levels 2 and 3: Have students read portions of Edith Hamilton's *Mythology*. Then have students write a brief essay that points out the human qualities and personalities that the Greeks gave their gods.
[English Language Learners]

TEACH OBJECTIVE 6

Level 1: Have students review in writing the progression of Greek government from kings to democracy. After the clear progressions are defined, divide the students into groups of aristocracy, tyrants, and supporters of democracy. Have representatives of each group propose the benefits of their rule and then open the forum for a debate.

[English Language Learners, Cooperative Learning]

Levels 2 and 3: Have students write a narrative of the account of the life of a woman in each of these governments and then the life of a slave.

REVIEW AND ASSESS

Have students complete **Review Section 2.** Then have each student write a 10-item quiz based on information in the sections, exchange it with a classmate, and complete the quiz. Have students complete **Daily Quiz 5.1 and 5.2.**

RETEACH

Have students complete **Main Idea Activities 5.1 and 5.2.** Assign each student a **Reading Check** question from **Section 1 or 2.** Then have students create a drawing that illustrates the answer.
[English Language Learners]

CHALLENGE AND EXTEND

Have students read selections from the *Odyssey* and present orally. Discuss the epic hero and how his qualities and traits relate to some of the fictional heroes in current American culture (i.e., *Indiana Jones, James Bond*).

Lesson 2

(For use with Sections 3, 4, and 5, pp. 113–127)

OBJECTIVES

1. Analyze the society of Sparta.
2. Explain the development of democracy in Athens.
3. Explain the basis of Athens' economy.
4. Explain how the Persian Wars began and what the results of those wars were.
5. Explain how the Peloponnesian War began and its results.

BELLRINGER

As students enter the classroom, ask them to describe the types of government that developed in the Greek city-states. (*First Greek city-states were governed by kings. The kings were overthrown by aristocrats. Eventually the aristocrats were overthrown by tyrants who, in turn, were overthrown by citizens who set up popular governments*). Explain to students that in Section 3 they will learn about the government and society of two of the most important city-states: Sparta and Athens.

TEACH OBJECTIVE 1

Level 1: Assign students to one of the following categories of Sparta's inhabitants: half-citizens, helots, equals, ephors, boy soldiers, and Spartan girls. Have students write a journal entry in the role of their assigned character, describing daily life, Sparta, their role in Spartan society, and what the character thinks about that role.
[**English Language Learners**]

Levels 2 and 3: Have students write a newspaper editorial that explains the connections between the beginnings of Greek democracy and our own.

TEACH OBJECTIVE 2

Level 1: Write the names of the following Athenians on the chalkboard: Draco, Cleisthenes, Solon, and Peisistratus. Ask students to write in their journals what each leader added to the government. Discuss the responses.
[**English Language Learners**]

Levels 2 and 3: Ask students to compare the basic features of direct and representative democracies. (*All citizens participate in making the decision in a direct democracy, while citizens elect representatives to run the government for them in a representative democracy.*) Ask students if they think a direct democracy would work well in the United States, and why or why not.
[**English Language Learners, Cooperative Learning**]

TEACH OBJECTIVE 3

Level 1: Make a web diagram on the chalkboard with Athenian Economy at the center.

Then write Agriculture and Trade, circle each, and connect them to the first circle. Have students read the paragraphs on the Athenian economy and complete the web. (*Agriculture: poor soil, terracing, olives, grapes, figs, olive oil, wine. Trade: set up colonies, imported grain and foodstuff; exported vases and household items.*)
[**English Language Learners**]

Levels 2 and 3: Discuss with students the Athenian practice of setting up overseas colonies. Have them research the trade routes and colonies established. (*Some of the major ones: Magna Graecia, in southern Italy and Sicily, were the first areas of settlement. Corinth founded Syracuse; Tarentum was founded by Sparta; and Cyrene on the coast of Africa was founded by Massilia.*) Have students research what the colonies produced. (*They were largely farming communities, as the shortage of fertile land in Greece was the main reason for their existence.*)

TEACH OBJECTIVE 4

Level 1: Ask students if the final Greek victory successfully ended the conflict with Persia. (*Students should recognize that victory was incomplete because the threat from Persia continued.*) Have students identify the effects of the ongoing tensions between Greece and Persia. (*Greek city-states worked toward unity; Athens and other city-states formed Delian League.*)
[**English Language Learners, Cooperative Learning**]

Levels 2 and 3: Have students create an illustrated time line showing the significant events of the Persian Wars. (*546 B.C.: Persia conquers Greek colonies in Asia Minor; c. 500 B.C.: Greek colonies rebel/Athens becomes involved; 492 B.C.: Persia conquers Thrace and Macedonia; 490 B.C.: Athens defeats Persians at Battle of Marathon; 480 B.C.: Spartans inspire Greeks in loss of Battle of Thermopylae; Persians destroy Athens; 479 B.C.: Athens and Sparta defeat Persia*) Tell students that they should try to make their time line self-explanatory so that someone looking at it can understand the events of the Persian Wars and who took part in them.

TEACH OBJECTIVE 5

Level 1: Before students read about the Peloponnesian War, discuss with them the quotation by Thucydides on page 124. Ask students if they can think of other reasons that young Greeks might be eager to go to war. Then tell students that war finally broke out between Athens and Sparta. Lead a discussion about who students think will win the Peloponnesian War. Close by having them read about the war.
[English Language Learners, Cooperative Learning]

Levels 2 and 3: Present information on the influential Athenian leader, Pericles (*c. 495–429 B.C. He was one of the greatest Greek statesmen and was responsible for building the Parthenon and the Acropolis.*) Have students think about his political success in conjunction with the war with Persia. Ask them to read pp. 123–124 and then discuss in their groups what the connection is between the Greeks' victory over Persia and Athens' peak of power, culture, and wealth. (*Students should note that the unity among the city-states, the Delian League, and the defeat of the Persians gave the Greeks confidence.*) Have each group present its ideas to the class.
[Cooperative Learning]

REVIEW AND ASSESS

Have students complete **Review Sections 3, 4, and 5.** Then have groups of students construct a crossword puzzle using all of the terms and individuals mentioned in the Section Reviews. Have students complete **Daily Quiz 5.3, 5.4, and 5.5.**

RETEACH

Have students complete **Main Idea Activities 5.3, 5.4, and 5.5.** Then pair students to answer the **Reading Check** questions in **Sections 3, 4, and 5.**
[English Language Learners, Cooperative Learning]

CHALLENGE AND EXTEND

Organize students into groups representing Athenians and Spartans or other members of the Delian League. Have groups discuss ways to settle the disagreements among the city-states and present their solutions to the class.

Greek Discoveries

GOAL

In this activity, students will learn more about the significant historical archaeological discoveries in Mycenae.

PLANNING

- **Purpose** This activity may be used in combination with teacher-directed lessons, as an enrichment activity, or as a performance-based assessment of content mastery.

- **Suggested Time** Plan to spend two lesson blocks and one homework assignment on this activity. Provide time for the presentation of the narratives at the end of the lesson.

- **Teaching Team** At least one social studies teacher and one language arts teacher should take part in teaching this activity.

- **Group Size** This activity will work as a small group activity or for individual students.

- **Materials and Resources** Read a brief account of Heinrich Schliemann's life and discoveries. Have students consult the text on Mycenae. Allow them to research the dig and the city on their own in preparation for the creative, first-person narrative they will write.

IMPLEMENTATION

1. Give students an overview of the activity by explaining that they will first hear the accounts of Heinrich Schliemann's contribution to Greek history. Then they will each be asked to research additional information on Mycenae. Finally, they will each be asked to write a creative, first-person narrative of Schliemann's discovery of the golden death mask in Mycenae, incorporating the historical information they have researched.

2. Read these brief accounts: Born in Germany in 1822, Heinrich Schliemann, the son of a poor pastor, adored the stories of the Homeric legends of Greek heroes. Schliemann worked his way from being a penniless errand boy to a wealthy entrepre-

neur. Though he had to leave his formal classical studies because of lack of money, when he became wealthy, he determined to spend his fortune finding the remains of the Greek heroes he loved in Homer. In 1876, in Mycenae, Schliemann discovered (among many other treasures) the golden death mask he declared to be the face of Agamemnon.

3. Ask the students to read pages 108–109 and to do additional research on the archaeological dig in Mycenae. After they have compiled a list of facts and artifacts from the dig (which should include extensive quantities of gold masks, cups, jewelry, and weapons), instruct them on writing a first-person narrative of the account of the dig.

4. Instruct students on the elements of a well written narrative. Remind them to include dialogue, to describe the setting using all five senses (taste, touch, smell, hearing, and seeing), and to create tension and character. Remind students to write their narrative as if they are Heinrich Schliemann. Have them review the facts of Schleimann's life and his fascination with the Greeks.

5. Remind students to incorporate their research into their account. Have them research what happens at an archaeological dig by consulting an introductory guide to archaeology. They should use details about a "dig" in their narrative. They also should research information about the Mycenaen site, noting, for example, Mycenae's proximity to the sea, the olive groves, the elevation of the site, etc. Students may even want to look for descriptions in the *Odyssey* by Homer to find details for their narrative.

6. Have students exchange essays and read for editorial purposes.

7. Conclude by calling on volunteers to read their creative account to the class. Then discuss with students the differences of the approaches, but that the central evidence that bears that the Mycenaean palaces were centers of political and economic control with a considerable degree of sophistication.

ASSESSMENT

1. Assess students' work by their use of historical information, combined with their ability to fulfill the creative writing components.

2. Additional grades can be based on students' participation in the presentation.

Golden Age and Hellenistic Time Line

Have students look at the time line on pages 128 and 129. Write column headings on the chalkboard that relate to the following categories on the time line: *Global Events, Daily Life, The Arts, Politics, Business and Finance, and Science and Technology).* Have students, in turn, fill in each column with the events listed on the time line for each category. Tell students that in this chapter they will learn about the development of Greek culture and how that culture was spread throughout the ancient world.

Lesson 1
(For use with Sections 1 and 2, pp. 127–137)

OBJECTIVES

1. Explain why the 400s B.C. are considered the golden age of Greek art and architecture.

2. Examine how Greek art of the golden age reflected the Greeks' view of themselves and the world.

3. Explain the basic ideas of Socrates, Plato, and Aristotle.

4. Identify the achievements of Greek mathematicians and scientists of the golden age.

5. Identify the literary forms that originated or flourished during Greece's golden age.

BELLRINGER

As students enter the classroom, write the term "golden age" on the board. Ask what mental images are evoked when this term is used to describe a period in history. *(Responses should suggest a cultural high point.)* Ask what qualities in the arts must be present for a period in a society's history to be called a "golden age." *(possible responses: high status for the arts, excellence in design and craft, enduring value)* Tell students that in Section 1 they will learn about the arts in the golden age of Greece.

TEACH OBJECTIVE 1

Level 1: Copy the following examples of art and architecture on the board: Parthenon; vases; Myron's *The Discus Thrower;* statues by Praxiteles. Ask the students to write the characteristics of each example. *(Parthenon: balanced proportions, columns; vases: everyday life and myths, graceful, natural movement, light and shade show contour and depth; Myron's* The Discus Thrower: *almost 40-feet high, one of the "Seven Wonders of the World"; statues of Phidias: lifelike and natural bodies)*
[**English Language Learners**]

Levels 2 and 3: Show students photographs of Greek sculpture. Ask them what they notice about the poses and physical shape of the bodies of the sculpture. Have them write what ideals the Greeks must have valued from their art. *(the human body, fitness, beauty, strength)* Ask them to make connections with today's values. What similarities do they see in our "Nike" culture? How have we inherited some of the Greek's values? *(glorification of the body, exercise)*
[**English Language Learners, Cooperative Learning**]

TEACH OBJECTIVE 2

Level 1: Have students discuss the ideals expressed in the Parthenon. *(perfectly balanced proportions, usefulness, beauty, pride in the city-state)*
[**English Language Learners, Cooperative Learning**]

Levels 2 and 3: Have students select a piece of Greek art and explain how it expresses the four basic Greek ideals.

TEACH OBJECTIVE 3

Level 1: Organize students into three groups and assign each group to study and represent the ideas of Socrates, Plato, or Aristotle. Students may decide whether to vote on one spokesperson or to allow any member to speak as the philosopher. Ask questions such as: How

do you view education? The world? What special views do you hold? What are your views on the government? (**Socrates:** *believed that education is the key to personal growth; he insisted that students be trained to think for themselves, forced students to test their own values and ideas; based his teachings on asking questions, not memorization.* **Plato:** *Founded the Academy; believed that all material things were imperfect expressions of perfect and universal ideas, or forms; believed perfection could never be reached in the physical world; saw the human being as consisting of two parts—the soul and the body; thought the ideal government was an aristocracy.* **Aristotle:** *believed everything had to be studied according to organization; collected, described, and classified plants and animals; thought monarchy, aristocracy, and democracy were equally good forms of government, however, they could easily be corrupted.*) You may want students to role-play among themselves the philosophers discussing the last question.
[**English Language Learners, Cooperative Learning**]

Levels 2 and 3: Engage students in a dialogue by asking such questions as "What is philosophy?" "With what questions is a philosopher concerned?" and "What is the difference between philosophy and science?" Tell students they have just taken part in the Socratic method of teaching. Challenge them to carry on a short lesson with a particular theme, such as honesty or happiness, using the Socratic method. They should take turns playing the role of Socrates.
[**English Language Learners**]

TEACH OBJECTIVE 4

All Levels: Ask students to write down the contribution the following men made to Greek science and medicine: Pythagoras, Aristotle, Hippocrates.
[**English Language Learners, Cooperative Learning**]

TEACH OBJECTIVE 5

Level 1: Write the following literary genres on the board: *History, Tragedy, Comedy.* Ask stu-

dents what the Greeks contributed to the development of each. Conclude by asking how all three contribute to our knowledge and understanding of ancient Greeks. (*Histories record important events. Tragedies and comedies give insights into values.*)
[**English Language Learners, Cooperative Learning**]

Levels 2 and 3: Have students choose a play written by one of the Greek dramatists discussed in this section, and report to the class on its theme, plot, and characters.
[**English Language Learners**]

REVIEW AND ASSESS

Have students complete **Review Section 2.** Then have each student write a 10-item quiz based on information in the sections, exchange it with a classmate, and complete the quiz. Have students complete **Daily Quiz 6.1 and 6.2.**

RETEACH

Have students complete **Main Idea Activities 6.1 and 6.2.** Assign each student a **Reading Check** question from **Section 1 or 2.** Then have students create a drawing that illustrates the answer.
[**English Language Learners**]

CHALLENGE AND EXTEND

Have students access the Internet through the HRW Go Web site to find information about a Greek mathematician or scientist. Learn how his ideas were developed and are used today. Then ask students to prepare a short report that summarizes their findings.

Lesson 2

(For use with Sections 3, 4, and 5, pp. 138–145)

OBJECTIVES

1. Detail how Philip II of Macedon paved the way for cultural change.

2. Examine what Alexander the Great accomplished.

3. Identify the factors that contributed to the breakup of Alexander's empire.

4. Describe how society changed during the Hellenistic Age.

5. Explain how philosophers of the Hellenistic Age viewed ethics.

6. Identify how Hellenistic scientists added to the existing body of knowledge.

BELLRINGER

As students enter the classroom, ask what it means when we say that the United States is a multicultural or pluralistic society. *(Many different ethnic and racial groups live in one nation.)* Discuss the concept of one general American culture in this multicultural society and how the subcultures help create it. Tell students that in Section 4 they will learn about the spread of "Greek-like," or Hellenistic culture throughout Alexander's empire.

TEACH OBJECTIVE 1

Level 1: Have students list the events that led to Philip's conquest of Greece. *(Greek city-states are weakened by war and disunited; Philip becomes king of Macedon; recruits paid army and applies Greek idea of phalanxes; takes control of northern Athenian colonies; moves into Greece; some, like Demosthenes, oppose; Athens fights, but city-states remain disunited; one by one city-states fall; Thebes and Athens defeated at Chaeronea in 338 B.C.)*
[English Language Learners]

Levels 2 and 3: Ask students to explain the irony of Philip's conquering the Greeks. *(He had been a hostage in Greece when young; he borrowed the idea of phalanxes from the Greeks.)* Then ask them to choose a point of view about Philip—whether he was a savior who could unify Greece or someone who would threaten its freedom. Have them write a paragraph identifying and supporting their point of view.

TEACH OBJECTIVE 2

Level 1: Write the following goals of Alexander on the board: (1) Conquer the world, (2) Spread Greek culture, (3) Manage an empire. Organize the class into pairs or triads. Have each group use these goals as a basis for a chart that records what Alexander did to accomplish each goal and that assesses whether or not he accomplished it. Call on volunteers to explain their charts to the class.
[English Language Learners]

Levels 2 and 3: Ask students to consider the Greek influence over the countries Alexander the Great conquered. In what ways would the culture of these other countries be changed? *(art, language, architecture, literature, government, religion, etc.)* Read to students the quote from the Greek traveler Plutarch, who said, "Because of Alexander Homer became widely read [in Asia] . . . the Gedrosians sang the tragedies of Euripides." Have several groups of students research one aspect of Grecian influence on Persia and report their findings to the class.
[English Language Learners, Cooperative Learning]

TEACH OBJECTIVE 3

Level 1: Discuss whether Alexander's empire really was "one world." Ask how its size and composition may have undermined its unity. *(Its people were diverse, and ultimate authority was distant.)* Ask what other factors led to the empire's breakup. *(fighting among generals, the Roman invasion)*
[English Language Learners]

Levels 2 and 3: Ask students to consider how Alexander's ambition ultimately worked against him after his death. Have them write about the difference of Alexander's goals with the Greek beliefs in harmony, balance, order, and moderation.

TEACH OBJECTIVE 4

Level 1: Call on students to identify ways in which Greek society changed during the Hellenistic Age. List responses on the board. *(growth of trade, cities as centers of trade and learning, thriving middle class, widespread* education, new values, more rights for women, new idea of "Greek") Then explore with the class how some of the changes are related.

TEACH OBJECTIVE 5

Level 1: Write the following philosophical approaches on the board: Cynicism, Skepticism, Stoicism, Epicureanism. Ask students to write down characteristics of each. *(Cynicism: live simply, no regard for wealth, pleasure, or status; Skepticism: changing universe, uncertain knowledge, acceptance; Stoicism, divine reason directs world, acceptance of fate; Epicureanism: seek pleasure, avoid pain, limit desires to avoid suffering)*
[**English Language Learners, Cooperative Learning**]

Levels 2 and 3: Ask students to think about how women having property rights would change society. *(Women could have economic independence, inheritances, etc.)* What changes will occur after women have property? Have them write a first-person narration of a woman who has just purchased her first piece of property.
[**Cooperative Learning**]

TEACH OBJECTIVE 6

Level 1: Have students work in pairs to note the various scientists discussed in the text and the accomplishments of each. You might also want students to prepare questions for the presenters in the Level 3 activity for this objective.
[**Cooperative Learning**]

Level 2: Ask students to discuss or write a paragraph describing Hellenistic science as largely "knowledge for knowledge's sake." Then have them discuss or write a second paragraph predicting how this concept might have changed if slavery were not so prevalent in the empire. Students should support their point of view.
[**Cooperative Learning**]

Level 3: Have students play the roles of Euclid, Archimedes, Aristarchus, Hipparchus, and Eratosthenes. Ask each to explain the scientist's work to the class and discuss how it spread to other cultures (*Euclid: contributed important work to the development of geometry; Archimedes: calculated the value of pi, the ratio of the circumference of a circle to its diameter; explained how levers work and invented many machines, including the compound and the pulley, and the Archimedes screw; Aristarchus: believed that the earth moved around the sun; Hipparchus: used trigonometry to predict eclipses and the sun and the moon to calculate the length of the year; Eratosthenes: calculated the distance around the earth with amazing accuracy)*
[**Cooperative Learning**]

REVIEW AND ASSESS

Have students complete the **Review Sections 3, 4, and 5.** Have them complete the graphic organizer or the speech exercise in Section 6.3 and **Daily Quiz 6.3, 6.4, and 6.5.**

RETEACH

Have students complete **Main Idea Activities 6.3, 6.4, and 6.5.** Then pair students to answer the **Reading Check** questions in **Sections 3, 4, and 5.**
[**English Language Learners, Cooperative Learning**]

CHALLENGE AND EXTEND

Organize students into groups to create maps of the Hellenistic world. Each group should draw its map and add illustrations of sculptures, buildings, reliefs of rulers, and other period art and artifacts at appropriate locations. Each image should include a descriptive caption.

Greece's Lasting Influence

GOAL

In this activity, students will learn how Greece's Hellenistic period remains a major touchstone for poets of the past and present.

PLANNING

- **Purpose** This activity may be used in combination with teacher-directed lessons, or as an enrichment activity.

- **Suggested Time** Plan to spend two lesson blocks and one homework assignment on this activity. Provide time for the presentation of the narratives at the end of the lesson.

- **Teaching Team** At least one social studies teacher and one language arts teacher should take part in teaching this activity.

- **Group Size** This activity will work as a small group activity or for individual students.

- **Materials and Resources** Jonathan Keats' "Ode on a Grecian Urn" and Section 1 on Grecian vases.

  Additional library sources on Greek art and poets who have been influenced by these works.

IMPLEMENTATION

1. Give students an overview of the activity by explaining that they will first read and discuss Keats' famous poem "Ode on a Grecian Urn." Then they will each be asked to write about Keats' poem. After they have completed their first response to Keats, they will be asked to compose their own poem based on Grecian art, philosophy, and religion. Then they will be asked to research another poet who has used Greek art, literature, or thought for inspiration. (A list of poets could include: Alfred Lord Tennyson, H.D., William Butler Yeats, e.e. cummings, Percy Bysshe Shelley, etc.) Finally, they will each be asked to write a paper describing the Greek influence on the poet of their choice and they will present their ideas to the class.

2. Hand out Keats' poem and read aloud. Ask students to describe in writing what they are visualizing in each stanza. (*Students should note young lovers about to kiss, a boy piping a song, a priest leading a cow to sacrifice.*) Then have them look at actual Hellenistic vases that depict similar images. Explain that Keats is looking at a Grecian Urn and finds the piece inspirational and meaningful.

3. Ask the students to answer these important questions about the poem in context to what they have learned about Grecian ideals. Is beauty truth and truth beauty? (*The Greeks and Keats would say yes. Do students agree with this?*) Why does Keats value this vase? (*Because of its immortality. The art will never suffer from change or ultimately death. It will exist after his death and our own.*) How is the vase like his verse? (*It, too, is immortal.*) Is it true that "heard melodies are sweet, but those unheard/Are sweeter?" What does Keats mean by that line? (*Sometimes experiencing something in art is superior to experiencing it in life.*) Do the students agree with Keats' view? Why is it significant that the vase has young lovers, a musician, and a priest? (*represents several facets of life: love, religion, art*)

4. Bring in a photograph of an object of Greek art. (*Suggestions: winged Nike, the Caryatids, the statue of Dionysus, the Elgin Marbles*) Ask the students to begin by describing the work with descriptive language. Then ask them to create three metaphors and three similes about the work. Ask them if the piece evokes an emotion or thought like Keats had on the Grecian urn. Explain rhyme scheme and rhythm. Ask them to create a poem from their observations of the piece and share it with the class.

5. Finally, ask students to research an individual poet who was also influenced by the

Greeks. Present them with a beginning list of poets: Tennyson, H.D., William Butler Yeats, e.e. cummings, Percy Bysshe Shelley. Ask them to select and research the work of one poet and the influence Greek art, thought, or philosophy had on one of the poet's poems. Have them write a paper on their discoveries tracing the Greek influence on the particular work.

6. Conclude by calling on volunteers to present what they have discovered to the class. Then discuss with students their findings.

ASSESSMENT

Assess students' work by their participation in class discussion, the quality of their poems, and the quality of their research, writing, and presentation skills.

Interpreting the Map of Ancient Italy

Have students examine the map on page 150. Have students locate Rome on the map. Ask them to use this map and the information on page 150 to list advantages to Rome's location.

Lesson 1

(For use with Sections 1 and 2, pp. 146–158)

OBJECTIVES

1. Identify the role geography played in the development of Italy and Rome.

2. Describe the form of government of the Roman Republic.

3. Explain the Conflict of the Orders and how it changed the early Roman Republic.

4. Compare and contrast the roles of citizens and noncitizens as Rome expanded its power.

5. Discuss the Punic Wars and how Rome gained control over Carthage.

6. Explain how expansion changed the Roman Republic.

BELLRINGER

As students enter the classroom, ask them to write down Greek advances in the arts, architecture, medicine, mathematics, and the sciences during the Classical and Hellenistic periods. Students should write a brief description of each advance and explain how it contributed to the civilization. Have volunteers share their responses with the class. Tell students that, in Section 1, they will learn how contact with these ideas helped the small but energetic culture of Rome to grow.

TEACH OBJECTIVE 1

All Levels: Have students recall how Athens' geographical significance influenced the cul-

ture and people. Have students write about the river Tiber's importance to the city of Rome.
[English Language Learners, Cooperative Learning]

TEACH OBJECTIVE 2

Level 1: Have students work in pairs to create an organizational chart of the Roman Republic government. Instruct them to include all governing bodies and officials.
[English Language Learners, Cooperative Learning]

Levels 2 and 3: Have students list duties of the assemblies and write an explanation of how the tribunes influenced assembly decisions.

TEACH OBJECTIVE 3

Level 1: Copy the following graphic organizer on the board, omitting the italicized answers. Call on students to identify characteristics of these two groups of Romans before the Conflict of the Orders. Discuss what rights the plebeians gained over time.
[English Language Learners, Cooperative Learning]

Levels 2 and 3: Ask students the importance of the plebeians' victory in forcing the patricians to engrave their laws on tablets and to place them in the public forum. What can the students infer about what life was like for the plebeians? Have them write their thoughts in their journals and then read them allowed.
[English Language Learners]

TEACH OBJECTIVE 4

All Levels: Ask students to write down the roles and rights of citizens and non citizens under Roman rule.
[English Language Learners, Cooperative Learning]

TEACH OBJECTIVE 5

Levels 2 and 3: Ask each student to write the answer to the question, "How did Rome gain control over the Mediterranean?" Ask that the following be explained in the essay: Punic Wars, Hannibal, Scipio, and Spartacus.
[English Language Learners]

TEACH OBJECTIVE 6

Level 1: Have students list changes that resulted from Roman expansion. Then ask them to identify the challenges posed to Rome by its expansion and to suggest possible solutions.

REVIEW AND ASSESS

Have students complete **Review Sections 1 and 2.** Have students work in pairs and create a graphic organizer that demonstrates how the main ideas of the two sections are related. Have students complete **Daily Quiz 7.1 and 7.2.**

RETEACH

Have students complete **Main Idea Activities 7.1 and 7.2.** Assign each student a **Reading Check** question from Section 1 or 2. Then have students work in pairs to create a timeline that notes the major events of the early Roman Empire.
[English Language Learners]

CHALLENGE AND EXTEND

After students read *History Maker: Spartacus,* have them produce short skits about one aspect of the slave revolt. Encourage props and/or costumes if time permits.

Lesson 2

(For use with Sections 3 and 4, pp. 158–167)

OBJECTIVES

1. Identify the political events in Rome during the first century B.C. that helped weaken the Roman Republic.

2. Explain how the reign of Julius Caesar served as a transition between the Roman Republic and the Roman Empire.

3. Describe the events and conditions that marked the first two centuries of the Roman Empire.

4. Explain how the Romans built a strong and unified empire.

5. Describe the daily lives and occupations of Roman citizens.

6. Explain the role of science and the arts in the Roman Empire.

BELLRINGER

As students enter the classroom, ask them to write a list of the challenges that faced Rome as it expanded after the Punic Wars. Ask students how they think these problems might have weakened the Roman Republic. Tell students that, in Section 3, they will learn that these challenges ultimately brought about the end of the Roman Republic and the rise of the Empire.

TEACH OBJECTIVE 1

Level 1: Copy the following cause-and-effect flowchart on the board, omitting the italicized answers, and have students complete it after reading Section 3.

- Gracchus brothers introduce reform = *Angry senators kill both Gracchus brothers*

- Violence/primary tool of Roman politics = *Leaders recruit personal armies*

- Sulla marches on Rome: civil war = *Sulla establishes dictatorship*
[English Language Learners]

Levels 2 and 3: Ask students to expand on the flow chart by writing the opening to a book on Roman history. Ask them to be creative in their writing style, but to use the facts they have already learned from Section 3.

TEACH OBJECTIVE 2

Level 1: As students read the section "Caesar in Power" on page 159, have them complete a web diagram that includes characteristics and events related to Caesar. Then draw a web on the board and fill it in with students' responses.
[English Language Learners]

Levels 2 and 3: Ask students to discuss why Caesar became a great leader. What foundations did he lay for the Roman Empire? With this established, have students write an essay on how Julius Caesar's reign was a transition between the Republic and the Empire.
[**English Language Learners, Cooperative Learning**]

TEACH OBJECTIVE 3

Level 1: Have students create a scrap book of the important events that marked the first two centuries of the Roman Empire.
[**English Language Learners**]

Levels 2 and 3: Assign pairs of students to study a Roman leader of this time and to write a profile that explains the leader's significance. Encourage students to use their textbooks, the library, the Internet, and other sources.

TEACH OBJECTIVE 4

Level 1: Ask students to list the important contributions that these three items had to the strength of the empire: Roman Army (*kept peace, stationed along frontiers, soldiers became citizens*), Government and Law (*revised Twelve Tables, provincial officer, strong emperor, enforced law, kept order*), and Trade and Transportation (*encouraged widespread trade, made roads and bridges*)
[**English Language Learners, Cooperative Learning**]

Levels 2 and 3: Ask students to choose one of the three aspects (Government/Law, Trade/Transportation, or Roman Army) and research more in depth about the contribution their topic had on the growing Empire. Have students share their findings with the class.
[**Cooperative Learning**]

TEACH OBJECTIVE 5

Group students and inform them that they are creative consultants for a movie to be set in the Roman Empire during the Pax Romana. Tell them that creative consultants advise filmmakers on the historical aspects of a movie. Their job is to check for historical accuracy and to offer plot advice. Each group is to work together on one aspect of daily life or contribution to the arts and sciences in the Roman Empire. Groups should put together a portfolio of images, diagrams, and narrative descriptions. Encourage students to be creative by building models or developing illustrative materials and costume designs. Detailed information should be included to help the prop and set builders, make-up artists, wardrobe specialists, and others working on the film.

TEACH OBJECTIVE 6

Level 1 and 2: Have students discuss how life in the Roman Empire presented a complex picture of great progress and achievement contrasted against corruption, injustice, and violence. Be sure they support their views with specific examples.

REVIEW AND ASSESS

Have students complete the **Review Sections 3 and 4**. Then have groups of students construct a crossword puzzle using all of the terms and individuals mentioned in the Section Reviews. Have students complete **Daily Quiz 7.3 and 7. 4**.

RETEACH

Have students complete **Main Idea Activities 7.3, 7.4**. Then pair students to answer the **Reading Check** questions in Sections 3 and 4 and 5.
[**English Language Learners, Cooperative Learning**]

Lesson 3

(For use with section 5 and 6, pp. 168–177)

1. Describe how the conditions that the Jews faced in Judaea contributed to the rise of Christianity.

2. Identify the difficulties early Christians experienced in the Roman Empire.

3. Discuss the changes that occurred during the late Roman Empire that helped establish Christianity and stabilize the church.

4. Identify the problems the Roman Empire had to deal with during the A.D. 200s.

5. Describe how the reigns of Diocletian and Constantine slowed the decline of the empire.

6. List the factors that led to the final decline of the Roman Empire in the West.

BELLRINGER

As students enter the classroom, have them look again at the map of the Roman Empire on page 263 of their textbooks. Ask students what they know about Roman religion and the religion of groups in the areas Rome controlled. Tell students that, in Section 5, they will learn about the rise of Christianity in the Roman Empire.

TEACH OBJECTIVE 1

Level 1: Have students draw time lines and enter the events that signaled increasing problems between the Roman government and the Jews of Judaea.

TEACH OBJECTIVE 1 AND 2

Level 3: Have students write an analysis of the message of Christianity and relate it to the spread of the religion. Remind them to use standard grammar, spelling, sentence structure, and punctuation.

TEACH OBJECTIVE 3

Level 1: Have students write down the major figures/events in the development of Christianity. (*Jesus, Spread of Christianity, Acceptance and Organization*) Then have them explain the importance of each.

TEACH OBJECTIVE 4

Level 1: Draw a chart on the board titled *Problems in Roman Empire* and have students

complete it as they read "Troubled Times Arise" on page 172. Then ask students to use a problem-solving process to determine whether they think these problems were insurmountable.

TEACH OBJECTIVE 5

Level 3: Discuss how to use a problem-solving process. Then have students write edicts for both Diocletian and Constantine to deliver to the Roman people announcing new policies and reforms that the emperor hopes will solve the problems facing the Roman Empire. If time permits, have some of the students give their speeches to the class.

TEACH OBJECTIVE 6

Level 1: Discuss the role that the barbarian invasions played in the fall of Rome. Have students compare the map on page 174 with the map on page 170. Ask students for the results of the invasions.

REVIEW AND ASSESS

Have students complete the **Review Sections 5 and 6**. Have students complete **Daily Quiz 7.5 and 7.6**.

RETEACH

Have students complete **Main Idea Activities 7.5 and 7.6**. Then pair students to answer the **Reading Check** questions in Sections 5 and 6. Have each student create an annotated time line of the fall of the western empire.
[**English Language Learners, Cooperative Learning**]

CHALLENGE AND EXTEND

Have students create collages that highlight Roman legacies in the modern world, including contributions to the arts and sciences.

A Roman Newspaper

GOAL

In this activity, students will learn how to analyze and incorporate persuasive devices in the creation of a newspaper about the life of Julius Caesar and the political circumstances surrounding his death. In creating features, articles and graphics for the newspaper, students will demonstrate an understanding of Roman history and culture.

PLANNING

- **Purpose** This activity incorporates teacher-directed lessons and individual and group assignments. It could be used as a teaching model for the study of the Roman Republic or as an enrichment activity.

- **Suggested Time** Plan to spend two lesson blocks and two homework assignments on this activity. Provide time for students to share and discuss their newspapers.

- **Teaching Team** At least one social studies teacher and one language arts teacher should take part in teaching this activity.

- **Group Size** This activity will work as a small group activity or for individual students.

- **Materials and Resources**

  - Copies of *Julius Caesar* by William Shakespeare

  - Background notes for the teacher on the life and career of Julius Caesar

  - Student photocopies of Rubric 23: Newspapers from *Portfolio and Performance Assessment for Social Studies*

  - Variety of illustrated reference books from the library on Roman art and culture

IMPLEMENTATION

1. Give students an overview of this activity by explaining that, while they read Shakespeare's play *Julius Caesar*, they will study the history and culture of the Roman Republic leading up to Caesar's death. Then they will produce a newspaper incorporating historical information and persuasive techniques in news and feature articles, editorials, and graphics.

2. Focusing on Section 1 of Chapter 7, have students draw a diagram of Roman government, including all governing bodies and officials, power of each body or official, method of selection for each body and lines of command. Lead a discussion of the impact of expansion on the Roman Republic. Some questions to consider are: How did the acquisition of grain, slaves, and wealth both benefit and harm the Roman Republic? What was their impact on Roman social structure and government? How did this change set the stage for Caesar's career and death?

3. Before reading *Julius Caesar* by Shakespeare, ask the students to consider some ethical issues surrounding the play's themes.

4. Assign parts and read excerpts of *Julius Caesar* aloud, or obtain an audiotape of the play to listen to with the class. Introduce students to the persuasive techniques of emotional appeals (including appeals to pity, pride, and national interest), logical appeals, and verbal irony. While reading the persuasive speeches in Act III (Brutus' speech to the Romans, scene 2, lines 12–26; Antony's speech to the Romans, scene 2, lines 63–217), have students list the uses of these persuasive techniques and their impact on the Romans in the play.

5. Using Sections 1–4 of Chapter 7 and available reference books, have students create a special edition newspaper from Rome, dated March 16, 44 B.C. Each student should be responsible for contributing one news article, one feature article, one editorial, and one graphic. News articles should accurately report on an actual event occurring within the one hundred years of Roman works, advice columns, birth and wedding announcements, obituaries, surveys, recipes, and fashion notes. Editorials should comment on problems facing the

Roman Republic and must include the use of persuasive techniques. Graphics might include advertisements, puzzles, poems, comic strips, and illustrations accompanying articles. All information and graphics must be historically accurate. Students could produce newspapers in groups or as a whole class. Have each student or group share their best example of a persuasive technique and the most interesting fact they learned about Roman culture.

ASSESSMENT

1. Assess students' presentations, use Rubric 23: *Newspaper in Portfolio and Performance Assessment for Social Studies.*

2. Additional grades can be based on class participation, diagrams of Roman government, lists of persuasive techniques in *Julius Caesar,* and written responses to selected discussion questions.

Interpreting the Map of Africa

Have students locate the Congo Basin on the map on page 183. Prompt them to discuss how natural barriers, such as a river that is hard to navigate, a rain forest, mountains, and deadly insects might affect the culture of a region.

Lesson 1

(For use with Sections 1 and 2, pp. 182–190)

OBJECTIVES

1. Identify the cause-effect roles that geographic features had on early Africa's human cultures.
2. Describe how historians have learned about the migrations of early African peoples.
3. Explain the predominant patterns of life in early African societies.
4. Explain how geographic, economic, and cultural factors helped Kush develop as an independent kingdom.
5. Analyze the geographic, economic, and cultural factors that helped Aksum develop as an independent kingdom.

BELLRINGER

As students enter the classroom, ask them to write some of the methods scientists use to learn about the history and culture of early civilizations. Students should also write a brief description of each method. *(excavating cities and buildings, studying artifacts, and analyzing the spread of languages)* Tell students that, in Section 1, they will learn how scientists have learned about the cultures and civilizations of early sub-Saharan Africa.

TEACH OBJECTIVE 1

Level 1: Draw a large outline map of Africa. Divide the class into three groups and assign one of the following regions to each: desert, savanna, and tropical rain forest. Have each group choose a color to code its region on the map and design symbols to represent the natural vegetation, crops, and livestock suited to the region. *(rain forest: green/trees and yams; savanna: brown/grasses, sorghum, millet, rice; desert: yellow/cattle)* Have each group complete its part of the map.
[English Language Learners]

Level 2: Referring to the map on p. 183, have students write descriptions of the Sahara Desert, the savannas, tropical rain forests, and the jungle. Ask them to describe the physical conditions of each area, the amount of rain, or lack of rain, the vegetation, and the weather patterns. *(The Sahara covers one-fourth of the continent. One thousand years ago it was fertile, but over the course of centuries, the area has become dry and barren; rainfall is sparse; and farming is difficult. The savannas are dotted with few trees; farming includes grains, such as sorghum, millet, and rice; the land has vast stretches of dry grasslands. Tropical rain forests receive 100 inches of rain a year; dense tangles of plants are located in central and western Africa; farmers grow root crops, such as yams.)*
[English Language Learners, Cooperative Learning]

Level 3: Ask students to recall the influence trade routes had on other cultures they have studied. *(Greece, Rome, etc.)* How were those countries changed because of the trade routes? *(economic wealth, exchange of ideas, their culture spread over a large geographical area)* How does this region differ from the two mentioned above? *(The mountains and rain forests were barriers between groups of people and the rivers were blocked by rapids which prevented trade.)* Ask students to write a one-page paper on the value of the oral traditions in the sub-Saharan Africa culture to historians and archaeologists. Remind them to create a thesis statement: the central idea of the paper that expresses the author's idea about the subject. Encourage students to use specific facts to support their thesis.

TEACH OBJECTIVE 2

Level 1: Have students create an inverted tree diagram that will help them to remember some of the methods scholars use to analyze limited evidence from early Africa civilizations. Instruct them to include examples of language, cultural exchange, and other evidence. Use the following sample diagram to help students get started:

Language: *spread of languages, oral tradition, new words, stories, songs, poems.* **Cultural Exchange:** *music, styles of art.* **Other:** *spread in cultivated plants, changes in climate, excavation of artifacts*
[**English Language Learners, Cooperative Learning**]

Level 2: Have students research some well known languages in Africa (Zulu, Makua, Shona, Bemba, Swahili, Ganda, Kongo, or Fang). Have them explain in an essay the development of the language. Consult go.hrw.com, keyword: SP3 WH8.

Level 3: Ask students to research important phrases in one African language. Have them memorize how to greet others, how to say thank you and goodbye. Have them do this in front of the class. Finally, ask them to create a phrase/vocabulary book for their chosen language.

TEACH OBJECTIVE 3

Level 1: Lead students in a class discussion about patterns of life in early Africa. Discussion should include the village as the basic unit of society, the role of women as farmers, matrilineal inheritance of property, religions with gods linked to nature and human activities, and the role of the village elders.
[**English Language Learners, Cooperative Learning**]

Levels 2: Have students expand on their in-class discussion on the patterns of life in Africa. Have them write a short essay on one of the following: the role of women as farmers, matrilineal inheritance of property, religions with gods

linked to nature and human activities, or the role of village elders.
[**English Language Learners**]

Level 3: Have students research the role of women in Africa today. Have them identify where matrilineal inheritance is practiced today. Then ask them to write how they think this would influence the way women are viewed. How does it differ from other cultures where women take on the husband's family name, or where having a son to carry on the family business is considered preferable? Have them present their ideas to the class.
[**English Language Learners, Cooperative Learners**]

TEACH OBJECTIVE 4

All Levels: Have students read the material titled "Kush Arises" on pages 187–188 of the text. Then have them construct a chart that lists the geographic, economic, political, and cultural factors that led to Kush's development and fall. (*Kush thrived as an important place of trade, and then became a distinct kingdom. It maintained close economic and cultural ties to Egypt and was governed by the pharaohs. Communication between Kush and Egypt diminished. Kush conquered Upper Egypt and ruled for about 50 years. Assyrians invaded and weakened the kingdom.*)
[**English Language Learners, Cooperative Learning**]

Levels 2 and 3: Have students take one of the topics above (geography, economic or political systems, or cultural factors) and have them research the topic in detail and present a short speech on the importance of the feature to the rise or fall of the Kush society (*relationship with Egypt, trade, Assyrians*)

TEACH OBJECTIVE 5

Level 1: Make a chart titled Aksum, similar to the one for Kush, on the chalkboard. Have students read the section about Aksum on pages 188 and 190 and study the map on page 188. Then ask students to complete the chart by working alone or in pairs to identify geo-

graphic, economic, political, and cultural factors in the development of the independent kingdom of Aksum.
[**English Language Learners, Cooperative Learning**]

Level 2: Ask students what geographic factors are important for the growth of trade. _(location on a river, seaports, clear routes for trade)_ Have students look at the map on page 188 and make a list of ways Aksum's location helped it become a trading kingdom. Have students discuss how Aksum's power increased by conquering Kush. _(Aksum took control of the trade in eastern Africa. With Kush conquered, Aksum could freely trade with Egypt.)_ Have them draw their own map of Egypt, Kush, and Aksum on the Red Sea and write a description of the importance of the Red Sea to the trading practices of Aksum.
[**English Language Learners**]

Level 3: Ask students to research Aksum's exports, including gold, rhinoceros horns, ivory, incense, and decorative obsidian stone. Have them find photographs of the goods and discuss how they were used in Egypt. Have them present their findings and photographs to the class.

REVIEW AND ASSESS

Have students complete the **Review Sections 1 and 2.** Ask students to make note cards of important events. Have students complete **Daily Quiz 8.1 and 8.2.**

RETEACH

Have students complete **Main Idea Activities 8.1 and 8.2.** Assign each student a **Reading Check** question from **Section 1 or 2.** Then have students create a drawing that illustrates the answer.
[**English Language Learners**]

CHALLENGE AND EXTEND

Have students work in small groups to use the process of historical inquiry to conduct research on the ivory trade in Africa in about

A.D. 100. Then ask them to research what has happened to the ivory trade in recent years. Finally, ask them to write a persuasive essay either supporting or opposing the selling of ivory.

Lesson 2
(For use with Section 3, pp. 191–196)

OBJECTIVES

1. Discuss the roles played by the Islamic religion and by migrating peoples in the development of trade along the East African coast.

2. Examine how the kingdoms of Ghana, Mali, and Songhai became rich and powerful as a result of trade.

BELLRINGER

As students enter the classroom, have them look at the map on page 192. Ask them to write the location of the areas highlighted on the map in relation to the kingdoms of Kush and Aksum. _(southeast and west)_ Tell students that, in Section 3, they will learn about trading kingdoms that developed along the East Coast of Africa and in West Africa.

TEACH OBJECTIVE 1

Level 1: Discuss the development of the Swahili states and Great Zimbabwe. On the board, draw a circle labeled Swahili States. From this circle, extend lines labeled People, Cities, Religion, Trade Partners, and Goods Traded. Draw another circle at the other end of each line. Have students fill in the circles. Then help students proceed in the same manner to learn about trade in Great Zimbabwe.

TEACH OBJECTIVE 2

Level 1: Ask students to read the material entitled West Africa. Divide the class into four groups. Assign the introductory paragraphs to one group; assign Ghana, Mali, and Songhai each to the other groups. Ask each group to compile a summary that includes geographic

areas covered, goods traded, important events in sequence, rulers, cities, and accomplishments. Have a representative from each group present the summary to the class.
[English Language Learners]

Level 2: Have students discuss the role of Islamic traders in the development of trade in Ghana, Mali, and Songhai. Then assign groups of students to conduct research on trade routes, goods traded, and the impact of Islam on one of the West African trading kingdoms *(Groups of Muslim settlers from Arabia and Persia began to move onto the East African coast. At the same time, people from Indonesia settled on the island of Madagascar, off the coast of East Africa. These groups were influenced by the ideals of Islam, and formed a new, trade-based society in coastal East Africa that combined elements of African, Asian, and Islamic culture.)* Have students present their research as the class takes notes.
[English Language Learners, Cooperative Learning]

Level 3: Ask students to research the current role of Islam in Africa today. Have them write their findings in a report and present it to the class.

Levels 2 and 3: Have students research Islamic religion, art, and culture in Chapter 11. Ask them to research how Africa's culture was influenced by the Islamic world. Then have students write an essay on their findings and share it with the class.
[Cooperative Learning]

REVIEW AND ASSESS

Have students complete **Review Section 3.** Ask students to ask five questions about section three and to form groups to discuss the answers. **Daily Quiz 8.3.**

RETEACH

Have students complete **Main Idea Activities 8.3.** Then pair students to answer the **Reading Check** questions in **Section 3.**
[English Language Learners, Cooperative Learning]

CHALLENGE AND EXTEND

Have students work in small groups to conduct research on the gold trade in Africa in the A.D. 900s and present the information in a written or visual form.

The Value of Oral Tradition

GOAL

In this activity, students will read tales that exemplify Africa's oral history. They will also create their own moral tale in the style of the African stories.

PLANNING

- **Purpose** This activity may be used in combination with teacher-directed lessons, as an enrichment activity, or as a performance-based assessment of content mastery.

- **Suggested Time** Plan to spend two lesson blocks and one homework assignment on this activity. Provide time for students to tell their stories.

- **Teaching Team** At least one social studies teacher and one language arts teacher should take part in teaching this activity

- **Group Size** This activity should be completed by individual students. You may wish to assign the activity as an extra credit option for individual students.

- **Materials and Resources** Provide students with copies of "Blind Man and Lame Man" on page 94 of *Readings in World History*. Also provide students with pages 96 through 99 of Chinua Achebe's *Things Fall Apart*. Students should be given Rubric 37 as well.

IMPLEMENTATION

1. Give students an overview of the activity by explaining that they will read two ancient African stories and use them as models to create their own tales.

2. Remind students that part of the information about the history and cultural development of Africa comes from the study of oral traditions. Such poems, songs, and stories are passed by word of mouth from one generation to the next. The tales usually hold some moral lesson or talk about

past kings and heroes. As review, you may want to have students read the text below the heading "Rediscovering the African Past" on page 184 of their textbook.

3. Direct students' attention to the story "Blind Man and Lame Man" on page 94 of *Readings in World History.* Explain that the story is an example of that which would be passed on through oral tradition. After reading the story, discuss the following questions: How did Blind Man solve the problem of Lame Man not being able to walk to hunt the monkeys? Who do you think was right, Blind Man or Lame Man? Give reasons for your answer. What is the moral of the story? In other words, why would this story be passed down from generation to generation? How might the tale of Blind Man and Lame Man be applied to modern-day Africa?

4. Then ask students to refer to the legend on pages 96 through 99 of Chinua Achebe's *Things Fall Apart.* You may want to tell the story as a storyteller might instead of having students read silently. Explain that long ago, this is the way people would hear of the stories. Once the tale has been read/told, ask a student to briefly summarize the plot. Then discuss the following questions: What are the similarities between this story and "Blind Man and Lame Man"? What is the moral of this story? Why would this tale be appropriate especially for children? Does the story have more than one function? *(Students should recognize that it also relates the origin of the cracked tortoise's shell.)* Ask students if they remember such stories that they learned as a child, either teaching a moral or relating the origin of something in particular.

5. Then tell students that they will write their own story in a style similar to those already read. Their stories should teach a moral, include animals, and be simple enough for children to understand. After students have written their drafts, they should engage in

peer editing. At least two students should read a story, editing for spelling, grammar, punctuation, sentence structure, flow, and clarity. Authors should revise their work based upon their peer editors' comments.

6. Ask students to share their stories with the class. They must tell their stories as a storyteller would—no reading!

ASSESSMENT

1. To assess students' speeches, use Rubric 37: Writing.

2. Additional grades can be based on students' participation in the discussions following each story as well as the skill they demonstrate in telling their own tale to the class.

The Migration to America

Ask students to create a map that shows the migrations from Asia to North America. Have them note specific geographical areas, including the Pacific Northwest, the Southwest, the Great Plains and the Eastern Woodlands. Ask them to write an explanation of the migrations and attach to their map. Present their maps to the class.

Lesson 1

(For use with Sections 1 and 2, pp. 200–207)

OBJECTIVES

1. Explain how people first arrived in the Americas.

2. Describe changes that the development of agriculture brought to the Americas.

3. Explain how geography and climate affected life in different regions of North America.

4. Distinguish between the early American cultures in the Pacific Northwest, the Southwest, the Great Plains, and the Eastern Woodlands.

BELLRINGER

As students enter the classroom, ask them to list several basic material needs that people have. *(food, water, shelter, and clothing)* Ask students what early people did when they could not meet needs in a particular place. *(They migrated to another place.)* Tell students that, in Section 1, they will learn how the first Americans migrated from Asia to North America, and then spread throughout the Americas.

TEACH OBJECTIVE 1

LEVEL 1: Discuss why the land bridge may have encouraged people from Asia to move into North America. Ask students to recall other societies they studied who migrated to other areas. How did this movement change the his-

tories of other lands? Ask students to record their thoughts in their journals and share them with the class.
[English Language Learners, Cooperative Learners]

LEVEL 2: Have students research the Ice Age for specific information on the Bering Strait. Ask them to write a report on the physical changes the strait has experienced since the Ice Age. They can include sketches or photographs with their work. Ask them to present their findings to the class.
[English Language Learners, Cooperative Learners]

LEVEL 3: Have students read "The Nomadic Life" from *Readings in World History.* Ask them to learn the characteristics of a Nomadic life. Then have them create a first person narrative describing the journey from Asia into North America. Remind them to use descriptive language *(language that uses the senses of hearing, touch, sight, smell)* and historical facts *(the people were hunters and gatherers; they may have followed animal herds across the land bridge; changes in climate may have forced them to leave Asia).* Have them present their creative piece to the class.
[English Language Learners, Cooperative Learning]

TEACH OBJECTIVE 2

LEVELS 1 AND 2: Have students compare the differences between hunting and farming to a culture. *(hunting: nomadic groups; farming: communities, settled towns)* Ask them to think about how these changes would affect the daily life of the people and their view of the world. Record answers on the board for further discussion.
[English Language Learners, Cooperative Learning]

LEVEL 3: Begin by asking students these questions: "When a group of people must worry about feeding themselves daily, are they able to

pursue other endeavors, like education, art, and architecture? *(No, the people are consumed by trying to survive and do not have time for other things.)* Have students use page 202 to write a two- or three-paragraph essay describing how agriculture changed the lives of early Americans. *(Food became abundant, lasting settlements were created, advancements in farming equipment and other activities other than farming took place.)* Ask them to then research further the influence agriculture had on other societies. *(Greeks traveled to establish agricultural centers and this increased their geographical area, along with an exchange with other peoples and cultures.)* Ask them to compare and contrast another society with the beginnings of these societies. Have them share their reports with their groups.
[English Language Learners, Cooperative Learning]

TEACH OBJECTIVE 3

LEVEL 1: Have students match each region's geography and climate with a way of life by responding to these different regions:

- Seacoast: *fishing*
- Desert: *irrigated farming*
- High plains: *hunting buffalo*
- Forest region: *hunting, fishing, farming*

Ask them to consider what specific things would be different among the lives of the people in these regions. *(types of shelter, clothes, what they held sacred, how they enjoyed their free time, their life expectancy, etc.)* Keep this on the board for further discussion.
[English Language Learners, Cooperative Learning]

LEVEL 2: Discuss in greater detail how climate and geography affected the cultures of these regions. *(These factors helped determine types of food and clothing, art, and religious beliefs in cultures of the regions.)* Have students choose a particular area and find one example of their way of life that was determined by their geographical surroundings. Ask them to write their findings and present them to the class.
[English Language Learners]

LEVEL 3: Instruct students on making a lesson plan. Explain objectives, teaching, review, and extending information. Ask them to create a lesson plan for fifth graders based on the information in Section 2 on pages 203–207, "The Cultures of North America." Divide students into small groups to exchange their ideas, notes, and approaches. Ask them to write up their lesson plan with the Objective, Implementation, Review and Extend. Tell them that hands-on activities and visual aids will be beneficial to their lesson as well. Then have them present their lessons to the class.
[English Language Learners, Cooperative Learning]

TEACH OBJECTIVE 4

LEVEL 1: Lead a brainstorming discussion about the different cultures the students think might develop from the different geographical areas in the Americas. Record answers on the board and refer to them as students read Section 2.
[English Language Learners]

LEVEL 2: Tell students to imagine they are curators for a museum. Inform them they are presenting a show entitled "Cultures and Art of North America." Assign a specific culture from the map on page 204 to students working in groups. Have each group develop a detailed list of artifacts, photographs, and historical information they are going to use to present their cultures to the public. *(Some items may include photographs of a tumi, a ceremonial knife for the Chimu people, ruins of mud brick walls, The Gateway of the Sun, Guaman Poma de Ayala, The Temple of the Sun.)* Ask students to write several paragraphs for each artifact or photograph that will describe the historical significance of the piece. In addition, have them create posters for the show and plan an opening party complete with the food and music from their civilization. Have them construct the show in the room and have other classes visit.
[English Language Learners, Cooperative Learning]

LEVEL 3: Ask students to research the lasting influence these beginning cultures had on the

current cultures located in those geographical places. Have them write a report on their region's past and present culture. Ask them to exchange reports with other students to have a full understanding of the all regions.
[English Language Learners, Cooperative Learning]

REVIEW

Have students complete **Review Sections 1 and 2.** Have students work in pairs and create a graphic organizer that demonstrates how the main ideas of the two sections are related. Have students complete **Daily Quiz 9.1 and 9.2.**

RETEACH

Have students complete **Main Idea Activities 9.1 and 9.2.** Assign each student a **Reading Check** question from **Section 1 or 2.**
[English Language Learners]

CHALLENGE AND EXTEND

Have students research a particular Native American culture to find out what daily life was like for young people living in that culture. Have students write and illustrate a journal entry based on their research.

Lesson 2

(For use with Section 3, pp. 208–211)

OBJECTIVES

1. Identify the characteristics of the Olmec, Toltec, and Maya cultures.

2. Explain how the Aztec and Inca built and strengthened their empires.

BELLRINGER

Write the following questions on the board: How does geography affect locations of cities? Why might a calendar be important to societies based on agriculture? How might the conquest of a region affect cultures of the conquered peoples as well as the conquerors? Have students suggest responses. *(Sample responses: must sustain large populations; can determine*

when to plant and harvest crops; shared ideas could influence social development) Tell students that in Section 3 they will study how these factors shaped patterns of life in the empires of Mexico and Peru.

TEACH OBJECTIVE 1

LEVEL 1: Draw three triangles on the board and label them Olmec, Maya, and Toltec. Ask students to identify the earliest and latest civilizations. *(Olmec, Toltec)* Have students write details about each culture in the blanks at the bottom of the triangles.
[English Language Learners]

LEVEL 2: Have the students create a concept map on the information they have learned about the difference in the three cultures (include political, social, and religious differences).

LEVEL 3: From the information gathered from the cultures of the Olmec, Maya, and Totec, have students write a newspaper article appropriate for the travel section. Include climate, geography, culture, religion, etc. Include photographs of the region in article.

TEACH OBJECTIVE 2

LEVEL 1: Have small groups list characteristics of Aztec and Inca civilizations. Suggest that students consider government, social organization, religion, communications, and military organization. *(Aztec: settled on an island in Lake Texcoco, wandering warriors, conquered peoples paid tribute or taxes to rulers, worshipped Quetzalcoatl and the sun god, used calendars and mathematics, borrowed from cultures of the people they conquered, military-dominated society; Inca: located in the Andes Mountains of South America, worshipped the sun and moon, expanded empire to Peru, Ecuador, Bolivia, and Chile, incorporated the people they conquered into their culture, emperor had absolute power, built irrigation systems and roads, domesticated animals, had an educational system)* Put the items on the board and discuss the similarities and differences.
[English Language Learners, Cooperative Learning]

LEVEL 2: Divide students into groups. Have students imagine they are members of either the Inca or Aztec civilizations. (Make sure they are from different social and economic groups, including priests, ruling class, conquered people, artisans, warriors, women, farmers, etc.) Ask them to imagine that these two groups have come in contact with one another and want to explain their individual culture to the other. Have them prepare a speech on the accomplishments of their society and have one member of each group present the speech to the class.
[English Language Learners, Cooperative Learning]

LEVEL 3: Ask students to write a short essay comparing and contrasting the Aztec and Inca civilizations. Have them create a thesis statement and specific evidence of the similarities and differences. Allow them to consult outside sources.
[English Language Learners, Cooperative Learning]

REVIEW AND ASSESS

Have students complete **Review Section 3.** Ask them to create note cards and quiz one another on main ideas and concepts. Have students complete **Daily Quiz 9.3.**

RETEACH

Have students complete **Main Idea Activities 9.3.** Have students prepare notes for an oral summary of the section.
[English Language Learners, Cooperative Learning]

CHALLENGE AND EXTEND

Show a documentary on one of the Olmec, Maya, or Toltec civilizations. Discuss the elements of making a good documentary. *(historical fact, interesting presentation with visuals, music, engaging narration)* Organize students into groups and have them choose Olmec, Maya, or Toltec civilizations. Inform them that they are responsible for creating a historical documentary on the civilization. Have them first research their civilization in detail. Then have them write a script for the documentary. Finally have them find visual aids of artifacts, ruins, and geographical points of interest that they can use in their presentation. Documentaries can be videotaped or performed live and then shared with the class as a whole.

Team Teaching Strategy
The Americas

Children of the Sun

GOAL

In this activity, students study in depth the Inca religion and the importance it played in the culture and daily lives of the people. In addition, they will practice their descriptive writing skills.

PLANNING

- **Purpose** This activity may be used in combination with teacher-directed lessons, as an enrichment activity, or as a performance-based assessment of content mastery.

- **Suggested Time** Plan to spend two lesson blocks and one homework assignment on this activity. Provide time for the presentation of the narratives at the end of the lesson.

- **Teaching Team** At least one social studies teacher and one language arts teacher should take part in teaching this activity.

- **Group Size** This activity will work as a small group activity or for individual students.

- **Materials and Resources** "The Incas: Worshippers of the Sun" in *Readings in World History.*

  Library sources, Internet sources

IMPLEMENTATION

1. Give students an overview of the activity by explaining that they will first read about the Inca's ancient religion from a variety of sources. Then they will be asked to imagine that they, like the Jesuit priest who wrote "The Incas: Worshippers of the Sun," saw firsthand the religion of the Incas. Ask them to write an account of the rituals they saw, the hierarchy of the religion, the buildings for worship and the art created for the sun god, and the tenets of the religion.

2. Instruct students on the elements of a well-written descriptive essay. Ask them to use vivid language that evokes the sights,

smells, sounds, and textures, of the ancient Inca world. Ask them to organize their details in a thoughtful, well-organized way.

3. Ask the students to read about the Inca's religion from library sources and from the selection from *World Literature.* Ask them to take notes on specific artifacts they have read about. *(the golden-faced sun, sculptures of figures up to 25-feet high, the ornate places of worship, the dress of the priests, The Gateway of the Sun, the largest and most ornately decorated portals at Tiahuanaco. The frieze depicts a central figure, dressed in an elaborate tunic, who holds a staff in each hand. He is surrounded by winged attendants, etc.)* Ask them to note specific tenets of the religion. *(blood sacrifice—animal and human; a hierarchy of worship—priests and women designated to worship; the concept that the moon is the sun's wife and the stars his children; the rituals of worship, etc.)* Ask them to include attributes of the sun god. Why did the Incas think the sun represented goodness? *(the light, looks like gold, the sun's role in agriculture)*

4. Have the students write a rough draft of the essay. Instruct them to organize their descriptive details in a way that will make sense to their readers. Remind them to use past or present tense throughout the paper and correct grammar. Avoid weak verbs and descriptions that are not concrete and visual. Stress the importance of an interesting opening to pull the reader in and a conclusion that effectively closes the piece.

5. Divide students into groups and ask them to read each others' papers. Give them the rubric you will use to grade their papers. Ask them to grade each others' work. Ask them to look for coherency, language that they can visualize, and correct historical information.

6. Have students revise their essays according to the suggestions their peers made. Explain that the best writing is revised many times. They may want to rearrange

facts, paragraphs, write a new introduction, or conclusion, or include other descriptions that they left out. Give them time to revise and improve their draft.

7. Ask the students to now take their papers and make them look like a document from the time of the Incas. They can make their paper look like a scroll, or journal, or letter. Have them attach a note to the piece saying where it was found and who found it. Encourage creativity. Ask them to draw sketches of the things they have witnessed and add to their paper.

8. Collect papers and have individual students read their accounts to the class.

ASSESSMENT

1. Assess students' work by their use of correct historical information, combined with their descriptive writing skills. Also note their creative covers and sketches.

2. Additional grades can be based on students' participation in the presentations.

Mapping the Byzantine Empire

Have students examine the map on page 223. What is the subject of the map? Have students list the areas Emperor Justinian conquered.

Lesson 1

(For use with Section 1, pp. 222–228)

OBJECTIVES

1. Identify the factors that contributed to the growth and strength of the Byzantine Empire.

2. Explain how the Christian church came to be divided.

3. Analyze the cultural contributions made by the Byzantines.

4. Explain the factors that contributed to the downfall of the Byzantine Empire.

BELLRINGER

Have students think about the legal system in the United States today. Ask them why it is important to have laws that are fair to all. Tell students that, in Section 1, they will learn about the legal code of the Byzantine Empire.

TEACH OBJECTIVE 1

All Levels: Have students create a chart titled *Strengths of the Byzantine Empire* with the following headings: *Political Strengths, Military Strengths,* and *Economic Strengths.* Tell students to fill in their charts as they read their textbook. After students have completed their charts, have them discuss which of the strengths they have listed might be important in making a nation strong today. Students should also analyze which of these strengths are comparable to those of the United States today.
[**English Language Learners**]

All Levels: Have students use their textbooks to make a list of the political, military, and eco-

nomic strengths of the Byzantine Empire in one column of a two-column chart. In the other column, tell students to write why this strength was important to the empire.

TEACH OBJECTIVE 2

Level 1: Ask students to explain the Iconoclastic Controversy. *(It was the debate between the opponents and defenders of icons.)* How were the Byzantines different from the Western church? *(They did not recognize the pope's authority; some of them venerated icons.)* What caused the Christian church to split? *(The pope's council threatened to excommunicate iconoclasts.)*
[**English Language Learners**]

Level 2: Have students create a time line that illustrates how the Christian church came to be divided.

Level 3: Review with students the Iconoclastic Controversy. Then have each student write a speech expressing either an Iconoclastic or anti-Iconoclastic point of view. You may then set up a debate and have students use their speeches as support of their group's viewpoint. Students may also simply read their speeches to the class and then discuss which was the most convincing and why.

TEACH OBJECTIVE 3

All Levels: Ask students to list social improvements that benefited women during Justinian's reign. *(Women gained greater benefit from divorce laws and could own property.)* Ask students to keep in mind the other empires they have studied while generating a short written response to the following statement: *Women were better off in Justinian's time than any previous time in history.* Remind students that their responses should include details and facts. After students have completed their responses, discuss their ideas as a class.
[**English Language Learners**]

Level 3: Have students read the paragraphs under the "Byzantine Culture" heading on pages 226 and 227. Then ask them what seems to be the unifying theme among these different elements of the Byzantine culture. *(importance of religion)* Organize the class into three groups: creators of the Cyrillic alphabet, Byzantine artists, and architects who built Hagia Sophia. Tell each group to prepare a debate speech in which the students will explain why their group has made the most important contribution to Byzantine culture. Members of the opposing groups should ask questions from the floor. **[Cooperative Learning]**

All Levels: Ask students what other systems of law had been developed by early civilizations. *(Babylonians and the Code of Hammurabi, Hittites, Greece and Draco's code of laws, and Solon's reforms)* Ask students in what way each of the four parts of the Justinian Code would have contributed to the overall system of laws in the Byzantine Empire. *(The Code reorganized Roman law; the Digest could be used when a law was not fully understood; the Institutes could be used for making new laws; the Novellae contained the updated laws.)* Close by asking students how we know that the Justinian Code was successful and efficient. *(It was the basis of many European legal systems.)*

TEACH OBJECTIVE 4

Level 1: Draw five boxes on the chalkboard and, as a class, fill in each box with one important turning point that led to the decline of the Byzantine Empire. **[English Language Learners, Cooperative Learning]**

Levels 2 and 3: Have students create a time line extending from 1000 to 1500, labeled with events that contributed to the decline of the Byzantine Empire. Under each event, have students write a statement that explains its significance. *(Possible answers: early 1000s—Saljuq Turks capture most of Asia Minor which weakened the empire; 1096–1099—Western European armies recaptured western Asia Minor for the Byzantines, which restored and ensured the sta-*

bility of Constantinople; 1204—Western Europeans captured Constantinople the empire's most important city; 1261—the Byzantines recaptured Constantinople which restored the empire; 1453—Ottoman Turks captured Constantinople, ending the Byzantine Empire.)

REVIEW AND ASSESS

Have students complete **Review Section 1** on p. 228. Have students complete **Daily Quiz 10.1**. As Alternative Assessment, you may want to use one of the chart exercises in this section's lessons.

RETEACH

Have students complete **Main Idea Activity 10.1**. Then have them list the main ideas of each heading and subheading in the section. **[English Language Learners]**

CHALLENGE AND EXTEND

Have interested students locate primary and secondary sources to find out what kinds of goods and merchandise came through Constantinople. Then have students plan a creative way to share their findings with the class.

Lesson 2

(For use with Sections 2 and 3, pp. 229–235)

OBJECTIVES

1. Explain why different peoples settled in Eastern Europe.

2. Describe how Kievan Russia differed from the Byzantine Empire.

3. Identify the ways in which Mongol rule affected Kievan Russia.

4. Describe the effects of Moscow's growing power and independence.

BELLRINGER

Ask students to think about the importance of trade. Have them list some goods Americans can buy because of trade with other countries. *(Students may list goods such as foreign cars, and fruits and vegetables that do not grow in the*

United States.) Tell students that, in Section 2, they will learn about trade in Kievan Russia.

TEACH OBJECTIVE 1

All Levels: Have students read the paragraphs under the "Religion" heading on page 231. Then have students create a cause-and-effect chart and fill it in with facts about Kievan Russia and Christianity. Ask students how Kievan Russia's religion differed from that of the Byzantine Empire. *(Kievan religion was both Christian and pagan.)*
[**English Language Learners**]

Level 3: Have students look at the map on page 230. Ask them what is the most outstanding feature of Kievan Russia. *(Many Viking trade routes cut through the territory.)* Ask them what benefit this might have had for the people who lived in this region. *(It gave them access to other goods as well as an outlet for trading their own goods.)* Ask students why they think Kiev and not Novgorod became the most important city. *(Answers will vary, but students might suggest that, because Kiev was closer to southern Europe and Asia Minor, its inhabitants were more easily able to trade goods and learn about new ideas.)*

TEACH OBJECTIVE 2

Level 1: Ask students to describe the Pravda Russkia. *(A legal code written by Yaroslav I, it combined elements of Slavic tribal customs with older laws and traditions and outlined lawful responses in cases of violence and other harmful activity.)* How was the Pravda Russkia similar to the Justinian Code? *(They both contained elements of older laws.)* How was it different? *(It also included elements of Slavic tribal customs.)*
[**English Language Learners**]

Levels 2 and 3: Have students create a chart with the column headings *Kievan Russia* and *Byzantine Empire*. Students should compare and contrast the two using the chart as an organizational tool.

TEACH OBJECTIVE 3

All Levels: Ask students how the Mongols influenced Russian culture. *(Mongol words became part of the Russian language; Mongols built roads and improved methods of taxation and communication)* Then ask how these influences make sense in terms of the Mongols' goal in Russia. *(Good roads, communication, and systems of taxation ensured that the Russians delivered taxes to the Mongols.)*

Level 2: Ask students to list the positive and negative effects of Mongol rule on Kievan Russia. *(positive: built roads, improved methods of taxation and communication; negative: taxed people heavily, prevented Slavs from keeping their own government and customs unless paid money)*

All Levels: Have students imagine that they are teenagers living in Kievan Russia under Mongol rule. Have students write a short journal entry that describes their daily lives.

TEACH OBJECTIVE 4

Level 1: Have students create a chart with the following headings: *Ivan I, Ivan III,* and *Ivan IV.* Tell students to fill in their charts with characteristics and accomplishments of each leader. After students have completed their charts, have them discuss who was the best ruler.
[**English Language Learners**]

Levels 2 and 3: Have students list elements that contributed to Moscow's rise. Discuss the positive and negative aspects of each contributing factor.

All Levels: Have students discuss the beliefs and actions of Ivan the Terrible. Why was he referred to as "terrible?"

REVIEW AND ASSESS

Have students complete **Review Sections 2 and 3**. Have students complete **Daily Quizzes 10.2 and 10.3**. As Alternative Assessment, you may want to use the chart or chain of events exercises in this section's lessons.

RETEACH

Have students complete **Main Idea Activities 10.2 and 10.3**. Then have them write three statements about each subsection.
[English Language Learners, Cooperative Learning]

CHALLENGE AND EXTEND

Have students study illustrations or slides of Russian art of the period to look for examples of Byzantine influence. Students should make a chart of elements that are common to both artistic traditions.

And the Verdict Is . . .

GOAL

In this activity, students will learn more about the *Pravda Russkaia*. They will examine an excerpt from the legal code and use sections of it in a creative writing activity.

PLANNING

- **Purpose** This activity may be used in combination with teacher-directed lessons, as an enrichment activity, or as a performance-based assessment of content mastery.

- **Suggested Time** Plan to spend two lesson blocks and one homework assignment on this activity.

- **Teaching Team** At least one social studies teacher and one language arts teacher should take part in teaching this activity.

- **Group Size** Students should be organized into groups of four.

- **Materials and Resources** Provide students with copies of the *Pravda Russkaia* from *Readings in World History* as well as Rubrics 14 and 33.

IMPLEMENTATION

1. Have students read the *Pravda Russkaia* on pages 60–62 in *Readings in World History*. Discuss the following questions: What in the excerpt suggests that Russian men placed a value on their beards? What is interesting about the punishments established for murder? What similarities are there between the *Pravda Russkaia* and other medieval legal codes? Also discuss which parts of the legal code students find most interesting. Which laws do students find just? Are there any laws that seem unjust?

2. Remind the class that they are examining these laws through the eyes of an American of the twenty-first century and may be biased. Then have students compare the crimes and their punishments to conse-

quences Americans of the twenty-first century might face for committing similar crimes. If time allows, students may even research a few of the crimes mentioned and the specific consequences to which offenders may be sentenced. Students could present their findings to the class and lead the discussion.

3. If time allows, have students compare and contrast actual American laws with those listed in the *Pravda Russkaia*. How are the laws different in their phrasing? Tone? Severity?

4. Divide the class into groups of four. Tell students that they will create a skit involving the following four characters: a defense attorney, a prosecuting attorney, a judge, and a defendant. Each student in a group should assume one of the four roles.

5. Ask students to create a five to ten minute skit in which a defendant is on trial for a particular crime. The crime should be one that is mentioned in the *Pravda Russkaia*. Remind students that they must first and foremost prove that the defendant is guilty. However, attorneys should present their cases and suggest consequences keeping this legal code in mind. If the defendant is found guilty, the judge must rule according to the punishment defined in the legal code. Each student will be responsible for writing his or her own lines; however, the entire group must work together to create a skit that is clear and flows well.

6. If time allows, have a few groups write a skit in which similar crimes are being tried, yet the punishment is based upon American law. Again, each student is responsible for writing his or her own lines.

7. Conclude by having students perform their skits for the class. If you wish, you may assign the members of the class the role of jury. Discuss which rulings were more or less consistent with those that might result from the American trials dealing with sim-

ilar issues. Ask students which trials seemed "fairer" and which appeared to be too lenient.

ASSESSMENT

1. To assess students' speeches, use Rubrics 14 and 33.

2. Additional grades can be based on students' participation in the concluding discussion.

Arabian Peninsula

Have students examine the map on page 240. Ask the following questions: Why do you think many people in Arabia became traders? What body of water formed a natural trade route between the Arabian Peninsula and the east coast of Africa? What geographic feature might have prevented the growth of cities in the southeastern part of the peninsula?

Lesson 1

(For use with Sections 1 and 2, pp. 240–247)

OBJECTIVES

1. Describe how geography affected the people of the Arabian Peninsula.
2. Explain how Islam began.
3. Identify the main beliefs of Islam.
4. Explore how the Muslims expanded their empire.
5. Explain why the Islamic community divided.

BELLRINGER

Write the following passage on the chalkboard or overhead projector: *Do unto all men as you would that they should do unto you.* Ask students to explain this statement and call on volunteers to identify its source. Many students may believe it comes from the Bible, as a similar passage is found in Matthew 7:12. Explain to the class that, in fact, the passage comes from the Qur'an, the holy book of Islam. (If students correctly attribute the passage, shift the discussion to its similarity with the biblical passage.) Tell students that, in Section 1, they will discover other similarities between the teachings of Islam and Judeo-Christian principles.

TEACH OBJECTIVE 1

Level 1: As a class, discuss the geography of the Arabian Peninsula. Then draw a two-column chart on the board or overhead projector. Label one column *Desert Arabs* and the other *Coastal Arabs.* Have students complete the chart by

listing the differences in geography and lifestyle of each.
[English Language Learners]

Levels 2 and 3: Tell students to review the text under the heading "Arabia: Its Geography and People." Ask students to explain how the lifestyle of the desert Arabs differed from the lifestyle of the Arabs who lived along the coasts.

TEACH OBJECTIVE 2

Level 1: Ask students to write a brief history of Islam. Ask them to point to specific important events.
[English Language Learners]

Level 2: Ask students to imagine that they are living during Muhammad's time. Have them write a historical account of what Muhammad was doing and what changes were occurring at the time. In doing so, students should relate the origins of Islam.

Level 3: Ask students to create an annotated time line of the development of Islam. Have volunteers use their time lines to explain how Islam began.

TEACH OBJECTIVE 3

All Levels: Ask students to describe the major beliefs of Islam. Have them list the five chief obligations of a Muslim.
[English Language Learners]

Level 3: Explain to students that oftentimes a fable and/or fairy tale can teach the reader a valuable lesson in morality. Ask students to write a fable or fairy tale in which they teach the reader one or two major values the Muslim people uphold. Tell students to be creative as possible. If time allows, students may share their stories with the class.

TEACH OBJECTIVE 4

Levels 1 and 2: Refer students to the map on page 244 of their textbook and ask how far

Islam spread under Muhammad. (*through much of the Arabian Peninsula*) Ask how much farther it spread under Abu Bakr and 'Umar. (*throughout the Arabian Peninsula and well into North Africa and Persia*) Ask how much farther it spread in the approximate 100 years after Muhammad's death. (*through Persia, and North Africa, and into India and Europe*) Have students identify two activities that contributed to the rapid spread of Islam. (*war and trade*) [**English Language Learners**]

Level 3: Have students identify how Abu Bakr and 'Umar helped to spread Islam. Ask students to look at the map on page 244. What years saw the greatest expansion of the Muslim Empire? How might the expansion of Islam have affected the history of areas such as North Africa and China?

TEACH OBJECTIVE 5

All Levels: Have students work in pairs to create two diagrams that illustrate how Sunni and Shi'ah Muslims differed over where religious and secular authority originate and the proper relationship between the two types of authority. Select volunteer pairs to duplicate their diagrams on the chalkboard or overhead projector and explain them to the class. [**English Language Learners, Cooperative Learning**]

Level 3: Form students into triads to decide which of the following was a more critical event for Muslims: the death of Muhammad, Abu Bakr, or 'Umar. (*Students should recognize that while Islam survived after Muhammad's death, his successors were faced with maintaining Muslims' political unity.*) Use the responses to launch a discussion of the divisions that arose among Muslims after 'Umar's death. Ask whether these disputes were about power or Islamic principles. (*power*) [**Cooperative Learning**]

REVIEW AND ASSESS

Have students complete **Review Sections 1 and 2.** Have students also complete **Daily Quizzes**

11.1 and 11.2. As Alternative Assessment, you may want to use the map or diagram exercises in this section's lessons.

RETEACH

Have students complete **Main Idea Activities 11.1 and 11.2.** Then ask them to create a flow-chart showing the succession of Islamic leaders. [**English Language Learners**]

CHALLENGE AND EXTEND

Have students form small groups and imagine that they are Arab merchants in Medina. Tell them that they have employees traveling throughout North Africa and Persia buying, selling, and trading goods. Have each group develop a written code of conduct for these employees while away from home and in dealings with non-Muslim customers that will strengthen the perception of Islam in those regions.

Lesson 2

(*For use with Section 3, pp. 248–253*)

OBJECTIVES

1. Describe how the location of Arabia affected trade in the Muslim Empire.

2. Explain what Muslim society and family life were like.

3. Identify Muslim achievements in science.

4. Explore how Islam influenced Arab art and literature.

BELLRINGER

Write the following words on the chalkboard or overhead projector: *algebra, almanac, apricot, cotton, damask, guitar, lemon, soda,* and *sofa.* Tell the class that all these words are derivations of Arab terms that over time have found their way into the English language. Ask students what this list suggests about contact between the Muslim world and Europe. (*Responses should include that a considerable trade existed between Europe and the Near East, and the Arab culture had a significant influence on Europeans.*)

TEACH OBJECTIVE 1

Level 1: Have students list some items that Muslims produced and traded. *(silk, cotton, and wool textiles, woven tapestries, carpets, metal products, jewelry, perfumes, leather goods)* In addition to goods, ask students what else Muslims exchanged with other cultures. *(ideas)* [**English Language Learners**]

Levels 2 and 3: Assign each student to create a three or four panel cartoon strip showing how Muslim culture was spread by the group's interaction with other peoples. Make sure students include at least five goods, which the Muslims traded.

TEACH OBJECTIVE 2

All Levels: Ask students what rights Muslim women had. *(Women could choose their husbands. Men had to treat all wives equally. Women could divorce, keep their own money, and remarry. Women could inherit money and own property.)* Explain to students that Muslim women still had restrictions placed upon them. Have a volunteer list some of these restrictions. *(Women had clearly defined positions. Men were responsible for women's behavior. Muslim men engaged in polygamy.)* [**English Language Learners**]

Level 2: Ask students to imagine that they are living in ancient Islamic civilization. First have students write a journal entry from the perspective of an Islamic woman. What was daily life like? What were women allowed to do? What were they forbidden to do? Then ask students to write a journal entry from the perspective of an Islamic man. Have them address similar questions. Have volunteers read their pieces aloud to the class. Conclude by discussing the differences between men and women in Islamic society.

Level 3: Ask students to explain how the principles of Islam factored into daily life. *(Muslims lived according to the Qur'an and there was no separation between religious and daily life. The Qur'an gave detailed instructions about how society should be organized; it also set down rules about slavery and marriage.)*

TEACH OBJECTIVE 3

Levels 1 and 2: Create a chart on the chalkboard titled *Muslim Culture*. Label the columns *Manufacturers, Science and Medicine, Mathematics,* and *Geography.* Call on class members to provide information to fill in the chart. Ask students why geography and mathematics would be emphasized in a society where trade was so important. [**English Language Learners**]

Level 3: Have students create a list of modern-day medical practices and techniques that would not exist without the discoveries of the Muslims. *(pharmaceutical drugs, techniques such as distillation, surgical instruments and processes, surgical techniques, diagnoses, schools of pharmacy, encyclopedia of known drugs.)*

TEACH OBJECTIVE 4

Levels 1 and 2: Ask students to create a piece of artwork that would be acceptable as Islamic religious art. *(No images of God, humans, or animals only geometric and floral designs)* Also ask students to name some topics of Islamic literature. [**English Language Learners, Cooperative Learning**]

Level 3: Read these words of Muhammad to the class: "The ink of scholars is more precious than the blood of martyrs." Ask students what they think Muhammad meant. Ask what this statement suggests about the value that Muslims put on knowledge and learning. *(writings were seen as a more permanent way of spreading the faith than was conquest, and knowledge was highly revered in Muslim society)* Have a volunteer explain how Islam affected Arab art. *(Religious art could not show the human form, so it emphasized geometric and floral patterns.)*

REVIEW AND ASSESS

Have students complete **Review Section 3** on page 253. Have students complete **Daily Quiz 11.3**. As Alternative Assessment, you may want to use the trade or chart exercises in this section's lessons.

RETEACH

Have students complete **Main Idea Activity 11.3**. Then have them write down three important Islamic achievements and describe why each was important.
[**English Language Learners**]

CHALLENGE AND EXTEND

Have interested students research Arabic music and bring in selections to play for the class. Students should explain the significance of each musical selection and describe the instruments used.

The Arts of the Islamic World

GOAL

In this activity, students will view a photograph of the Taj Mahal and read Muslim folktales from *The Thousand and One Nights.* Students will create a poem inspired by the photograph. They also will analyze the themes, characters, and style of the stories and apply them to their own writing.

PLANNING

- **Purpose** This activity may be used in combination with teacher-directed lessons, as an enrichment activity, or as a performance-based assessment of content mastery.

- **Suggested Time** Plan to spend two lesson blocks and one homework assignment on this activity.

- **Teaching Team** At least one social studies teacher and one language arts teacher should take part in teaching this activity.

- **Group Size** This activity works best if students work individually.

- **Materials and Resources** Provide students with access to a photograph of the Taj Mahal and *The Thousand and One Nights.* Students should also be provided with Rubric 39. Textbooks should be on hand for review.

IMPLEMENTATION

1. Review with students the section of the text entitled "The Arts" on page 252. Ask students to summarize the Muslims' contribution to this particular area. Make sure students mention architecture and explain the special religious and artistic significance of calligraphy to Islamic culture. If time allows, have students research Islamic calligraphy and create a chart showing several designs that are important to Islamic culture. Ask students to determine what each design means. Also ask students to locate photographs of prayer rugs and ask

them to discuss the designs and purposes of the carpets.

2. Locate a photograph of the Taj Mahal to show the class. Discuss why people consider the Taj Mahal to be such a majestic and important piece of architecture. Suggest that students use the photograph as inspiration to create a poem about the Taj Mahal. Tell students that their poem may be about the structure itself, the reason it was built, or the time and effort required to build it. Remind students to be aware of various poetic techniques such as rhyme, figurative language, symbolism, alliteration, tone, and meter.

3. Then ask students to choose one story from the collection *The Thousand and One Nights.* Possibilities include "Sinbad the Sailor," "Aladdin," and "Ali Baba and the Forty Thieves." Each student should read a different story. As students read, ask them to note the themes, style, and types of characters in their stories. They should prepare a brief summary of the plot and character sketches of at least three characters.

4. Have a few volunteers share their characters and summaries with the class. Try to reach some conclusions as to the main themes with which many of the stories deal. How might you describe the writing style of the stories? Are there types of characters that surface again and again?

5. Ask students to write their own stories that contain some of the same themes and character types as the stories in *The Thousand and One Nights.* Students should try to write their pieces in a style similar to that of the stories in the collection. Students should create a plot diagram and various character sketches to prepare them for their writing. Once students have completed their stories, have them participate in peer editing. Have one or two students read one piece, editing for spelling, grammar, sentence structure, style, flow, and clarity. Students should list three general areas upon which the writer could improve. They should also list three positive comments about the piece as a whole.

6. Students may also create pieces of art to be placed with their writing. Urge students to be as creative as possible.

7. Conclude by combining the students' stories into a book to be shared with each member of the class. Have each student read his or her poem and/or story to classmates.

ASSESSMENT

1. To assess students' pieces, use Rubric 39.

2. Additional grades can be based on students' participation in the discussions and presentations.

CHAPTER 12

Tang Dynasty

Have students examine the map on page 268. What was the Imperial capital of the Tang Dynasty? Along what waterway could Tang people travel between the cities of Tianjin and Hangzhou?

Lesson 1

(For use with Sections 1 and 2, pp. 266–275)

OBJECTIVES

1. Explain how Chinese civilizations advanced during the Sui and Tang dynasties.

2. Describe what daily life was like for the Chinese people during the Sung dynasty.

3. Explore how the Mongol invaders were able to conquer and rule so much of Asia.

4. Examine the effect Mongol rule had on China.

BELLRINGER

Ask students to think about city and rural life in America today. Have students list some differences between city and rural life. *(City dwellers have easier access to many goods and services. People who live in rural areas sometimes make a living by farming or raising livestock.)* Ask students which type of life they believe is more difficult and have them support their opinions. Tell students that, in Section 1, they will learn about city and rural life in China.

TEACH OBJECTIVE 1

Levels 1 and 2: Remind students that many cultural, political, and economic changes occurred in China under the Sui and Tang dynasties. Have students make web diagrams of these changes, filling in circles for *Arts, Economy, Government, Society,* and *Technology.* Organize students into pairs or triads to compare and discuss differences in their web diagrams and to revise their entries if necessary.
[**English Language Learners, Cooperative Learning**]

Level 3: Ask students to recall how Buddhism was brought into China. *(by missionaries from India)* Ask students why it flourished in Tang China. *(supported by Empress Wu and wealthy believers; similar to Daoism)* Have students explain how Buddhism's popularity caused problems for its followers. *(The government feared the growing wealth of Buddhist monasteries.)* Ask what other religions were popular at the time. *(Daoism, Neo-Confucianism)* Have students speculate whether the government would have reacted against Buddhism if it had been a "native" religion like Daoism or Neo-Confucianism. *(Answers will vary, but students should note that many Buddhist sects in China were uniquely Chinese.)*

TEACH OBJECTIVE 2

Levels 1 and 2: Have students work in pairs to complete four-cell charts that list how urban life and rural life in Sung China was similar to urban and rural life in America today. Column headings should read *Urban Life in China* and *Rural Life in China.* Row headings should read *Similar in America* and *Different from America.*
[**English Language Learners, Cooperative Learning**]

Level 3: Discuss with students the developments during the Sung dynasty that improved life for the Chinese people and those that made life worse. Then have students imagine that they are living during the rule of the Sung dynasty. Ask them to write a journal entry about a typical day. Students may write from the point of view of a peasant or city dweller.

TEACH OBJECTIVE 3

Level 1: Have students create a flowchart that shows important events in the Mongol conquest of Asia. *(Answers should include the following: capture of Beijing, conquest of Central Asia, conquest of most of Persia, conquest of Tibet, conquest of part of Southeast Asia.)*
[**English Language Learners**]

Levels 2 and 3: Have students compare the map on page 273 with maps in the Reference Section to list modern nations that were once part of the Mongol Empire. (*China, Mongolia, Russia, North and South Korea, Pakistan (part), Afghanistan, Iran, Iraq, Azerbaijan, Turkey (part) Armenia, Georgia, Turkmenistan, Uzbekistan, Kazakhstan, Ukraine, Poland, and Hungary*) Ask how the Mongols were able to establish and govern so vast an empire. (*well-organized armies and superior troops, military technology, and tactics; divided empire into four parts*)

TEACH OBJECTIVE 4

All Levels: Have students suggest headlines for a news story on the political, economic, or cultural consequences of the Mongols' rule of China. List responses on the board. (*Mongols Restore Peace and Prosperity; Khan Extends Grand Canal; New Roads Improve Trade; Heavy Taxes Burden Nation*) Then have students choose one of the headlines and write a short news article to accompany it.

Level 3: Have students prepare to hold a mock trial of Kublai Khan for alleged crimes against the Chinese people. Pairs of students should serve as prosecution and defense teams. Other students should be witnesses for the prosecution and the defense. Remaining class members should serve as jurors, evaluating Khan's political choices and decisions and voting on the defendant's guilt or innocence. To involve jurors actively during the trial, require each to write an explanation of his or her vote, citing the testimony that influenced it.
[**Cooperative Learning**]

REVIEW AND ASSESS

Have students complete **Review Sections 1 and 2**. Have students complete **Daily Quizzes 12.1 and 12.2**. As Alternative Assessment, you may want to use the map or flow chart exercises in this section's lessons.

RETEACH

Have students complete **Main Idea Activities 12.1 and 12.2**. Than have students write a para-

graph that summarizes what they have learned in Section 1.
[**English Language Learners**]

CHALLENGE AND EXTEND

Have students work together to create a comic book, storyboard, or multimedia presentation about the Mongols' conquest or rule of China using computer software, biographies, and artifacts to acquire information.

Lesson 2
(*For use with Section 3, pp. 276–283*)

OBJECTIVES

1. Investigate how the geography of Japan influenced its development.

2. Analyze how China influenced the early development of Japan.

3. Describe how changes in government influenced society in feudal Japan.

4. Examine how Southeast Asia was influenced by China and Japan.

BELLRINGER

Ask students what effects geographic isolation can have on the development of civilizations and nations. (*People may have little contact with foreigners and the nation may develop unique legal systems and culture.*) Have students name a culture they have already studied that developed in isolation. (*China*) Tell students that in this section they will learn about the effects of geographic isolation on Japan.

TEACH OBJECTIVE 1

Level 1: Write the following questions on the board: *What geographic similarities do Korea and Japan share? How are Korea and Japan different geographically? How did those similarities and differences influence the development of each?* Pair students and ask them to prepare and answer to each question. Have pairs share their answers with the class.
[**English Language Learners, Cooperative Learning**]

Levels 2 and 3: Ask students to examine the map on page 277. Have students answer the following questions: *At the narrowest point, approximately how much distance separates Korea from Japan? How might this affect the relationship between the two countries?*

TEACH OBJECTIVE 2

Levels 1 and 2: Ask students to list the ways China influenced the development of Japanese society. *(writing, Buddhism, art, science, government, fashion)* Then have students research and present Japanese writings and artwork that reflect these influences. Students may perform research in groups of two or three. For example, students may find ancient Chinese and Japanese writings and compare the characters used in each. Students may also find illustrations of Chinese and Japanese clothing and, once again, compare and contrast them.

Level 3: Ask students to summarize various ways in which China influenced the development of Japanese society. List responses on the board. *(artistic designs, Buddhism, fashion, government methods, writing)* Then hold a class debate over which item on the list was the most important influence. *(Positions will vary, but students should support their point of view. Buddhism was very influential, but Shinto remained popular. Chinese writing allowed literature to develop, but Japan eventually adopted its own writing system.)*
[English Language Learners]

TEACH OBJECTIVE 3

Levels 1 and 2: Ask students to identify the two general sources of power within the Japanese feudal system. Then ask students to list the characteristics of each group within the feudal system.
[English Language Learners]

Level 3: Have five students take the roles of emperor, shogun, daimyo, samurai, and peasant. Have each class member, in turn, direct a "yes" or "no" question to one of the five students. *(Do not allow direct questions about a stu-*

dent's identity, such as "Are you the peasant?") When all class members have had a chance to ask their question, have each write out his or her prediction of the identity of each role player. See how many students can correctly identify all five. Conclude the activity by discussing what each role player's answers reveal about power in feudal Japan.

TEACH OBJECTIVE 4

Levels 1 and 2: Have students think about Chinese influences on the development of Japanese and Korean civilizations. Ask them to list the similarities that Vietnam's development shares with either of these countries. *(Japan and Vietnam: Buddhism, Chinese writing system, Chinese influences on government. Korea and Vietnam: conquest by China, Buddhism, Confucianism, Chinese influences on government.)*
[English Language Learners]

Level 3: Have each student develop a diagram or chart that shows the similarities and differences in China's influence on the development of the Japanese, Korean, and Vietnamese cultures. Select students to copy their diagram or chart on the chalkboard and explain it. *(Charts should include the following influences: religion, writing system, government/political structure, technology, fashion, and literature.)*

REVIEW AND ASSESS

Have students complete **Review Section 3.** Then have students complete **Daily Quiz 12.3.** As Alternative Assessment, you may want to use the geography or feudal Japan exercises in this section's lessons.

RETEACH

Have students complete **Main Idea Activity 12.3.** Then ask them to write a question and answer that covers the main idea for each subsection in the section.
[English Language Learners]

CHALLENGE AND EXTEND

Have students access the Internet through the HRW Go Site to conduct research on painting in China, Japan, and Korea. Ask students to present their findings to the class in an illustrated brochure emphasizing the similarities and differences in the art of these three cultures.

Team Teaching Strategy

The Civilizations of East Asia

Japan's Feudal System

GOAL

In this activity, students will learn more about the type of life led by a Mogul Emperor. Students will create a diary entry documenting a day in the life of an individual within the feudal system. Students will also compare the Japanese feudal system to the American government.

PLANNING

- **Purpose** This activity may be used in combination with teacher-directed lessons, as an enrichment activity, or as a performance-based assessment of content mastery.

- **Suggested Time** Plan to spend two lesson blocks and one homework assignment on this activity.

- **Teaching Team** At least one social studies teacher and one language arts teacher should take part in teaching this activity.

- **Group Size** This activity works best if students work individually. You may wish to assign the activity as an extra credit option for individual students.

- **Materials and Resources** Provide students with copies of "A Day in the Life of a Mogul Emperor" on page 70 in *Readings in World History*. Also provide students with a copy of Rubric 37. Have students use their textbooks to help them find information about Japan's feudal system.

IMPLEMENTATION

1. Have students read "A Day in the Life of a Mogul Emperor" on page 70 in *Readings in World History*. Discuss the types of activities in which Akbar indulged. Also discuss the following questions: What in the excerpt suggests that Akbar believed in equal justice for all? How does the author illustrate Akbar's inquisitive nature? Do you think that Binyon admired Akbar? Why or why not? Allow students to lead the class discussion. One student may be responsible for one question.

2. Referring to the textbook, review the nature of Japan's feudal system. *(emperor, shogun, daimyo, samurai, and peasant)* Have students identify each level of the system as well as the responsibilities and lifestyles of each position. *(emperor: figurehead, not the most powerful position; shogun: general, controlled military, finances, and laws; daimyo: local lords, extremely powerful, promoted trade, taxed; samurai: warriors trained in sword fighting, archery, and martial arts; peasant: farmers, not much power)* You may want to record students' answers on the chalkboard or overhead projector.

3. Ask students to imagine that they occupy one of the above positions of power within the feudal system. Keeping the previous readings in mind, have students write diary entries for their chosen roles for a typical day in their life. Students should write their pieces in first person. Tell students that they may include descriptions of the following: typical duties, ways of entertaining oneself, relationships with others in the feudal system, and/or thoughts about the future. Once students have completed their pieces, ask them to engage in peer editing. One or two students should read one piece and edit for spelling, grammar, punctuation, sentence structure, style, flow, and clarity. Peer editors should also list three general areas upon which the author might improve. Finally, students should list three positive comments about the piece as a whole.

4. Ask students to share their writing with the class. Discuss how accurately they represent the life of a certain group within the feudal system.

5. Conclude by having students create an organizational chart, like the one on page 279 of their textbooks, that shows the structure of the United States government. Compare this chart with the figures on page 279 noting similarities and differences between the American government and the Japanese feudal system. If time allows, have students research the structure of another country's government and create a similar organizational chart. Then compare the chart with those representing the Japanese and American systems.

ASSESSMENT

1. To assess students' writing, use Rubric 37. Also assess peer editors work by reviewing their suggestions and comments.

2. Additional grades can be based on students' participation in the concluding discussion. You may grade the organizational charts created in the concluding portion of the activity.

Charlemagne's Empire and the Frankish Kingdoms

Have students examine the maps on page 291. Ask students to name those areas under Louis the German's Kingdom. Whose kingdom after 843 A.D. claimed the most major cities?

Lesson 1

(For use with Sections 1 and 2, pp. 288–299)

OBJECTIVES

1. Describe how Frankish rulers gained control of Europe.

2. Explain what caused the decline of Charlemagne's empire.

3. Explore how feudalism helped shape political and social development in Europe during the Middle Ages.

4. Identify the ways in which the manorial system influenced economic growth in Europe during the Middle Ages.

BELLRINGER

Ask students what comes to mind when they think of Vikings. *(invaders, brutality, conquest)* Write students' responses on the board or overhead projector. Tell students that in Section 1, they will learn more about the Vikings.

TEACH OBJECTIVE 1

Level 1: Have students draw time lines that trace the Frankish rulers' involvement in the Christian faith from Clovis to Charlemagne. *(The following events should be included: Clovis converts to Christianity after victory; the pope crowns Pepin III "king by the grace of God"; Pepin aids the pope in defending Rome; Pope Leo III crowns Charlemagne "Emperor of the Romans.")* Ask students why they think this friendly relationship between church and state developed. *(Students may note that the relation-*

ship was of mutual benefit.)
[English Language Learners]

All Levels: Organize students into five groups and assign each group one of the following Frankish kings or mayors of the palace: Clovis, Pepin II, Charles Martel, Pepin III (Pepin the Short), or Charlemagne. Tell students to develop one-page biographical profiles of their assigned leaders. Encourage each group to find and include an image with their profile. When students have completed their profiles, arrange and display them in chronological order and have students take notes from one another's profiles.
[English Language Learners, Cooperative Learning]

TEACH OBJECTIVE 2

Level 1: Have students create a list of factors that contributed to the decline of Charlemagne's empire. Ask students which factor they believe contributed most heavily to the decline. Have students justify their answers.
[English Language Learners]

Levels 2 and 3: Charlemagne's vast empire did not last long after his death. Ask students why. *(Frankish practice of dividing the kingdom among the king's sons, numerous invasions)* Have students use their textbooks to list the most prominent invading peoples. *(Muslims, Magyars, Vikings)* Have students use computer software to learn more about Vikings, the most-feared invaders. Have students write short stories about Viking characters in the 800s. Stories should be creative, but settings and characters should be based on historical facts.

TEACH OBJECTIVES 3 AND 4

Level 1: Have students create a chart with the column headings *Poverty in Feudal Europe* and *Poverty in the U.S. Today.* Have students, either independently or with guidance, find at least three details from the text that describe peasant life. Then, in small groups, have students fill in the other side of the chart, comparing poverty in feudal Europe to poverty in the United States today. Discuss and debate conclusions.

Level 2: Tell students to imagine that they work for a time travel agency. They need to develop a brochure explaining feudalism and the manorial system to travelers who wish to visit medieval Europe. Students' brochures should include the following: definitions of terms, such as *vassal, fief,* and *lord;* information about feudal justice and warfare; and a brief note about chivalry. Encourage students to include illustrations and graphic organizers to help clarify the system of feudalism; a graphic representation of the feudal hierarchy would be particularly helpful. Tell students to remember that the purpose of their brochure is to prepare travelers to exist within the political system they will encounter during their expedition.

All Levels: Have students read the subsection entitled "Chivalry" on pages 298 and 299. Discuss the characteristics of the code of chivalry. *(Knights had to be brave, fight fairly, be loyal, keep their word, treat conquered foes gallantly, and be courteous to women.)* Show students sample images of medieval or modern coats of arms and point out the unique symbolism of each. Then have students create coats of arms for themselves, considering events, people, places, or animals that were or are significant in their lives or represent themselves.
[**English Language Learners**]

REVIEW AND ASSESS

Have students complete **Review Sections 1 and 2.** Have students complete **Daily Quizzes 13.1 and 13.2.** As Alternative Assessment, you may want to use the time travel or contract exercises in this section's lessons.

RETEACH

Have students complete **Main Idea Activities 13.1 and 13.2.** Then ask them to write a ques-

tion and answer that covers the main idea for each subsection.
[**English Language Learners**]

CHALLENGE AND EXTEND

The mutual-dependency relationships basic to manorialism may remind students of a term from science class: *symbiosis.* Ask a group of students to research symbiotic relationships in nature and report on some of these to the class. Have them point out parallels with feudal-manorial society.
[**Cooperative Learning**]

Lesson 2
(For use with Sections 3 and 4, pp. 300–309)

OBJECTIVES

1. Describe how the church hierarchy fit into society.

2. Explain how the practices of monasticism changed.

3. Explore how the church influenced life in medieval Europe.

4. Explain how the kingdom of England was formed.

5. Identify the achievements of William the Conqueror and his successors.

6. Describe how Parliament and common law evolved.

7. Explore how the French kings gained power over their nobles.

BELLRINGER

Ask students to consider the separation between church and state in the United States. Ask them what this separation means. *(The government cannot attempt to control religious beliefs, and the church cannot interfere in matters of the state.)* Have students state whether they think the separation is positive or negative and explain why. Tell students that, in Section 3, they will learn about the role of the church in medieval society.

TEACH OBJECTIVE 1

All Levels: Have students create a chart that demonstrates the hierarchy of the medieval church.
[**English Language Learners**]

TEACH OBJECTIVE 2

Level 1: Have students explain the beliefs of those committed to Monastic lifestyles. Ask students to describe the Benedictine Rule. How did Saint Benedict change monasticism?
[**English Language Learners**]

Levels 2 and 3: Ask students why they think monastic life appealed to so many during the Middle Ages. *(Monasteries and convents offered a feeling of stability.)* Have students use their textbooks to summarize the Benedictine Rule as a bulleted list in their notes.

TEACH OBJECTIVE 3

Level 1: Ask students to put themselves in the shoes of a medieval European. Who would they fear more, church or king? Have students compare powers of church and king. Guide them to the idea that the powers of excommunication and interdict often seemed more mighty and frightening than the powers of the monarch. True, a king might imprison or even execute, but if the church excommunicated a person, he would not only be shunned in life but also doomed to eternal damnation.
[**English Language Learners**]

Levels 2 and 3: Have students create a chart with the following column headings: *Political Influence, Economic Influence,* and *Social Influence.* Ask students to note underneath each heading how the church influenced each area in medieval life.

TEACH OBJECTIVE 4

All Levels: Ask students to look at the series of maps on page 308, which represent the growth of France. In their textbooks, students should read about the shifting of power in England between the 400s and the 1100s. Then have stu-dents create a map progression for England. Students should create three to five rough maps colored and keyed appropriately to show major shifts in boundaries and power between the Anglo-Saxons, the Danes, and the Normans. Encourage students to consult additional sources in order to complete their maps as accurately as possible.
[**English Language Learners**]

TEACH OBJECTIVE 5

Level 1: Ask students to create a flowchart illustrating William the Conqueror and subsequent leaders. Have students include each ruler's accomplishments within the chart. Students may work in groups.
[**English Language Learners, Cooperative Learning**]

Levels 2 and 3: Have students read about the Norman Conquest and the policies of William the Conqueror and his successors. Then have them write letters to the editorial section of a fictional medieval newspaper evaluating the changes brought about by William and his successors. The letters should be written from the perspective of commoners who have lived under the rule of one or more of these Norman kings.

TEACH OBJECTIVES 6 AND 7

Levels 1 and 2: Ask students to list the goals of William the Conqueror and successors and the Capetian kings. Ask them to support their point of view on how well these rulers accomplished their goals.
[**English Language Learners**]

Level 3: Organize students into four groups. Assign two groups to study English politics and the other two to study French politics between 1000 and 1350. Each group will prepare a multimedia presentation outlining the evolution of royal power in their assigned kingdom. Presentations on England should include information about rulers and their policies, the Magna Carta and its impact on English society, Parliament, and common law. Presentations on

France should include information on rulers and other interesting items they find.
[**Cooperative Learning**]

REVIEW AND ASSESS

Have students complete **Review Sections 3 and 4.** Have students complete **Daily Quizzes 13.3 and 13.4.** As Alternative Assessment, use map or presentation exercises in this section's lessons.

RETEACH

Have students complete **Main Idea Activities 13.3 and 13.4.** Have partners outline the section and compile a chapter glossary, using an outline and a glossary to create flashcards to quiz each other on correct social studies terminology.
[**English Language Learners**]

CHALLENGE AND EXTEND

Have each student choose and read a tale from Chaucer's *The Canterbury Tales* and prepare a shortened, modernized version for dramatic reading, using standard grammar, spelling, sentence structure, and punctuation. Encourage audience questions.

Lights, Camera, Action!

GOAL

In this activity, students will gain a deeper understanding of the code of chivalry by reading parts of Geoffrey Chaucer's *The Canterbury Tales*. Students will rewrite an assigned tale in the form of a skit.

PLANNING

- **Purpose** This activity may be used in combination with teacher-directed lessons, as an enrichment activity, or as a performance-based assessment of content mastery.

- **Suggested Time** Plan to spend two to three lesson blocks and one homework assignment on this activity. Provide time for the groups to perform their skits.

- **Teaching Team** At least one social studies teacher and one language arts teacher should take part in teaching this activity.

- **Group Size** This activity works best by organizing students into groups of three to five. You may wish to assign the activity as an extra credit option for individual students.

- **Materials and Resources** Provide students with copies of tales from Geoffrey Chaucer's *The Canterbury Tales*. Also provide students with Rubric 33. Have students use their textbooks to help them find information about the code of chivalry.

IMPLEMENTATION

1. Give students an overview of the activity by explaining that they will first read one tale from Geoffrey Chaucer's *The Canterbury Tales*, a collection of stories told by a group of pilgrims on their way to a holy shrine at Canterbury. If time allots, provide students with some background information on Chaucer and his work. Tell students that they will use the tale as a model for a skit they will produce.

2. Review the English code of chivalry using the text under "Chivalry" on page 298 of the textbook. Ask students the following questions:
   - What is the definition of chivalry?
   - From where does the word originate?
   - How might one become a knight?
   - What is the significance of the coat of arms?
   - How were knights expected to behave?

3. Divide students into groups and assign one story to each group. After students have completed the reading, ask them to write the following:
   - A plot outline of the story
   - Character sketches of the main characters
   - At least three examples of chivalry
   - At least three themes of the story
   - At least one literary technique used by Chaucer

4. Each group should rewrite their particular tale in modern-day English to create a skit of about five to ten minutes in length. Ask students to emphasize those parts of their tale that illustrate the code of chivalry in action. Students may stage their scene in the context of a popular television show or may even use slang to assist other students in relating. Encourage students to create costumes and props for their skits.

5. Each group will then perform their skit for the class. Conclude by asking students if they believe that Chaucer's stories are still entertaining in today's society. Why or why not? Also ask students if the nature and content of the stories were what they had expected.

ASSESSMENT

1. To assess students' skits, use Rubric 33.

2. Additional grades can be based on students' participation in the discussion of chivalry and the concluding discussion. Students may evaluate their own performances if time permits.

The Major Crusades, 1096–1204

Have students examine the map on page 319. Ask students the following questions: Near what city did the routes of the four crusades cross? Which crusade brought armies from the farthest distance to the Holy Land?

Lesson 1

(For use with Sections 1 and 2, pp. 318–326)

OBJECTIVES

1. Identify the causes of the Crusades.

2. Describe the outcome of the First Crusade.

3. Describe the outcomes of the other major crusades.

4. Explain how the Crusades affected Europe.

5. Explain the factors that led to the revival of trade in Europe.

6. Describe goods traded in Europe and explain why fairs began.

7. Identify important business developments that resulted from the growth of trade.

BELLRINGER

Ask students to locate Dover and Acre on the map on page 319. Have them use the scale to estimate the distance of the route crusaders took from Dover to Acre. *(about 4,000 miles)* Have students speculate about why the crusaders might have gone to war so far from home. Tell students that in Section 1 they will learn why the crusaders went to the Holy Land.

TEACH OBJECTIVE 1

Level 1: Have students create a graphic organizer that illustrates the chain of causes and effects that led to the First Crusade.
[**English Language Learners**]

Levels 2 and 3: Ask students to list the causes and effects that led to the First Crusade. Then

have students read the two quotations in bold print on page 320. Ask students to write a journal entry from the point of view of a Muslim or Jewish inhabitant of Jerusalem who was present at the crusaders' conquest of the city.

TEACH OBJECTIVE 2

All Levels: Have students work in pairs to create a chart of the political, economic, and cultural effects of the First Crusade. *(political: Europeans control Holy Land, European institutions spread, crusaders set up small states; economic: feudalism spread, trade between Europe and the Holy Land, Italian shipping business grew; cultural: Europeans wore Eastern clothes and ate Eastern foods, Christians grew to respect Muslims)* [**English Language Learners, Cooperative Learning**]

TEACH OBJECTIVE 3

Level 1: Have students create a chart with the following column headings: *Second Crusade, Third Crusade, Fourth Crusade, Children's Crusade.* Ask students to list the outcomes of each crusade under its heading.
[**English Language Learners**]

Levels 2 and 3: Have students write five false statements about the outcomes of the other major crusades on a sheet of paper. Ask them to skip spaces between each statement. Then tell students to exchange papers with a partner and correct the partner's false statements in the spaces provided.
[**Cooperative Learning**]

TEACH OBJECTIVE 4

All Levels: Ask students to imagine a reunion of elderly crusaders. Then have them write speeches that the attendees might give about their lives since the Crusades. Tell students to use information under "Results of the Crusades."

TEACH OBJECTIVE 5

Level 1: On the chalkboard, draw a web diagram so that *Revival of Trade* is surrounded by five ovals. Tell students to fill the ovals with reasons for the revival of trade in Europe.
[**English Language Learners**]

Levels 2 and 3: Ask students how the geographic locations of Italy, Kiev, and Flanders and the power of the Hanseatic League revived trade in Europe. Ask students to examine the map on page 324. Who controlled most of the trade routes in Europe? Why did they not control trade in the North Sea and Baltic Sea?

TEACH OBJECTIVE 6

All Levels: Organize the class into groups of four. Assign each group the role of either medieval merchants or rulers. Have the merchants plan how to attract more buyers for their goods. Have the rulers plan how to profit from the increased trade in their kingdoms. Have each group present its plan to the class.
[**English Language Learners, Cooperative Learning**]

TEACH OBJECTIVE 7

All Levels: Ask students to identify the three major areas that developed as a result of the growth in trade. Then have students use the information in the section to create a chart comparing the characteristics of a barter economy with those of a market economy.
[**English Language Learners**]

REVIEW AND ASSESS

Have students complete the **Review Sections 1 and 2**. Have students complete **Daily Quizzes 14.1 and 14.2**. As Alternative Assessment, you may want to use the growth of trade graphic organizer or the comparison activity in this section's lessons.

RETEACH

Have students complete **Main Idea Activities 14.1 and 14.2**. Then have them rewrite the section's headings as questions and answer the questions with main ideas from the section.
[**English Language Learners**]

CHALLENGE AND EXTEND

Have students use the medieval illustration on page 326 as a model to create their own illustrations of another aspect of business in the Middle Ages.

Lesson 2

(For use with Sections 3 and 4, pp. 327–335)

OBJECTIVES

1. Identify rights townspeople gained during the late Middle Ages.

2. Explain how merchant and craft guilds contributed to their communities.

3. Describe how the growth of cities helped lead to the decline of serfdom.

4. Analyze changes in language and literature during the Middle Ages.

5. Examine changes in education during the Middle Ages.

6. Identify developments made in philosophy and science.

7. Describe the characteristic architecture of the later Middle Ages.

BELLRINGER

Tell students that the approximate present-day populations of Paris and London are 2 million and 7 million, respectively. Have them predict their size in the 1200s. Ask volunteers to write their predictions on the chalkboard. Tell students that, in Section 3, they will learn the actual size of these cities in the Middle Ages.

TEACH OBJECTIVE 1

Level 1: On the chalkboard, write the four basic rights of medieval townspeople. *(freedom, exemption, town justice, and commercial privileges)* Then tell students to use the reading to explain each one. Ask students to compare

these rights with those of American citizens.
[**English Language Learners**]

Levels 2 and 3: Ask students to imagine that they are townspeople in the Middle Ages. Ask them to write a statement analyzing the rights given to them. Are they satisfied with these rights? Are there any rights not mentioned that students believe they should possess?

TEACH OBJECTIVE 2

Levels 1 and 2: Ask students to identify and define the guilds founded during the Middle Ages. Ask students how a guild might help a young person who wanted to work.
[**English Language Learners**]

Level 3: Have students compose letters that members of a merchant or craft guild might write to townspeople who question the worth of guilds. Tell students to explain how the existence of guilds helps the entire community.

TEACH OBJECTIVE 3

All Levels: Create a chart of two columns on the board and title it *The Decline of Serfdom.* Have students list the factors that contributed to the decline of serfdom in the left column. Then ask the class to rank the importance of each factor and write the result in the right column.
[**English Language Learners, Cooperative Learning**]

TEACH OBJECTIVE 4

All Levels: On the chalkboard, create a chart of three columns and title it *Vernacular Literature in the Middle Ages.* Use the following for column headings: *Kind of Literature, Characteristics,* and *Example.* Have students fill in the chart using the text under the heading of "Language and Literature."
[**English Language Learners**]

TEACH OBJECTIVE 5

All Levels: Ask students to summarize how education changed during the Middle Ages. What new institutions formed? What did students study? How were medieval universities like guilds?
[**English Language Learners**]

TEACH OBJECTIVE 6

All Levels: Write the following on the chalkboard: *Thomas Aquinas argued that science and reason were in conflict with faith.* Organize students in groups and tell the groups to decide whether they agree or disagree with Thomas Aquinas. Have each group explain its decision.
[**English Language Learners, Cooperative Learning**]

TEACH OBJECTIVE 7

All Levels: Show students exterior pictures of a Romanesque church (Pisa Cathedral) and a Gothic church (Notre Dame in Paris). Have them point out the Gothic church and list the features that identify it as Gothic architecture.
[**English Language Learners**]

REVIEW AND ASSESS

Have students complete **Review Sections 3 and 4.** Have students complete **Daily Quizzes 14.3 and 14.4.** As Alternative Assessment, you may want to use the Summarizing graphic organizer or the Supporting a Point of View exercise at the end of Section 4.

RETEACH

Have students complete **Main Idea Activities 14.3 and 14.4.** Then have students make an outline of this section using the headings as main ideas.
[**English Language Learners**]

CHALLENGE AND EXTEND

Tell students to imagine they are troubadours who will perform a poem in the court of an important noble. Have them research one of the medieval ideals of chivalry or courtly love and write the poem.

Lesson 3

(For use with Sections 5 and 6, pp. 336–343)

OBJECTIVES

1. Identify ways the Hundred Years' War affected England and France.

2. Analyze how Spain's rulers both strengthened and weakened their nation.

3. Explain why the Holy Roman Empire remained weak throughout the later Middle Ages.

4. Identify the factors that led to the decline of the Catholic Church in the later Middle Ages.

5. Describe how the Babylonian Captivity and the Great Schism affected the church.

6. Explain why great teachers and priests challenged the church during the later Middle Ages.

BELLRINGER

Have students scan Section 5 for dates. Have them arrange the dates on a time line leaving space beside each year. Tell students that in Section 5 they will learn about events that united nations during the period on their time line.

TEACH OBJECTIVE 1

All Levels: Divide the class into two groups. Assign one group to represent England and the other to speak for France. Have students list the ways in which the Hundred Years' War affected their particular country and present the information to the other group. Is it possible to determine which country suffered most?

TEACH OBJECTIVE 2

All Levels: Organize the class into two groups and plan a panel discussion. Have the members of one group defend the actions of Isabella and Ferdinand from 1479 to 1515. Ask the students in the other group to criticize the rulers' policies. **[Cooperative Learning]**

TEACH OBJECTIVE 3

All Levels: Have students create a time line documenting every major event that contributed to the weakening of the Holy Roman Empire. **[English Language Learners]**

TEACH OBJECTIVE 4

All Levels: Organize students into two groups to present arguments why the French clergy in 1300 should or should not pay taxes. **[English Language Learners, Cooperative Learning]**

TEACH OBJECTIVE 5

All Levels: Have students write four cause-and-effect relationships about the Babylonian Captivity and the Great Schism.

TEACH OBJECTIVE 6

All Levels: Ask the class to create a Venn diagram showing how John Wycliffe and Jan Hus were alike and different. **[English Language Learners]**

REVIEW AND ASSESS

Have students complete **Review Sections 5 and 6**. Have students complete **Daily Quizzes 14.5 and 14.6**. As Alternative Assessment, you may want to use the cause-and-effect chart of Venn diagram exercise in this section's lessons.

RETEACH

Have students complete **Main Idea Activities 14.5 and 14.6**. Then have students work in pairs to list the people in the section, the actions of each, and how the actions affected the church.

CHALLENGE AND EXTEND

Have students research and write a newspaper article about the actual trial of a heretic. Articles should contain standard grammar, spelling, sentence structure, and punctuation.

A Medieval Romance

GOAL

In this activity, students will demonstrate their understanding of the elements of medieval romance and medieval culture by writing an original romance.

PLANNING

- **Purpose** This activity incorporates teacher-directed lessons and individual and group assignments. It should be used as a culminating activity for a study of the European Middle Ages.

- **Suggested Time** Plan to spend two lesson blocks and one or two homework assignments on this activity. Provide time for students to share and discuss their romances.

- **Teaching Team** At least one social studies teacher and one language arts teacher should take part in teaching this activity.

- **Group Size** This activity can be adapted for either individuals or groups.

- **Materials and Resources** Provide students with copies of one or several versions of Arthurian legends (Alfred Lord Tennyson, Sir Thomas Malory, T. H. White, et. al.). Also provide students with white drawing paper and copies of Rubric 20. Give students a variety of illustrated references on illumination such as *Medieval Ornamental Styles* (written by W. and G. Audsley, published by Chartwell Books, Inc., Secaucus, New Jersey, 1988) or *Alphabets and Numbers of the Middle Ages* (written by Henry Shaw, published by Crescent Books, New York, 1988).

IMPLEMENTATION

1. Give students an overview of the activity by explaining that, after studying the Middle Ages and reading Arthurian legends, students will write an original medieval romance and illustrate its pages. Each student's romance will include elements of the medieval romance as well as specified historical and cultural detail.

2. Focusing on Chapters 13 and 14, review the changing social structure of medieval Europe. Some questions to consider are: What was the social structure of feudal Europe? What role was played by each class of people? How could land be acquired? How was land governed? Why did trade revive? How did the revival of trade affect the social structure? How were the newly emerging towns governed?

3. Have each student or group of students invent a royal family around which to base their romance. On the large drawing paper provided, each student or group should depict an idealized setting for their romance. Although idealized, this drawing must include the basic elements of a medieval manor as described in "The Manorial System" in the text.

4. Read one or several versions of the Arthurian legends. As a class or in groups, identify and list elements that comprise a medieval romance. *(Student lists should include the following: royalty, chivalric heroes, mystery, magic and the supernatural, theme of good versus evil, lofty language, and idealized setting, disguise or concealment of identity, and courtly love.)*

5. Assign individual students or groups of students the task of creating an original medieval romance. The romance should revolve around their invented royal family and include all elements listed above. The plot of each romance should also include at least four of the following aspects of medieval life: guilds or craftsmen, banquet or feast, tournament, crusades, peasant life, power of the church, monasticism, medieval weaponry, plague, knight's proof of worthiness, troubadours, pilgrimage. In addition, pages of the romance should be illuminated in the medieval style. Share romances by having each student read and identify at least five elements of romance or medieval life in another student's romance.

ASSESSMENT

1. To assess students' romances, use Rubric 39.

2. Additional grades can be based on students' participation in class discussion and student diagrams of medieval manors using Rubric 20.

Renaissance Italy: A Patchwork of States

Have students examine the map on page 354. Ask students what the divisions on the map mean. *(Renaissance Italy was made up of many separate city-states.)* Ask why they think major city-states grew rich from trade and industry. *(The many ports and strategic trade routes in Italy encouraged trade and cultural exchange.)*

Lesson 1

(For use with Sections 1 and 2, pp. 352–363)

OBJECTIVES

1. Identify the factors that led to the Italian Renaissance and describe the characteristics of Renaissance thought.

2. Explain how Renaissance writers combined classical teachings and Christian doctrine.

3. Describe how Renaissance art differed from art of the Middle Ages.

4. Explain how the ideas of the Italian Renaissance spread to other parts of Europe.

5. Describe how northern Renaissance writers differed from Italian humanists.

6. List the principal characteristics of northern Renaissance art.

BELLRINGER

Display examples of medieval and Renaissance art, such as Pietro Caallini's *Birth of the Virgin* for medieval and Raphael's *School of Athens* for Renaissance. Have volunteers compare these works. *(Medieval art portrays ideal type, hides human form; Renaissance art focuses on human form and individuality.)* Explain that, in Section 1, students will learn more about the ideals and values of the Renaissance.

TEACH OBJECTIVE 1

Level 1: Have students work in pairs to create a list of factors that led to the Renaissance

(ruins of the Roman Empire a reminder of Roman glory; contact with Byzantine civilizations through Crusades and trade; knowledge of Arab and African achievements in science and medicine; an artistic awakening; the study of classical Greek and Roman literature and life; scholars' search for new knowledge) Then ask students to copy Renaissance Thought on their papers. Work with students to describe the nature of thought during the Renaissance. *(education important, critical approach, admiration for individual achievement, supporting the arts, belief in human dignity, one should lead a meaningful life)*
[**English Language Learners**]

Levels 2 and 3: Ask students what they recall of the Greek art, literature, and philosophy that they studied. What were some of the values of the Greeks *(education, art, human mind)* Ask them to write several paragraphs on the same ideas present in the Renaissance from Section 1. Share with the class.
[**English Language Learners, Cooperative Learning**]

TEACH OBJECTIVE 2

Level 1: Ask students to name the Renaissance writers that are mentioned in this section. *(Francesco Petrarch, Niccolo Machiavelli, Baldassare Castiglione)* Ask students to explain how Renaissance writers were able to combine classical teachings with their Christian beliefs. *(showed concern for spirituality, wrote with regard for morality)* Ask students if a concern for morality was true in the work of all Renaissance writers. *(not in Machiavelli's The Prince)*
[**English Language Learners, Cooperative Learning**]

Levels 2 and 3: Ask students to read several Petrarchan sonnets. Have them identify some of the themes. *(unrequited love, idealization of women, unworthiness of the poet, worthiness of his verse)* Discuss the themes in class in terms of Renaissance thought.

TEACH OBJECTIVE 3

All Levels: Have students list features of medieval art. Then have them list features of Renaissance art. Have them work in groups to make a comparison chart on posterboard. (*for example: medieval art stressed religion and world beyond everyday life, depicted formal and stylized figures, depicted the Holy Land; Renaissance art depicted religious and non-religious subjects, depicted realistic and lifelike human figures, depicted the rugged Italian countryside)*
[Cooperative Learning]

TEACH OBJECTIVE 4

Level 1: Have students imagine that no method of printing has ever been invented and that all written material must be copied by hand. Ask students how their lives might be different in this scenario. (*education would be difficult; fewer people would read; people would know less about distant places)* Discuss how the invention of the printing press affected learning, culture, and the spread of ideas in Europe.
[English Language Learners, Cooperative Learning]

TEACH OBJECTIVE 5

Level 1: Help students describe the characteristics shared between the Italian Humanist and the Northern Humanist. Write their answers on the board.
[English Language Learners, Cooperative Learning]

TEACH OBJECTIVE 6

Level 3: Ask students to describe characteristics that differentiate northern Renaissance art from that of the Italian Renaissance. (*Northern art has more realistic depiction of figures and everyday subject matter.)* Draw attention to Holbein's *The French Ambassadors.* Have volunteers identify objects in the painting that make the ambassadors seem down-to-earth. (*guitar-like instrument, open book, etc.)* Now have students write a paragraph describing how they would set up a studio shot to depict a classmate or friend. Encourage them to pay attention to

props they might use to make the subjects seem easy to know.

REVIEW AND ASSESS

Have students complete **Review Sections 1 and 2**. Have students work in pairs and create a graphic organizer that demonstrates how the main ideas of the two sections are related. Have students complete **Daily Quiz 15.1 and 15.2**.
[English Language Learners]

CHALLENGE AND EXTEND

Ask students to write an essay describing how Italian Renaissance art, literature, and thought were reflective of the period. (*Essays should include the combination of religious themes with the humanistic values of the era, and cite specific examples.)*

Lesson 2

(For use with Sections 3 and 4, pp. 158–177)

OBJECTIVES

1. Discuss the developments that led to the Reformation.
2. Describe how Martin Luther protested against the Roman Catholic Church and began a new church.
3. Identify the factors that caused the spread of Protestantism.
4. Explain the role that Calvinism played in the Reformation.
5. Describe how the Catholic Church responded to the Reformation.
6. Discuss the results of the Reformation and the Counter-Reformation.

BELLRINGER

As students enter the classroom, ask them how they would feel if they had worked hard for a good grade, and then were told that they could get that grade only if they paid for it. Have students relate this system to the Catholic Church's selling of indulgences—the practice of selling pardons for sin—in the 1500s. Prompt students to speculate what might happen if many people became outraged about indulgences. *(They might revolt.)* Explain that, in Section 3, students will learn about a religious revolution called the Reformation.

TEACH OBJECTIVE 1 AND 2

Level 1: Have students work in pairs or groups and have them list the events leading up to the excommunication of Martin Luther. Then have them write a list of events that lead up to his expulsion until the formation of the Lutheran Church.
[**English Language Learners**]

Levels 2 and 3: Ask students to expand on the ideas in Level 1. Have them research each statement that was in Martin Luther's 95 theses. Have them choose five of the statements and rewrite them in their own words.

TEACH OBJECTIVE 2

Level 1: Have students research Martin Luther's thesis. What were some of his complaints against the Catholic Church? Lead a discussion based on the thesis he nailed to Wittenburg Cathedral.
[**English Language Learners**]

Levels 2 and 3: Ask students to write a paper on the historical significance of Martin Luther to the Reformation.
[**English Language Learners, Cooperative Learning**]

TEACH OBJECTIVE 3

Level 1: Work with students to create a list of factors that led to the spread of Protestantism. *(many Europeans' desire for a simpler, more direct religion; German rulers' establishment of the Lutheran Church with their states; Charles V's inability to defeat Protestant princes; Peace of Augsbury; Henry VIII's divorce and subsequent creation of the Anglican Church)* Then discuss how these events, though they took place at different times in various parts of Europe, all contributed to what has become known as the Protestant Reformation.

[**English Language Learners**]

Levels 2 and 3: Ask students to research one element that contributed to the Reformation. Have them write an essay on the topic and present it to the class.

TEACH OBJECTIVE 4

Level 3: Ask students to write an essay describing Calvinism and its role in the Reformation. Remind them to use standard grammar, spelling, sentence structure, and punctuation. *(Essays should include some discussion of Huldrych Zwingli, John Calvin, predestination, theocracy in Geneva, Huguenots, and wars in France.)* Ask volunteers to read their essays to the class.

TEACH OBJECTIVE 5

Level 1: Ask students to detail the ways in which the Catholic Church responded to the growth of Protestantism. Have them list the main goals of the Church along with the methods used to achieve those goals. Students should work in pairs or groups.
Goal: Revive spirituality
Method: Ended abuses surrounding sale of indulgences, tightened discipline within clergy.
Goal: Combat heresy
Method: Brought the Inquisition to Rome, established *Index of Forbidden Books*
Goal: Define Catholic doctrine
Method: Supported dependence on priest, salvation through ceremonial actions and individual faith, notion of free will in every person
Goal: Slow the spread of Protestantism
Method: Better-educated priests worked more forcefully for the church, old and new religious orders, such as the Jesuits, spread Catholicism
[**English Language Learners, Cooperative Learning**]

TEACH OBJECTIVE 6

Level 1: Have students list long-term results of the Reformation and Counter-Reformation. *(many different churches in Europe, strong interest in education, growth in university enrollment, reading more important, remaining lack of toler-*

ance for new ideas, increased power for national governments, decreased power for the Pope)

REVIEW AND ASSESS

Have students complete **Review Sections 3 and 4**. Then have groups of students construct a crossword puzzle using all of the terms and individuals mentioned in the Section Reviews. Have students complete **Daily Quiz 15. 3 and 15.4**.

RETEACH

Have students complete **Main Idea Activities 15.3 and 15.4**. Then pair students to answer the **Reading Check** questions in **Sections 3 and 4 and 5**.
[**English Language Learners, Cooperative Learning**]

CHALLENGE AND EXTEND

Have students research the Inquisition and present their findings to the class. Encourage them to use their textbooks, the library, the computer software, and other sources of information on the subject.

Lesson 3

(For use with Sections 5, pp. 372–377)

OBJECTIVES

1. Explain why Europeans believed in superstitions.

2. Describe the characteristics of daily life that were typical in Europe during the Reformation.

3. Explain how knowledge spread to European villages.

4. Identify the factors that caused changes in the daily lives of Europeans.

BELLRINGER

As students enter the classroom, ask them what they think life was like for peasants during the Renaissance. *(War, famine, and plague affected*

many people. They looked to superstitions to explain and control their lives.)

TEACH OBJECTIVE 1

Level 1: Have students share some common superstitions. Ask them why they think some people believe in such things. *(Superstitions help people believe they can control fate.)* Discuss the superstitious nature of European villagers during the Renaissance and Reformation. Ask why superstitions were so widespread during this era.

TEACH OBJECTIVE 2

Level 2: Have students examine the painting by Pieter Brueghel the Younger on page 376. Ask them to write down what they can conclude about peasant life as they observe how the pethe activities. Have volunteers read their observations to the class.

TEACH OBJECTIVE 3

All Levels: Ask students to identify and describe the main ways in which village people learned about the world outside of their villages. Divide the class into small groups. Have each group create a broadside, an almanac page, or the message brought by a traveling preacher. Then have the groups share their work with the class.

TEACH OBJECTIVE 4

Level 3: Have students detail before and after charts comparing Europe in about 1400 and Europe in about 1600. Remind students to list the differences and explain the reasons for them. Close by asking students what remained the same.

REVIEW AND ASSESS

Have students complete the **Review Section 5** on page 377. Have students complete **Daily Quiz 15.5**. As Alternative Assessment, you may want to use the before-and-after chart of a magazine article exercise in this section's lessons.

Petrarchan and Shakespearean Sonnets

GOAL

In this activity, students will learn more about the poetic form of the sonnet and the connection to Renaissance thought.

PLANNING

- **Purpose** This activity may be used in combination with teacher-directed lessons, as an enrichment activity, or as a performance-based assessment of content mastery.

- **Suggested Time** Plan to spend two lesson blocks and one homework assignment on this activity. Provide time for the presentation of the sonnets at the end of the lesson.

- **Teaching Team** At least one social studies teacher and one language arts teacher should take part in teaching this activity.

- **Group Size** This activity will work as a small group activity or for individual students.

- **Materials and Resources** Examples of Petrarchan and Shakespearean sonnets:

  Student copies of Rubric 26: *Poems and Songs* from *Portfolio and Performance Assessment for Social Studies.*

  Paints, markers, or map pencils

  Butcher paper cut into different sizes

  Paper for book pages

IMPLEMENTATION

1. Give students an overview of the activity by explaining that they will first read a selection of Petrarchan and Shakespearean sonnets. After they have learned the poetic devices and themes of the sonnets, they will be asked to compose their own sonnet series.

2. Read several sonnets aloud to students. Ask students to first discuss the themes in the sonnet. *(unrequited love, the pain of love, the conflicting feelings of love—joy/ pain, Petrarch's oxymorons—fire/ice)*

3. Ask the students to look for any particular rhyme scheme. *(Petrarchan sonnets: abaabba, cdcdee; Shakespearean sonnets: abab/cdcd/efef/gg).* Then ask them if they notice how many beats there are in each line. *(10 beats in each line.)* Then explain stressed and unstressed syllables. Show the students the iambic pentameter *(5 stressed and unstressed syllables in each line).* Ask the students to count the number of lines in the poems *(14 lines).* Ask them to identify metaphors, similes, conceits and the couplet. Explain that a couplet is supposed to wrap the sonnet up, to solve the problem of love in a poetic way.

4. Ask students why they think the Renaissance mind would enjoy a complicated form such as the sonnet? *(It appealed to their intellectual side and romantic side. They enjoyed the puzzle and form of the poem.)* What challenges does it give to the poet? *(It is difficult to write in such strict form.)* To the reader? *(Sometimes it is hard to figure out the poem's meaning. It takes work and reason.)* How is the form reflective of the subject? *(It's complicated, like love.)* Explain to the students that sonnets became the rage in the Renaissance. Every young lover wrote his beloved a sonnet. Ask them to write one sonnet in class.

5. Ask students to write a sonnet series and to make a book of the poems. Encourage them to be creative in their books. Explain that they must write the sonnets by hand (publishing before the printing press) and decorate the pages like a Renaissance book. They may cover the books in velvet, or cloth, and embroider buttons, jewels, initials. Cut the butcher cloth in the sizes of the pages and place them over the paper to look like vellum.

6. In each sonnet, have students identify the poetic devices they used. Make note of metaphor, simile, and alliteration.

ASSESSMENT

1. Assess students' work by their use of historical information, combined with their ability to fulfill the creative writing components.

2. Additional grades can be based on students' participation in the presentation.

Exploration and Expansion Time Line

Have students look at the time line on pages 380 and 381. Ask which event they think had the most significant impact on the world as we know it today. *(Have students justify their answers. They will likely answer Columbus's voyage to the Americas.)* Ask what they think would have happened if Columbus had not made his voyage in 1492 and landed in the Americas.

Lesson 1

(For use with Sections 1 and 2, pp. 380–391)

OBJECTIVES

1. Identify the factors that contributed to the Scientific Revolution.

2. Explain how Copernicus, Kepler, and Galileo challenged traditional thought.

3. Describe some of the important scientific discoveries of this period.

4. Identify technological advances that made European exploration possible.

5. Describe the effect of the Commercial Revolution.

6. Explain the role mercantilism played in the colonies.

BELLRINGER

As students enter the classroom, ask them to divide a sheet of paper into two columns headed *Magical* and *Scientific*. In the Magical column have them write words that describe how people who believed in magic tried to learn about nature. *(alchemy, astrology, ancient texts)* In the Scientific column have them write words describing how scientists learn about nature. *(observation, mathematics, measurement, instruments)* Note any responses that fall in both columns. Tell students that, in Section 1, they will learn how belief in magic contributed to the beginnings of the Scientific Revolution.

TEACH OBJECTIVE 1

Level 1: Ask students to name causes of the Scientific Revolution and write their answers on the board *(questioning ancient beliefs, curiosity, observation, experiment, mathematics, scientific instruments)*
[English Language Learners]

Levels 2 and 3: Ask students to research one of the following scientific inventions: barometer, microscope, telescope, air pump, thermometer. Have them write an essay on the contribution the invention made to the Scientific Revolution. Have students share essays in class.
[English Language Learners, Cooperative Learning]

TEACH OBJECTIVE 2

Level 1: Explain the difference between the geocentric theory *(Sun, planets, and stars revolve around Earth.)* and the heliocentric theory. *(Earth and other planets revolve around sun.)* Then divide students into groups of three to six. Have each group plan and perform a short role-play about Copernicus, Kepler, or Galileo. Tell students their skit should explain the scientist's ideas in simple words and show how those ideas challenged traditional thought.
[English Language Learners, Cooperative Learning]

Level 3: Have students write an essay about how changing from geocentric to a heliocentric view of the universe might affect people's attitudes about other aspects of life. *(Essays will vary but might mention the idea that nature does not revolve around people, creation is like an impersonal machine, and what seems obvious is not necessarily true.)* Discuss the essays in class. Ask students if any modern scientific discoveries affect the ways people think about their lives. *(relativity, quantum theory, space exploration)*

TEACH OBJECTIVE 3

Level 2: Ask students to create a chart of discoveries made during the Scientific Revolution. Have them organize their ideas under the headings: *Astronomy, Physics, Anatomy, Chemistry,* and *Mathematics. (heliocentric theory; all objects fall at the same speed; laws of motion and universal gravitation; construction of human body; circulation of blood; oxygen; conservation of matter; calculus)* Then have students describe the significance of as many of these discoveries as they can. *(heliocentric theory—changed basic view of the universe; objects fall at the same speed—laid the foundation for modern science of mechanics; construction of human body and circulation of blood—laid basis for modern medicine)*

Levels 2 and 3: Ask students to read about Robert Boyle in go.hrw.com. Ask them to write a short essay describing his contribution to science.
[English Language Learners]

TEACH OBJECTIVE 4

Level 1: Have students create four-column charts about technology that aided overseas exploration in the 1300s. The first column should identify the technological advances. *(maps, compass, astrolabe, changes in ships, rudder, sails)* The second column should describe each advance and the third column should explain how it aided exploration. In the fourth column, students should rank-order the advances by their importance to exploration from "1" (most important) to "5" (least important). Select students to explain their rankings.
[English Language Learners, Cooperative Learning]

TEACH OBJECTIVE 5

Level 3: Ask volunteers to name ways expeditions were financed. *(bank loan, joint-stock company, monarch)* Have each student write and present a speech to persuade a banker, individual investor, or monarch to fund an expedition.
[English Language Learners, Cooperative Learning]

Levels 2 and 3: Ask each student to research the currency of Europe in the late 1400s. *(They should discover that different countries had different amounts of gold in coins and that this made trade difficult.)* Ask them to research the Euro dollar today. What are some of the common themes with both of these currency issues? Have students write a paper on the similarities.
[English Language Learners]

TEACH OBJECTIVE 6

Level 3: Have students draw a web diagram showing the reasons why Europeans established colonies. *Governments settled for markets, raw materials, gold and silver. Colonists settled for adventure, religious freedom, and overpopulation.*

REVIEW AND ASSESS

Have students complete the **Review Sections 1 and 2**. Have students work in pairs and create a graphic organizer that demonstrates how the main ideas of the two sections are related. Have students complete **Daily Quiz 16.1 and 16.2.**

RETEACH

Have students complete **Main Idea Activities 16.1 and 16.2.** Assign each student a **Reading Check** question from **Section 1 or 2.** Then have students work in pairs to create a time line that notes the major events of the chapter.
[English Language Learners]

CHALLENGE AND EXTEND

Have students draw political cartoons that illustrate one of the effects of mercantilism, such as accumulation of gold and silver, national self-sufficiency, or establishing an empire.

Lesson 2

(For use with Sections 3 and 4, pp. 392–407)

OBJECTIVES

1. Describe what the early Portuguese explorers accomplished.

2. Discuss how the voyagers of Christopher Columbus influenced the world.

3. Explain why the Atlantic slave trade prospered.

4. Describe how Spain extended its power abroad and at home.

5. Explain why the Dutch were successful in the 1600s.

6. Analyze why the Spanish Empire declined.

BELLRINGER

As students enter the classroom, ask them to list products from Asia that many people in America use. *(electronics, automobiles, watches, athletic shoes, clothing)* Ask how these products come to the United States. *(by ship or airplane)* Ask them to imagine what would happen if everything from Asia had to come almost entirely over land, crossing from Russia to Alaska at the Bering Strait. *(goods would cost more; Russia or China could interrupt trade)* Tell students that, in section 3, they will learn how the European desire for Asian products led Europeans to try to find sea routes to Asia so they would not have to depend on overland trade.

TEACH OBJECTIVES 1 AND 2

Level 1: To help students understand the economic motivations for the early voyages of exploration, lead a discussion using the following questions as a guide: What was the traditional way Asian goods moved west before the voyages of exploration? *(by various land and sea routes to the Middle East)* Why did Europeans begin to desire Asian goods? *(result of Crusades)* Before the voyages of exploration, what groups controlled the trade of these goods with Europe? *(Arab and Italian merchants)* Why did the trade process make Asian goods so expensive in Europe? *(high overland transportation costs, payments to Arab or Italian middlemen)* Have students refer to the map on pages 396–397 to answer the following questions: How did Dias and da Gama enable Portugal to trade directly with Asia? *(Dias found route to Indian Ocean; da Gama built on Dias's explo-*

ration and led to India) Why did Portugal take the lead in finding a sea route? *(location on the Atlantic; Prince Henry)* How did these explorations give Portugal a trade advantage over other European nations? *(allowed Portuguese to establish direct trade with Asian markets)*
[**English Language Learners**]

Levels 2 and 3: Ask students to create maps of the sailing and trading routes of the Portuguese. Attach to the maps a description of things traded at different ports.

TEACH OBJECTIVE 2

Level 3: Have students imagine they are European cartographers (map makers) around 1500 who have been hired by the rulers of Spain or Portugal to make a map of newly discovered territories. The rulers have asked them to illustrate the map with pictures of trade goods, scenery, or people from the regions shown. Invite students to present their maps to the class.
[**English Language Learners**]

Levels 2 and 3: Ask students to name the kinds of people who might be on a ship crossing the Atlantic Ocean in the 1500s. *(Answers will vary but might include explorers, map makers, sailors, slaves, slave merchants, and settlers.)* Then have students imagine they are on a ship crossing the Atlantic. Have them write a diary of the voyage. The first entry should explain who they are and why they are on the ship.
[**English Language Learners, Cooperative Learning**]

TEACH OBJECTIVE 3

Level 1: Divide students into four or more small groups. Have each group discuss any advantages and disadvantages of the slave trade from the point of view of one of these individuals: a plantation owner in the Americas, a slave, the owner of a slave ship, or the ruler of an African kingdom. Have each group prepare a skit or drawing about the slave trade from their character's point of view and present it to the class.

Level 2: Working as individuals or in pairs, have students create a chain of events chart of the origins of the transatlantic slave trade. (*Europeans wanted labor in the colonies, Europeans enslaved Native Americans; Native Americans died from European diseases; Europeans imported slaves from Africa to replace them*)

All Levels: Organize student into small groups to present skits about life in the colonies of Spain and the Netherlands. Each group should script a scene that would have been typical in the lives and interactions of the native people and the Spanish or Dutch colonists. Suggest that groups decide on their basic story line and assign characters before developing their scripts. After the groups complete their scripts, have them present their skits to the class.

TEACH OBJECTIVE 4

Level 1: Have students draw and color a map showing Spanish conquests in the 1500s. Then have them create a diagram showing how Spain directed colonial government.

Level 3: Ask students to imagine they are advisers to King Philip II of Spain. Have them write the advice they would give the king about how to improve the economy of Spain. As examples, suggest students consider possible changes in foreign policy, religious policy, or ways to become less dependent on imports. Have volunteers present their advice to the class, pretending that they are speaking to the king.
[**English Language Learners, Cooperative Learning**]

TEACH OBJECTIVE 5

Level 2: Have students work in small groups to make a web diagram with the following topics: *traders* and *seafarers*. Ask them for reasons for Dutch success in the 1600s. Ask them to extend the web diagram with ways these traits helped the Dutch succeed. (*Answers may include banking; the Dutch East India Company;*

didn't attempt religious conversions; good sailors; good ships.)
[**English Language Learners**]

TEACH OBJECTIVE 6

All Levels: Pair students and have them develop a "Top Ten" list of reasons for Spain's decline as a world power. Select pairs to present their lists to the class, working up from the tenth reason to the number one reason. (*Lists might include ineffective rulers, Dutch revolt, defeat of Armada, expulsion of Jews and Moriscos, lack of industrial development, inflation resulting from colonial gold and silver, and so on.*) Record each pair's number one reason on the board for comparison.
[**Cooperative Learning**]

REVIEW AND ASSESS

Have students complete **Review Sections 3 and 4.** Have groups construct a crossword puzzle using all of the terms and names mentioned in the Section Reviews. Have students complete **Daily Quiz 16.3 and 16.4**.

RETEACH

Have students complete **Main Idea Activities 16.3 and 16.4**. Then have students study the "Cause and Effects of Spain's Age of Empire" chart on page 406 and restate each part of the chart in their own words.
[**English Language Learners, Cooperative Learning**]

CHALLENGE AND EXTEND

Have students make time lines that illustrate how events in Spain's European empire relate chronologically to the growth of the Spanish and Dutch Empires overseas. Suggest they plot European developments on one side of the time line and colonial developments on the other. Suggest they color-code their time lines to distinguish Dutch from Spanish events.

CHAPTER 16

Modern Chapter **7**

Team Teaching Strategy
Exploration and Expansion

Galileo: Heretic or Genius?

GOAL

In this activity, students will learn more about the political and scientific environments during the life of Galileo and practice their creative writing skills.

PLANNING

- **Purpose** This activity may be used in combination with teacher-directed lessons, as an enrichment activity, or as a performance-based assessment of content mastery.

- **Suggested Time** Plan to spend two lesson blocks and one homework assignment on this activity. Provide time for the presentation of the one-act plays.

- **Teaching Team** At least one social studies teacher and one language arts teacher should take part in teaching this activity.

- **Group Size** This activity will work as a small group activity or for individual students.

- **Materials and Resources**

- *Galileo* written by Bertolt Brecht

- Internet and library sources

- Background notes from the teacher on the life and career of Galileo

- Student photocopies of "Rubrics for Creative Writing" from *Portfolio and Performance Assessment for Social Studies*

IMPLEMENTATION

1. Give students an overview of the activity by explaining that they will first read the play *Galileo*, which details the scientific discoveries of the telescope, his theory that Ptolemy's geocentric theory was incorrect, his persecution by the Inquisition, and his final renouncement of his discoveries. Then explain that they will choose a scientist (*Roger Bacon, Nicolaus Copernicus, Johannes Kepler, Isaac Newton, Andreas Vesalius, Rene Descartes, Francis Bacon, or Roger Boyle*) and write a one-act play based on the life and discoveries of their particular scientist.

2. Before students read the play, review the historical age in which Galileo lived. Ask them what changes were occurring in science. (*magic to science, the study of nature became organized, people felt freer to question old ideas and beliefs, they were no longer satisfied to explain the world in terms of religious thought*) Ask them what the Church's response to these developments were? (*the Inquisition*) Ask the students what themes they expect to find in *Galileo*.

3. After the students read the play, ask them to define describe Galileo's character. How does the playwright develop his character? Explain that conflicts are the heart of drama. Ask them what Galileo's conflicts are with the world and within himself? What did Galileo suffer because of his beliefs?

4. Instruct students on the elements of drama. (*characterization, conflict, tension, resolution*) Explain that, in drama, playwrights must show emotion and thought through acting and mere dialogue. Thornton Wilder once said that the dramatist is "one who from his earliest years has found that sheer gazing at the shocks and countershocks among people is quite sufficiently engrossing without having to encase it in comment." Ask the students what they think Wilder meant by that comment? How does this playwright get his point across without preaching at the audience?

5. Ask students to research the life of one of the scientists listed above. Ask them to choose one dramatic incident in the scientist's life and to brainstorm about what that person may have thought, said, and acted like in the face of his discoveries. What opposition do they think he came up against? Ask students to begin writing thoughts of what the scientist may have been thinking. From their research and notes, ask them to write a one-act play about the event. Have students divide into groups

and read their one-act plays aloud. Ask students to read and make suggestions for each other's plays. Is there tension, character development, interesting dialogue, and correct historical fact?

6. Ask students to revise their plays.

7. Have students perform their one-act plays for the class.

ASSESSMENT

1. Assess students' work by their use of historical information, combined with their ability to fulfill the creative writing components.

2. Additional grades can be based on students' participation in the presentation.

Ming Civil Service Exam

Discuss the significance of the civil service examination system to the Ming dynasty. Tell students that it was the only avenue to high office in the dynasty. Bring in information on the civil service examination that federal government employees in the United States are required to take. Ask students why they think this examination is required for people who want to work for the federal government.

Lesson 1

(For use with Sections 1 and 2, pp. 408–421)

OBJECTIVES

1. Explain why the Chinese showed little interest in overseas trade during the Ming dynasty.

2. Describe how the Qing dynasty came to rule China.

3. Discuss changes that occurred in the Chinese economy during Qing rule.

4. Analyze reasons for the decline of the Qing dynasty.

5. Characterize early contact between Portugal and China.

6. Explain why China and Great Britain went to war in the mid-1800s.

7. Describe how internal rebellions contributed to the decline of the Qing dynasty.

BELLRINGER

As students enter the classroom, ask them to write a paragraph discussing whether they think the United States would be better off or worse off if the government prohibited all immigration and world trade. *(Most students will suggest that the nation would be worse off.)* Have volunteers share their responses with the class. Tell students that, in Section 1, they will learn how a policy of isolation affected the Ming and Qing dynasties in China.

TEACH OBJECTIVE 1

Level 1: Organize the class into groups. Within each group, designate a student to be the emperor and divide the remainder of the group into two factions—one representing court officials who favor continued trade with the outside world and the other representing court officials who wish to end that trade. Each faction should present arguments in support of its position to the emperor. After hearing the arguments, the emperor must decide on a course of action regarding international trade and report his or her decision to the class. Discuss with the class the consequences each decision might have for China.
[**English Language Learners**]

Levels 2 and 3: Ask students what they think China's policy on trade reveals about its value system? *(The culture was considered more important than money gained from trade routes. The merchants were considered to be the bottom of the social order, as opposed to the scholars, farmers, and artisans.)* Likewise, ask them if China wanted to bring its culture and religion to other lands *(No, it did not.)* Have students write an essay on the different approach China took from the other European nations they have studied. How was the approach different from the Greeks, Romans, and Spanish?
[**English Language Learners, Cooperative Learning**]

TEACH OBJECTIVE 2

Level 1: Review with students how earlier Chinese dynasties fell. Then discuss with the class if the fall of the Ming dynasty and the rise of the Qing dynasty fit the pattern of Chinese political history.
[**English Language Learners, Cooperative Learning**]

Levels 2 and 3: Ask students to read about the White Lotus Rebellion in 1796. Ask them to write a newspaper article account of the rebellion and why it took place. *(discontent over increased taxes and growing government inefficiency)* Include in the article the effect the rebellion had on the Qing Dynasty. *(seriously weakened the dynasty and caused more rebellions)*

TEACH OBJECTIVE 3

Level 1: Have the class act as an advisory council to the Qing emperor and debate the following issue: Should Chinese merchants continue trading with peoples of Central and Southeast Asia, Russia, and India? How might such trade affect Chinese society?
[Cooperative Learning]

Levels 2 and 3: Ask students to discuss how other cultures they have studied have been changed by trade. *(the cultures spread over the world; the colonists and traders absorbed other cultures' art, religious beliefs, political outlooks, economic growth)* Ask students to write an essay about the positive and negative effects China's trade policy had on its people.
[English Language Learners]

TEACH OBJECTIVE 4

Level 1: Write *The Decline of the Qing Dynasty* on the board. Under the heading, write *Cause and Effect* and list the reasons. *(Cause: overpopulation, government inefficiency, natural disasters. Effect: lack of food for peasants, political unrest, social turmoil.)*

Level 2 and 3: Ask students to choose one of the causes or effects of the Decline of the Qing dynasty. Ask them to research the topic further and to write a short essay on the specific effect their topic had on the Dynasty. Ask them to present their thoughts to the class.
[English Language Learners, Cooperative Learning]

TEACH OBJECTIVE 5

Level 1: Have students write essays summarizing the establishment of Portuguese trade in China and events that followed. *(Students' essays should mention the trading station at Macao established in 1557, the presence of Jesuit mission-*

aries on Portuguese ships, how the Jesuits gained power in the imperial court, and how Qing leaders came to fear the Jesuits' power.) Then ask students to share and discuss their essays.
[English Language Learners, Cooperative Learning]

Levels 2 and 3: Ask students to think about how Catholic Portuguese leaders would have responded if Chinese visitors came to their country and taught their religion. How did the Roman Catholic Church respond to the teachings of other types of religious thought? *(the Inquisition, excommunication, imprisonment, death)* Ask them to write a short essay detailing their thoughts based on the historical facts they know about the Church and the similarities to the Chinese rule.
[English Language Learners]

TEACH OBJECTIVE 6

Level 1: Copy the following countries on the board: *India, Great Britain,* and *China.* Have students list the products traded among the countries.

TEACH OBJECTIVE 7

Level 2: Have students imagine they are participants in the Taiping Rebellion. As a class, have them discuss the problems they see in Chinese society under the Qing dynasty and possible courses of action to take. On the board, list the problems and courses of action that are discussed. Then have the class vote on the best course of action to take.

Level 3: Have students write three short editorial articles about the advantages or disadvantages of opening China to Western trade. One editorial should be from a perspective of a Western government, another from the Qing government's point of view, and the third from a Chinese merchant. Select students to share their editorial with the class.

REVIEW AND ASSESS

Have students complete the **Review Sections 1 and 2.** As Alternative Assessment, you may want to use the graphic organizer exercise in this section's lesson.

RETEACH

Have students complete **Main Idea Activities 17.1 and 17.2**. Assign each student a **Reading Check** question from **Section 1 or 2**. Then have students list the steps leading to the decline of the Qing dynasty.
[English Language Learners]

CHALLENGE AND EXTEND

Assign students specific time periods within the Ming or Qing dynasties. Have students research and record events in China on one side of a time line and important world events on the other side.

Lesson 2

(For use with Section 3, pp. 422–427)

OBJECTIVES

1. Explain how the Tokugawa shogunate came to power.

2. Discuss why Japan's rulers sought to isolate their nation from foreign influence.

3. Identify characteristics of society and culture under the Tokugawa shogunate.

4. Describe how Japanese isolation was brought to an end.

BELLRINGER

As students enter the classroom, ask them to write a brief paragraph telling what they know about the nation of Japan. Have students share their knowledge of Japan in a class discussion, writing key facts on the chalkboard as you go. Tell students that, in Section 3, they will learn about the history of Japan during the time of the Tokugawa shoguns.

TEACH OBJECTIVE 1

Level 1: Pair students to develop a diagram of the power structure of Japan under the Tokugawa shoguns. Select pairs to copy their

diagrams on the chalkboard and explain them to the class. Ask the class how the size of the Tokugawa landholdings increased the family's political power. *(Taxes from their lands would sustain a large army of samurai.)* Then have students make changes in the chalkboard diagrams to illustrate what could have happened if the Tokugawa shoguns had permitted daimyo alliances. *(Changes could create blocks of daimyo and their samurai that could have been used against the shogun.)* Ask students how the Tokugawa discouraged any such opposition.
[English Language Learners]

Levels 2 and 3: Ask students to read from go.hrw.com about Tokugawa Ieyasu. After reading more about the overlord on Holt Researcher, create at time line of the major events of his reign.

TEACH OBJECTIVE 2

Level 1: Ask students why a government might limit its people's trade and contact with other nations. *(Responses should include: maximize government's power and control; protect the nation's domestic businesses; protect the nation's culture.)* List responses on the chalkboard as you discuss them. Tell students to refer to the chalkboard list as they study the foreign policies of Japan's Tokugawa shoguns.
[English Language Learners]

Levels 2 and 3: Tell students to imagine that they are Portuguese traders in Japan. Have them write letters back home describing their lives in Japan and what they have observed about government and society there.
[English Language Learners, Cooperative Learning]

TEACH OBJECTIVE 3

Level 1: Call on students to identify changes that the Tokugawa shoguns made in Japan, and list responses on the chalkboard. *(expelled Portuguese, limited Dutch traders, banned shipbuilding and overseas travel, adopted Confucian ideal of social classes, educated warriors to be government officials, paid warriors' salaries, required*

each daimyo to live in his castle town) Next, organize the class into small groups and assign each group one of the chalkboard changes. Have each group discuss how its assigned change would help bring stability to Japan and report its conclusions to the class. Then ask the class why cities and the arts would be more likely to grow in a stable society. (*Lack of unrest would promote commerce and culture.*)
[English Language Learners]

Levels 2 and 3: Ask students whether they think that one's social and economic status is determined by his or her family. (*Some should say yes, some no.*) Ask them to write an essay expressing how it would be like to live in a society that is determined by heredity. Tell students to review the history of the Tokugawa shogun for their essays.

TEACH OBJECTIVE 4

Level 1: Invite the class to imagine that they are daimyo in the shogun's court at Edo. Have students assume the role of the shogun and ask for their advice on how to respond to Perry's demand for U.S. trading privileges in Japan. Have the daimyo debate whether opening trade with the United States is in Japan's best interest. Have the daimyo propose courses of action that might satisfy the United States but still pressure Japan's culture and isolation. (*offer only emergency shelter, rest stop, or better treatment of shipwrecked sailors; limit the ports where trade can occur*) Then ask them to weigh all this information and suggest a response to Perry. Conclude the activity by comparing the class's proposed response to the course the shogun actually took (*The shogun, worried about naval attack from the United States, reluctantly agreed*

to negotiate. *This led to the Treaty of Kanagawa in 1854, which opened two ports to let Americans obtain fuel, shelter, and supplies and permitted trade to begin between the two nations.*)

Levels 2 and 3: Ask students to write a persuasive essay on either supporting President Fillmore's decision to pressure Japan into opening ports and trade, or protesting this decision. Have them point to specific examples for proof of their theses.
[English Language, Learners Cooperative Learning]

REVIEW AND ASSESS

Have students complete the **Review Sections 3 and 4**. Have students complete **Daily Quiz 17.3**. As Alternative Assessment, have students complete the diagram exercise in this section's lesson.

RETEACH

Have students complete **Main Idea Activities for English Language Learners and Special Needs Students 17.3**. Have students discuss whether the Tokugawa shoguns' foreign policies benefited the Japanese people.
[English Language Learners, Cooperative Learning]

CHALLENGE AND EXTEND

Have students create a letter to the editor or a political cartoon about Commodore Perry's arrival in Japan. Tell students that their letter or cartoon can express the point of view of their choice, such as an American trader, or a samurai.

Emaki: A Japanese Scroll

GOAL

In this activity, students will demonstrate their understanding of the history of Japan from 1600 to 1868 by creating a long picture scroll and poetry in the Japanese tradition.

PLANNING

- **Purpose** This activity incorporates teacher-directed lessons and individual and group assignments. It should be used as a concurrent or culminating activity for a study of the Tokugawa shoguns in Japan.

- **Suggested Time** Plan to spend two lesson blocks and one homework assignment on this activity. Provide time for students to share and discuss their emaki and writings.

- **Teaching Team** At least one social studies teacher and one language arts teacher should take part in teaching this activity.

- **Group Size** This activity will work as a small group activity or for individual students.

- **Materials and Resources** Examples of Japanese haiku and senryu such as those found in *World Literature* (Holt, Rinehart and Winston, Inc.) or in library resources:

  Butcher paper cut into long rectangular strips

  Paints, markers, or map pencils

  Student copies of Rubric 3: *Artwork* and Rubric 26: *Poems and Songs* from *Portfolio and Performance Assessment for Social Studies*

  Variety of illustrated references on Japanese art and emaki, such as Japanese Art (written by Joan Stanley-Baker, published by Thames and Hudson Ltd., London, 1984)

IMPLEMENTATION

1. Give students an overview of this activity by explaining that they will create an emaki, a style of picture scroll used by the Japanese to depict the history of Japanese shrines, temples, legends, and military epics. These hand scrolls were meant to be unwound slowly from right to left, with the viewer observing the figures one by one in order to learn the history, legend, or epic. The students will also imitate the Japanese poetry form of haiku, a brief unrhymed nature poem of three lines and seventeen syllables, and the senryu, a type of poem with the same structure as the haiku but with a comic rather than serious tone.

2. Focusing on Section 2 of Chapter 18, review the Tokugawa period focusing on questions such as: By what methods did the Tokugawa gain and keep control of Japan? How did the Japanese react to foreigners? How did ending isolation affect Japan?

3. Introduce the Japanese poetic forms of haiku and senryu. Due to the isolation of Japan, the haiku form maintained its integrity, remaining a unique Japanese style with no western poetic influence, such as the use of simile, metaphor, or other figures of speech. Read and discuss some examples of haiku and senryu and discuss some of the masters of these art forms, including Matsuo Basho or Karai Hachiemon, who made senryu famous. Have students note the characteristics of each style, specifically the haiku's emphasis on nature and seasons and senryu's comic tone and emphasis on the everyday human condition.

4. Show students examples of Japanese emaki from reference sources. Individually or in groups, the students will produce original emaki depicting the history of Japan from 1600 to 1868. The scroll must begin with the ascent of the Tokugawa family to the shogunate (1600) and end with the Meiji Restoration (1868). It must include at least eight significant events. Students should be encouraged to choose events that they think are most significant. These might include holding daimyo families as hostages, establishing trade restrictions, expelling the Portuguese, limiting Dutch merchants to Nagasaki, negotiating with Matthew Perry, engaging in civil war, and

restoring the emperor's power. For ease of grading, have students list events they chose to depict on the back of the scroll.

5. After the scroll is complete, the student or group of students should compose a set of haiku and senryu to accompany their scrolls. The haiku might typically describe the setting of the historical events or the emotions associated with them, making particular reference to nature. The senryu, on the other hand, would focus on the problems of social class, education, living conditions, or occupations that these changes would have caused. When sharing their emaki and poetry with the class, students should explain the connections they made between the historical events and the poetry.

ASSESSMENT

1. Assess students' work by their use of historical information, combined with their ability to fulfill the creative writing components.

2. Additional grades can be based on students' participation in the presentation.

The Ottoman Empire

Ask students to refer to the map on page 433 and describe how the Ottoman Empire grew from its original boundaries. (*It expanded into eastern Europe, western Asia, and northern Africa.*) Ask students which time period on the map was the period of greatest growth for the empire.

Lesson 1

(For use with Sections 1 and 2, pp. 429–438)

OBJECTIVES

1. Explain how the Ottomans built and expanded their empire.

2. Describe how the Ottomans organized their government and society.

3. Discuss the role of religion on the development of the Safavid Empire.

4. Explain how 'Abbas the Great brought the empire to its height.

BELLRINGER

As students enter the classroom, ask them to write down what they recall about the Ottomans. (*Muslim Turks who created an empire in Asia Minor and Europe*) Tell students that they will learn about the Ottoman Empire's expansion, its government, and its society.
[**English Language Learners**]

TEACH OBJECTIVE 1

All Levels: Create a graphic organizer by writing *Ottoman Empire* in the center of the chalkboard and circling it. Write the names of the people and groups responsible for the growth of the Ottoman Empire around the circled term. Include dates with the people listed. (*ghazis; Janissaries; Osman, 1200s; Murad II, 1400s; Süleyman, 1500s; Mehmed II, 1400s*)
[**English Language Learners, Cooperative Learning**]

Level 3: Ask students to create a map of the Ottoman Empire. Ask students to then choose one country to study in depth to determine how the Ottoman Empire affected the country. Students should present their maps and findings to the class in an oral report.

TEACH OBJECTIVE 2

Level 1: Write Ogier Ghiselin de Busbecq's quote on the board: "No distinction is attached to birth among the Turks; the deference to be paid to a man is measured by the position he holds in the public service.... it is by merit that men rise in the service, a system that ensures that posts should only be assigned to the competent. Each man in Turkey carries in his own hand his ancestry and his position in life, which he may make or mar as he will." Ask students to write in their own words what they think this quote means. Ask them to then write in their journals why it is so significant that a person is not born into his or her social status. What similarities do they see in America?
[**English Language Learners, Cooperative Learning**]

Level 2: Ask students to consider the importance of the separate religious communities called millets. Write their responses on the board. (*freedom of religion, freedom to govern self*) Why do they think that this system made the empire strong? (*People were fighting less with one another so that they could be productive citizens.*) Ask students to research the millet system, write a short essay on its principles, and present to class.
[**English Language Learners**]

Level 3: Draw two columns on the chalkboard. Entitle one *Ottoman Society* and the other *U.S. Society*. Ask students to list details about Ottoman society and record those under the appropriate title. (*Ideas may include ruling class, reaya, personal ability, millets, and religious freedom.*) Then have students compare their list to aspects of U.S. society. (*Ideas may include the U.S. government, common citizens, citizens*

elected into office, state governments, and religious freedoms.)
[**Cooperative Learning**]

TEACH OBJECTIVE 3

Level 1: As students enter the classroom, ask them to write down several ways in which religion can affect a society. (*Ideas may include causing disagreements, prejudice, unity, friendship, etc.*) Students should expand on their ideas by writing specific examples of groups they have encountered or studied that have been affected by religion. Have volunteers share their ideas with the class. Ask how religious zeal helped unify and strengthen the Safavid Empire.
[**Cooperative Learning**]

Levels 1, 2, 3: Copy the following on the board, omitting the italicized answers. Use it to help students understand the role of religion in the development of the Safavid Empire. *Cause:* Esma'il's religious enthusiasm, *Effect:* Fought to control Persia. *Cause:* Safavids became Shi'ah in 1399, *Effect:* persecuted by Sunni. *Cause:* Forced conversion of Shi'ah, *Effect:* Gained distinction and national unity.
[**English Language Learners**]

Level 3: Explain to students that the Iranian (Persian) government has kept Shi'ah Islam as the state religion from the time of the Safavids up to the present day. Ask students to go to CNNfyi.com to explore how Iran's religion has shaped its policies with other countries. Ask students to write a report on their findings.
[**English Language Learners**]

TEACH OBJECTIVE 4

Level 1: Have students list reasons why they think Shah 'Abbas was called "the Great." (*military reforms, territory recovery, improvements to Esfahan, economic prosperity*) Then ask students to write a paragraph telling whether they think 'Abbas's activities qualify him for his epithet.

Level 2: Ask students to write a fictional interview with Shah 'Abbas. Tell them to include questions that pertain to the Shah's improvements to the Safavid Empire. Have students

make their interviews interesting and creative by describing the setting of the interview, how he looks, and his personality.
[**English Language Learners, Cooperative Learning**]

Level 3: Explain to students that, under 'Abbas, Esfahan became one of the most beautiful cities of the world. The new capital was full of splendid mosques, monuments, public baths, and open markets. Ask students to research one aspect of Esfahan (the art, architecture, commerce, etc.) and to write a short essay on the importance of their chosen topic.
[**English Language Learners**]

REVIEW AND ASSESS

Have students complete **Review Sections 1 and 2** on pages 435 and 438. Have students complete **Daily Quiz 18.1 and 18.2.** As Alternative Assessment, you may want to use the cause and effect graphic organizer or the homework exercise in this section's lesson.

RETEACH

Have students complete **Main Idea Activities for English Language Learners and Special-Needs Students 18.1 and 18.2.** Have each student write three questions and answers about the information in Sections 1 and 2.
[**English Language Learners**]

CHALLENGE AND EXTEND

Have students write a rebus for children that tells the story of the Safavid Empire. Encourage students to use more than one picture on each line.

Lesson 2

(*For use with Section 3, pp. 439–443*)

OBJECTIVES

1. Explain the events that led to the beginning of the Mughal.

2. Identify the policies that allowed for the expansion of the Mughal Empire.

3. Describe the Mughal Empire at its height.

BELLRINGER

As students enter the classroom, ask them to list the ways in which the policies of rulers like Süleyman's and Shah 'Abbas affected their empires. (*Süleyman's aggression helped expand the Ottoman empire; he tolerated others' religions and allowed various groups to govern themselves; he supported the arts and improvements such as roads, bridges, and mosques. Shah 'Abbas expanded his empire with a slave military force and improved the empire's capital and its economy.*) Tell students that, in Section 3, they will learn how the policies of rulers in India affected the success of the Mughal Empire.

TEACH OBJECTIVE 1

Level 1: Ask students to draw a three-column chart entitled *Mughal Origins.* In the first column, have students list the words *who, what, when, where, why,* and *how.* The second and third columns should be labeled *Rajputs* and *Babur.* Have students use the information on page 439 to complete their charts. (*Rajputs— who: Indian warrior princes; what: weakened power of sultans; when: 1500s; where: Delhi; why: gain power; how: challenged Delhi sultans. Barbur—who: Mongol leader, descendant of Timur; what: attacked Sultanate of Delhi; when: 1526; where: Panipat; why: build an empire; how: defeated sultan in battle*)
[English Language Learners]

Level 2: Ask students to list some of the essential ideas that Akbar brought to the throne. (*He married a Rajput princess and gave Rajputs positions of power; when harvest was poor, he did not require villagers to pay taxes; he was a great supporter of the arts; and perhaps, most importantly, he repealed the special tax that non-Muslims had to pay.*) What qualities do these reveal about his reign? (*He was inclusive, just, and fair to all religions.*) Ask students to define what they think a good leader is. Ask them to write a short essay on Akbar's leadership and whether they think he possessed ideal leadership qualities.

Level 3: Legend has it that Akbar would sometimes visit his subjects anonymously to gather information about their daily lives. He suppos-

edly learned the diversity that existed among his subjects through first-hand experience. Ask students to imagine that they are villagers who were visited by Akbar. Have them write a creative short story detailing the visit. Ask them to incorporate specific historical ideas into their accounts.
[English Language Learners]

TEACH OBJECTIVE 2

Level 1: Write the following terms on the chalkboard: *Rajputs, taxes, arts, religion,* and *economy.* Pair students to develop explanations of how each item helped Akbar expand his control in India. Tell each pair to decide which of the items was most important in expanding the Mughal Empire. Then select pairs to share their ideas with the class. Discuss any differences in the pairs.
[English Language Learners]

Level 2: Tell students to imagine that they are foreign ambassadors to India during the height of the Mughal Empire. Have them write a letter to an associate in their home country describing what they have seen and what is happening in the empire.
[English Language Learners, Cooperative Learning]

Level 3: Ask students to write a brief synopsis of the rise and fall of the Mughal Empire. Ask them to identify the following important people, places, and things in their synopses: Rajputs, Babur, Akbar, Shah Jahan, Taj Mahal, Sikh, and Aurangzeb. Have students present their papers to the class.
[English Language Learners, Cooperative Learning]

TEACH OBJECTIVE 3

Level 1: Ask students to write an essay that compares and contrasts the reigns of two of the Mughal rulers in this section. (*The reign of Akbar was marked by his sense of justice: he incorporated the Rajputs by marrying a Rajput princess, introduced an improved tax system that did not require taxes to be paid if harvest was poor, repealed unfair taxes on non-Muslims. The*

reign of Aurangzeb persecuted all other faiths, but Muslim. He forbade celebrations. He insisted on strict Muslim laws being enforced. When crowds protested, he ordered elephants to crush them. These widespread revolts weakened the empire.) Have them write their essays using a particular frame or reference. They should decide which ruler had the strongest character and how his character affected the empire. *(Students should use similar details from Section 3, though their decisions about character will vary.)*
[English Language Learners]

Level 2: Ask students the following question: Is the life of an empire most affected by the size and strength of its military, its leader's religious policies, or the personal character of its rulers? Divide students into groups of similar opinions and allow each group to define its position with details and examples from the text as support. Then ask students to write a report based on historical fact supporting their ideas. Have them present their reports in class.
[English Language Learners, Cooperative Learning]

Level 3: Ask students to write a paper on the importance of a just ruler to an empire. Ask them to refer to another era of history they have read and compare it to the rulers of the Mughal Empire. *(Students could compare Caesar, Alexander the Great, Ramses I, Constantine, Henry VII, Elizabeth I, etc.)*
[English Language Learners]

REVIEW AND ASSESS

Have students complete **Review Section 3** on page 443. Have students complete **Daily Quiz 18.3**. As Alternate Assessment, you may want to use the Mughal Origins chart or the letter-writing exercise in this section's lesson.

CHALLENGE AND EXTEND

Have students conduct research on the art or architecture of the Mughal Empire. Ask them to recreate by drawing or sculpting one work of their choice. Encourage students to consider what the piece tells them about the Mughal Empire. Then allow students to share their works of art and descriptions with the class.

The Ramayana

GOAL

In this activity, students read, discuss, and analyze the epic *Ramayana*. Students will look at the five episodes within the epic to provide substance for a discussion of dharma. Students will learn choices based on the Hindu concept of dharma and then will be asked to relate it to their own lives. Finally, students will be asked to create a book with the five moral dilemmas with illustrations of each.

PLANNING

- **Purpose** This activity incorporates teacher-directed lessons and individual and group assignments.

- **Suggested Time** Plan to spend two lesson blocks and one homework assignment on this activity. Provide time for students to share and discuss their writings.

- **Teaching Team** At least one social studies teacher and one language arts teacher should take part in teaching this activity.

- **Group Size** This activity will work as a small group activity or for individual students.

- **Materials and Resources**
  copies of the *Ramayana*
  bound paper
  colored pencils

IMPLEMENTATION

1. Give students an overview of this activity by explaining that they will read the ancient Indian epic the *Ramayana* (written down approximately 1300 A.D.). Then they will be asked to understand the concept of dharma and describe dharma's effect on major characters in the *Ramayana*. Ultimately, they will appreciate the differences in moral reasoning across cultures and relate the moral dilemmas of the *Ramayana* to their own experiences involving choices.

2. Begin by explaining the Hindu concept of dharma, which is a cosmic order, or law, including the natural and moral principles that apply to all beings and things. The dutiful observance of this law in one's life is essential to the Hindu religion. Ask students if there is any law in their lives that they can relate to? (*The Ten Commandments, the Beatitudes, the commandments to love your enemies, forgive those who sin against you, the laws of the state and school, etc.*)

3. Have students read the story of the *Ramayana*. After the entire story is read, divide the students into groups of four or five. Assign each group one of the five dilemmas: Dasaratha's choice of a successor, Lakshmana's loyalty to Rama (Leaving Sita in the woods), Rama's choice between Sugreeva and Vali, Hanuman burning Lanka, Sita's ordeal by fire. Ask students to review each dilemma and ask them to define the dilemma and the choice the character made. Then ask them to list the outcomes/consequences of each choice. (*Observations may include the following. Dasaratha's choice of successor: It is customary for the eldest son to inherit rule from his father and Dasaratha has publicly proclaimed to all Ayodha that Rama is the heir. However, Dasarataha is bound by the boons he promised Kaikeyi when she saved his life on the battlefield. Outcome: Dassartha keeps the oath made to Kaikeyi and breaks his promise to Rama. Lakshmana's Loyalty: Laksmana warns Rama not to fetch the golden deer that Sita desires. Rama ignores his brother's plea and goes anyway, making Lakshmana the guardian of Sita. Mareecha, calls for help in a voice disguised as Rama's. Upon hearing this voice, Sita pleads with her brother-in-law to save her husband. When Lakshamana goes to help his brother, Sita is captured. Outcome: Lakshamana breaks his vow to his brother to protect Sita and she is captured. Rama puts Sita through the ordeal by fire: Dilemma: Rama loves Sita and has*

gone to great lengths to rescue her, but he is jealous of the time she has spent with Lanka. He orders her to walk through fire to test her chastity. She pleads her innocence, but he will not be satisfied. His dilemma is that if she is guilty, she will die, and if she is innocent, he will be exposed as the jealous husband. She walks into the fire and comes out unscathed. The lotus in her hair is still fresh. Outcome: Rama is berated by the gods for sending Sita to the fire, yet he knows she was true to him.)

4. After students have defined the dilemmas and consequences on their own, ask them these specific questions about each sequence: What they would do in a specific situation like this one? Does their particular part of the epic remind them of any decisions they have had to make? What decisions would you have made in the situation and why?

5. Ask the students to write their responses to the epic and the moral dilemmas in each episode. Then ask them to illustrate the each of the five dilemmas. Show them historical illustrations of the *Ramayana* to use as examples.

6. Have students collect their written responses with their illustrations to create their own book of the *Ramayana*.

ASSESSMENT

1. Assess students' work by their analysis of the *Ramayana* and their responses to the moral dilemmas presented in their own lives combined with their creative illustrations of the five dilemmas.

2. Additional grades can be based on students' participation in class discussion and group work.

The Growth of France under Louis XIV

Have students examine the map on page 457. What is the topic of the map? What natural boundaries surrounded much of France? What city in southwestern France remained outside of Louis's control?

Lesson 1

(For use with Sections 1 and 2, pp. 454–464)

OBJECTIVES

1. Explain how Henry IV and Cardinal Richelieu strengthened France.

2. Analyze Louis XIV's strategy for strengthening the central government.

3. Identify Louis XIV's reasons for waging war and the results.

4. Identify ways Russia was isolated from western Europe.

5. Analyze how Peter the Great used his power to change Russia.

6. Identify how Catherine the Great expanded Russia's territory.

BELLRINGER

Ask students to predict what would happen if there were no government. Focus thinking by listing government services, such as law enforcement. Then ask students if they think people would exchange some personal liberty for security and peace. Remind them of the political and religious chaos in Europe caused by the decline of feudalism and the Reformation. Tell students that, in Section 1 they will learn how a strong central government headed by a monarch then evolved in France.

TEACH OBJECTIVE 1

All Levels: Have students create a chart with column headings that read *Henry IV* and *Richelieu.* Row headings should read *Economy, Religion,* and *Nobles.* Have students work in pairs to compare and contrast actions taken by Henry IV and Cardinal Richelieu to strengthen France. After pairs complete their charts, discuss which policy towards the Huguenots encouraged peace: compromise or conquest. **[English Language Learners, Cooperative Learning]**

TEACH OBJECTIVE 2

Levels 1 and 2: Have students write a series of newspaper headlines that report the course of Louis XIV's policies and actions as king.

Level 3: Ask students to prepare three oral presentations for the class showing how a peasant, a Huguenot, and a noble might have viewed Versailles. *(may have angered poor peasant class, may have been a symbol of excess and monarchical arrogance in the eyes of Huguenots, could have served as both palace and "prison" for nobles)*

TEACH OBJECTIVE 3

Level 1: Have students write the heads *Reasons* and *Results* on a sheet of paper. Ask students what Louis XIV hoped to accomplish by going to war and list these reasons. *(increase territory, establish natural border to the east)* Then prompt them to list the results of these wars on France. *(cost in money and lives)* **[English Language Learners]**

Levels 2 and 3: Divide students into two groups. Assign one group to be "pro-Louis XIV" and the other to be "anti-Louis XIV." Have students prepare arguments that either defend or condemn Louis XIV's decisions to go to war. Make sure students investigate both the reasons and results of the wars. Then begin a debate.

TEACH OBJECTIVE 4

All Levels: Remind students that both cultural and geographic factors separated Russia from Western Europe. Ask students to list these factors and summarize their effects. **[English Language Learners]**

TEACH OBJECTIVES 5 AND 6

All Levels: Have each student draw a slip of colored paper from a bag—one color will identify a student as a noble, another color as a serf. Have nobles sit on one side of the room, and serfs on the other to discuss how Peter and Catherine's absolutism and domestic policies affect them. *(nobles: mandatory shaving policy, European dress code, "service nobility" system, made to speak French, isolated from majority, yet also thrived; serfs: tied to land, tied to lord, continued poverty)* One serf and one noble should take notes and report. As a class, discuss whether such an imbalance of power and wealth lends itself to a stable society. **[English Language Learners, Cooperative Learning]**

Level 1: Refer students to the map on page 463. Note the territory that was gained under Catherine. On a world map, have students locate this same area as well as the Crimea and northern shore of the Black Sea, acquired by Catherine from the Turks. Finally, have students trace the eastern expansion of Russia across Siberia and into Alaska. **[English Language Learners]**

Level 3: Invite students to imagine they are French teenagers visiting Russia with a grandparent. Tell them their grandparent has visited Russia in the past, but this visit is the first since Czar Peter I tried to westernize the country. Ask students to create a travel journal, recording their observations as well as any surprises their grandparent encounters. Encourage them to use the library and the Internet for research. **[Cooperative Learning]**

REVIEW AND ASSESS

Have students complete **Review Sections 1 and 2.** Have students complete **Daily Quizzes 19.1 and 19.2.** As Alternative Assessment, you may want to use the travel journal or homework assignment in this section's lessons.

RETEACH

Have students complete **Main Idea Activities 19.1 and 19.2.** Then ask students to list five

ways in which Peter and Catherine changed Russia. **[English Language Learners]**

CHALLENGE AND EXTEND

Louis XIV adopted the sun as his personal symbol and considered himself the Sun King. Invite students to invent appropriate symbols and slogans for Peter the Great and Catherine the Great. They might make posters or create Web site pages.

Lesson 2

(For use with Sections 3 and 4, pp. 465–473)

OBJECTIVES

1. Explain how the Habsburgs gained and held power.

2. Explain how the Hohenzollerns rose to power.

3. Identify the factors that contributed to conflicts between Prussia and Austria.

4. Describe the rule of Mary Tudor in England.

5. Describe the rule of Elizabeth I.

6. Explain the problems James I faced in ruling England.

BELLRINGER

Ask students to write a summary in the form of a paragraph or graphic organizer of the conflicts and conquests that took place under Louis XIV, Peter the Great, and Catherine the Great. Explain that Central Europe saw struggles for territory and power similar to those that were taking place in France and Russia at about the same time. Tell students that, in Section 3, they will learn how the Habsburgs of Austria and the Hohenzollerns of Prussia vied for power in Central Europe.

TEACH OBJECTIVE 1

Levels 1 and 2: Have students use a map of Europe to locate the nations/regions that the Habsburgs controlled in 1740. *(include what are now Austria, Hungary, the Czech Republic, part* of the Balkans, part of the Italian peninsula, and the Netherlands) Ask students to summarize how Maria Theresa came to power over such a patchwork empire (was only successor of Holy Roman Emperor Charles VI, who had other rulers accept the Pragmatic Sanction, allowing a woman, Maria, to inherit Habsburg lands) [English Language Learners]

Level 3: Have students list some of the problems facing Maria Theresa. (gender prejudice, ethnic conflicts, scattered empire, resentment of power, alliances against Austria, growing rivalry with Prussia) Ask them to imagine how a ruler in her twenties faced with such problems might feel. Invite them to write a journal entry in which Maria Theresa expresses her thoughts and feelings.

TEACH OBJECTIVE 2

Level 1: Have students make a concept map for each Hohenzollern ruler that details his achievements.
[English Language Learners]

All Levels: Form students into triads to create a talk show called "Who's the Greatest?" The show's guests are Frederick William I and Frederick II. Have students compose questions to be asked by the interviewer and responses for the show's two guests. Invite triads to perform their talk shows for the class. After each performance, have the class vote to decide "Who's the Greatest?" —Frederick William I or Frederick II.
[English Language Learners, Cooperative Learning]

TEACH OBJECTIVE 3

All Levels: Have students make a time line of the events in Central Europe from 1740 to 1775.
[English Language Learners]

TEACH OBJECTIVE 4

Level 1: Draw a simple family tree to help students see that Mary I was the daughter of Henry VIII's first wife, Catharine of Aragon, a devout Catholic whom he divorced to marry Anne Boleyn. Anne gave birth to Elizabeth but

was later beheaded. Ask students what Mary did to earn the nickname "Bloody Mary."
[English Language Learners]

Levels 2 and 3: Ask students to explain why Mary I was nicknamed "Bloody Mary." Then have students write a speech from Mary's perspective in which she describes her beliefs and justifies her actions as the reigning queen.

TEACH OBJECTIVE 5

All Levels: Have students create a chart comparing how Mary Tudor and Elizabeth dealt with religious issues.
[English Language Learners]

Level 3: Have students evaluate Elizabeth's rule in a debate. (Pros might include support of the English navy, success against the Spanish, skillful dealings with Parliament, and patronage of the arts. Cons might include ordering the execution of Mary Stuart, persecution of non-Anglicans, and some struggles with Parliament.)
[Cooperative Learning]

TEACH OBJECTIVE 6

All Levels: As a class, list the problems James I faced. (belief in divine right of kings, unsupported by Parliament so raised money by selling titles and granting monopoly rights, unsuccessful negotiations with Spain led to war) Have students add James to the chart comparing/contrasting English monarchs' dealing with religion. (supported Anglican Church, problems with Puritans, King James version of Bible)
[English Language Learners]

REVIEW AND ASSESS

Have students complete **Review Sections 3 and 4**. Have students complete **Daily Quizzes 19.3 and 19.4**. As Alternative Assessment, you may want to use the compare/contrast chart or homework assignment in this section's lessons.

RETEACH

Have students complete **Main Idea Activities 19.3 and 19.4**. Then ask each student to create

three concept maps showing key details for Mary Tudor, Elizabeth, and James I.
[English Language Learners]

CHALLENGE AND EXTEND

Invite interested students to research some aspect of the Elizabethan Age, such as theater, politics, or historical figures.

Creating a Fan Club Newsletter

GOAL

In this activity, students will learn more about the lives, beliefs, and policies of Catherine the Great and Elizabeth I. Students will conduct research and determine which ruler they think was greater.

PLANNING

- **Purpose** This activity may be used in combination with teacher-directed lessons, as an enrichment activity, or as a performance-based assessment of content mastery.

- **Suggested Time** Plan to spend two lesson blocks and one homework assignment on this activity.

- **Teaching Team** At least one social studies teacher and one language arts teacher should take part in teaching this activity.

- **Group Size** This activity works best by organizing students into groups of four. You may wish to assign the activity as an extra credit option for individual students.

- **Materials and Resources** Provide students with copies of Rubrics 14 and/or 37. Students should have access to the Internet. Have them also use their textbooks to help find information about Catherine the Great and Elizabeth I.

IMPLEMENTATION

1. Give students an overview of the activity by explaining that they will conduct research on Catherine the Great and Elizabeth I. Students will determine which ruler provided a better environment in which to live.

2. Lead students in a discussion concerning the role of women during the seventeenth and eighteenth centuries. Make sure to point out that, although several powerful queens ruled during the time, women in general had few legal rights. Most were controlled first by fathers and then by hus-

bands. The majority of women faced a life of hard physical labor, in addition to bearing and rearing many children. Contrast the lives "average" women at the time with the lives led by Catherine the Great and Elizabeth I.

3. Using the information provided by the textbook, lead students in a discussion of the differing beliefs and actions of Catherine the Great and Elizabeth I.

4. Tell students that, in order to make an informed decision about whom they believe was a better ruler, they must conduct more research on the lives, beliefs, and policies of Catherine the Great and Elizabeth I. Students should focus their research specifically on the following topics: era of reign, main political focus, social reforms, challenges, and wars of the time. Students may begin their research online at www.go.hrw.com. Ask students to keep the following question in mind: Was Catherine really "great?" Be sure to discuss the meaning of the term as used historically to denote importance, strength, and power, and not necessarily goodness or merit.

5. After their research has been completed, ask students to decide who they believe is a better ruler. Ask students to form groups of four with others who share their choices. Tell students that each group will create a fan club newsletter honoring the ruler they have chosen. The newsletter should explain why one particular ruler is so great and include information found during research. Students may include the rulers' accomplishments, values, justifications of certain actions in the context of the time period, etc. Students should be as creative as possible, including all types of articles and graphic designs.

6. Conclude by having students present their newsletters to the class. Discuss which newsletters seemed to be the most persuasive in convincing students which was the better ruler.

ASSESSMENT

1. To assess students' newsletters, use Rubrics 14 and/or 37.

2. Additional grades can be based on students' participation in the discussions both before and after the activity.

The British Isles, 1707

Have students examine the map on page 488. What is the subject of the map? What small mountain range separates England from Scotland?

Lesson 1

(For use with Sections 1 and 2, pp. 478–489)

OBJECTIVES

1. Explore what led to the conflicts between Charles I and Parliament.

2. Examine how the rebellion in Ireland helped start the English Civil War.

3. Identify who would have supported the two sides in the English Revolution.

4. Investigate what led to the downfall or republican government in England.

5. Explain how religious attitudes affected the rule of Charles II and James II.

6. Describe how Parliament reduced the power of the monarchy after the Restoration.

7. Identify the principal features of Britain's limited constitutional monarchy.

BELLRINGER

Ask students to think about the issues that might divide a nation. List their responses on the board. *(Students might suggest disagreement over the form of government, who should rule, and religion.)* Tell students that in Section 1 they will learn about the issues that divided Great Britain and led to the English Civil War and Revolution.

TEACH OBJECTIVES 1 AND 2

Level 1: After students have read Section 1, ask them to create a visual organizer that illustrates the causes of the English Civil War. **[English Language Learners]**

Levels 2 and 3: Ask students to compose a short speech that Charles I might have read to Parliament. Then have students compose a response from members of Parliament. Discuss what factors led to the English Civil War and how the rebellion in Ireland contributed to it.

TEACH OBJECTIVE 3

Levels 1 and 2: Ask students to identify the groups who supported the king and those who supported Parliament. Have them describe the types of people who belonged to each group. **[English Language Learners]**

Level 3: Have each student give a very brief oral presentation defending one of the following statements:
(a) Charles I was within his rights when he entered the House of Commons to arrest radical leaders.
(b) Parliament's cause in the civil war was just.
(c) Charles I was guilty of arrogance, not treason, and he should not have been executed.

TEACH OBJECTIVE 4

All Levels: Using the diagram generated about the causes of the English Civil War, have students start a second list of characteristics of Cromwell's commonwealth and its effectiveness. Ask students the following question: Why was the monarchy restored to England? *(Students' answers will vary but should include that Cromwell's experiment with republican government failed. After his death, his son was named lord protector, but his weak leadership lost the support of the army. By 1660 the English people had undergone a change of feelings and even though they had once favored the execution of Charles I, they now believed that Cromwell's commonwealth had neither settled the nation nor solved its problems.)* **[English Language Learners]**

TEACH OBJECTIVE 5

Level 1: Ask students to explain how religious attitudes affected the rule of Charles II and James II. Write their responses on the board. *(led to suspicion, conflict with Parliament, opposition to kings' policies)*
[**English Language Learners**]

Levels 2 and 3: Ask students to list all the major historical figures mentioned in the section "The Restoration and the Glorious Revolution." Then have students note each figure's religious associations/sympathies/beliefs.

TEACH OBJECTIVE 6

Level 1: Ask students to define the following terms: Habeas Corpus Act, English Bill of Rights, Act of Toleration. Write their responses on the board. Then ask students how each document helped Parliament reduce the power of the monarchy.
[**English Language Learners**]

Levels 2 and 3: Have students create a chart with column headings that read *Safeguard* and *Purpose.* Underneath *Safeguard,* ask students to write the following row headings: *Habeas Corpus Act, English Bill of Rights, Act of Toleration.* Have students complete the right-hand column of the chart using their textbooks.

TEACH OBJECTIVE 7

All Levels: Review the definition of "constitutional monarchy." *(king or queen occupies the throne, but his or her powers are limited by the constitution)* Also ensure that students know how and why England became a constitutional monarchy. *(After centuries of conflict between royalty and Parliament, the English people wanted to avoid the possibility of any more tyrannical absolute rulers; however, they also wished to maintain the tradition of a monarch.)*
[**English Language Learners**]

REVIEW AND ASSESS

Have students complete **Review Sections 1 and 2.** Have students complete **Daily Quizzes 20.1**

and **20.2.** As Alternative Assessment, you may want to use the chart or constitutional monarchy exercises in this section's lessons.

RETEACH

Have students complete **Main Idea Activities 20.1 and 20.2.** Then have students use their textbooks to write a brief encyclopedia entry for each of the following: Charles II, Restoration, Tories, Whigs, James II, Glorious Revolution, William III and Mary II, Thomas Hobbes, John Locke, Habeas Corpus Act, English Bill of Rights, Act of Toleration, Act of Settlement, Act of Union, and constitutional monarchy.
[**English Language Learners**]

CHALLENGE AND EXTEND

Have students write two to three paragraphs expressing their feelings about the Act of Union, first in the role of an English noble, and then in the role of a Scottish person.

Lesson 2

(For use with Sections 3, 4, and 5, pp. 490–503)

OBJECTIVES

1. Investigate who the sea dogs were and what they accomplished.

2. Explore the results of the British mercantilist policy.

3. Identify the principal characteristics of Enlightenment thinking.

4. Analyze the similarities and differences in the ideas of important Enlightenment philosophers.

5. Explain how Americans responded to British policies after the French and Indian War.

6. Describe what type of government Americans set up after the American Revolution.

BELLRINGER

Tell students that Great Britain had a mercantilist economy, meaning it imported raw materials and exported manufactured goods. Ask students how the U.S. economy differs today. *(Students should point out that the United States imports and exports raw materials and manufactured goods.)* Tell students that, in Section 3, they will learn more about Great Britain's mercantilist economy.

TEACH OBJECTIVE 1

Level 1: Have students read the section entitled "Explorers and the Sea Dogs" and determine why Queen Elizabeth did nothing to stop the activities of the sea dogs. *(She profited from their piracy.)* Ask students what factors related to English naval exploits probably encouraged English rulers to establish colonies overseas. *(The navy showed supremacy over the Spanish Armada; adventurous captains explored new lands overseas; and Great Britain succeeded in challenging the Portuguese and Spanish monopolies on overseas trade.)*
[**English Language Learners**]

Levels 2 and 3: Have students imagine that they are Sir Francis Drake. Ask them to write a journal entry documenting one of Drake's conquests. Be sure to have them include what was accomplished from the piracy.

TEACH OBJECTIVE 2

All Levels: Ask students to define mercantilism. *(the belief that there is a fixed amount of wealth in the world and that one country must take wealth away from another country in order to gain more)* Then have them make a diagram to show the effects of this policy.
[**English Language Learners**]

Level 3: Tell students that English rulers embraced the idea of mercantilism wholeheartedly and aggressively sought to acquire new territories. Before long, Great Britain established itself as one of the world's most powerful empires. Have students create one or more political cartoons commenting on the early British colonial situation in India and/or the Americas. You may wish to collect examples of modern or historical political cartoons to share with students as models or for inspiration.

TEACH OBJECTIVE 3

Level 1: Ask students to name the major characteristics of the Enlightenment. *(belief that natural law governed human behavior, that truth could be determined by logic)* Ask students what these two characteristics have in common. *(orderliness, practicality, or interest in natural events)*
[**English Language Learners**]

Levels 2 and 3: Have students write an encyclopedia-style entry on a topic that would be of interest to someone studying the Enlightenment, such as one of its beliefs, characteristics, leading figures, or effects.

TEACH OBJECTIVE 4

All Levels: Have students construct a chart to list the characteristics and achievements specific to the philosophies of Diderot, Montesquieu, Voltaire, and Rousseau. Then have students identify philosophies shared by them. *(wanted to change society, disliked absolute monarchy)*

TEACH OBJECTIVE 5

All Levels: Provide students with a copy of the Declaration of Independence. After reading the document, students should list the main reasons that the colonists demanded independence. Then call on volunteers to review key ideas of the Enlightenment. Ask students which Enlightenment principles Thomas Jefferson incorporated into the Declaration. *(All people have natural rights; governments exist by the consent of the governed; when a government ceases to serve the people, the people have the right to change it.)*
[**English Language Learners**]

Level 2: Create a chart on the chalkboard. Have volunteers list British policies implemented in the mid-1700s and how the

American colonists reacted to them. Students should also fill in a column explaining why they think Britain enacted such a policy, even if an explicit reason is not provided in the chapter's text. After the chart is completed, ask students what actions these conflicts over policy led the American colonists to take. (*Patriot delegates met at the First Continental Congress and demanded the full rights of British people.*)

TEACH OBJECTIVE 6

Levels 1 and 2: Ask students to describe the government created by the Constitution and why the framers so devised it. (*The government created is a democratic one in which powers are separated between the federal government and state governments and, in the federal government, between the executive, legislative, and judicial branches. The Constitution also has a Bill of Rights. The framers wanted to create a strong government in which people would be free of unfair rule, to provide a system of checks and balances, and to protect the freedoms of individuals.*) Then write the following worlds on the chalkboard: *democracy, checks and balances,* and *Bill of Rights.* Ask students how these aspects of the Constitution reflect Enlightenment thinking. (*Democracy reflects the idea that popular government is the most acceptable form of government. A system of checks and balances reflects the idea that real liberty does not exist if one branch of government is more powerful than the others. The Bill of Rights reflects the idea that individuals have certain rights and that it is the task of the government to protect these rights.*)
[**English Language Learners**]

Level 3: Tell students to imagine that their government does not have the right to tax, coin money, or regulate trade, nor does it have a chief executive or a federal court system. Ask students what problems they can envision arising from such a situation. (*The government could run out of money; it would be difficult for merchants and consumers to conduct trade; lawmakers might have a hard time doing their jobs; punishment for crimes would differ greatly in different regions of the country.*) Tell students that such a situation existed in the early American states. Close by asking students how they would characterize the government created by the Articles of Confederation. (*ineffectual because there was no strong central government*)

REVIEW AND ASSESS

Have students complete **Review Sections 3, 4, and 5**. Have students complete **Daily Quizzes 20.3, 20.4, and 20.5**. As Alternative Assessment, you may want to use the Declaration of Independence or Constitution exercises in this section's lesson.

RETEACH

Have students complete **Main Idea Activities 20.3, 20.4, and 20.5**. Then ask students to write a question and answer that covers the main idea for each subsection in the sections. Have volunteers read their questions to the class. Have the class try to answer each question.
[**English Language Learners**]

CHALLENGE AND EXTEND

Encourage students to imagine they are cartoonists at the time of the American Revolution. Have them draw a cartoon from the colonial viewpoint of an incident or personality mentioned in the text. Display finished cartoons in the classroom.

Read All About It!

GOAL

In this activity, students will learn more about Charles I's execution. They will create a newspaper dated January 31, 1649, using the information they have learned.

PLANNING

- **Purpose** This activity may be used in combination with teacher-directed lessons, as an enrichment activity, or as a performance-based assessment of content mastery.

- **Suggested Time** Plan to spend two or three lesson blocks and one homework assignment on this activity. Provide time for student presentations.

- **Teaching Team** At least one social studies teacher and one language arts teacher should take part in teaching this activity.

- **Group Size** This activity works best by organizing students into groups of three or four.

- **Materials and Resources** Provide students with copies of "Charles I's Speech on the Scaffold" in *Readings in World History*. Also provide students with Rubrics 14, 27, and 37. Have students use their textbooks to help them find information about Charles I and issues of the time.

IMPLEMENTATION

1. Give students an overview of the activity by explaining that they will first read "Charles I's Speech on the Scaffold." Each group will then write an article to contribute to a class newspaper dated January 31, 1649.

2. Using the text as a guide, review the conflict between Charles I and Parliament. Ask the following questions: What led to the conflicts? How did the rebellion in Ireland contribute to the English Civil War? Why was Charles I executed? Furthermore, why might Parliament have chosen to execute him "in the open street before Whitehall," an important and centrally located govern-ment building? What if Charles and Parliament had been able to compromise on control of the army in 1640? Do you think the civil war and revolution would have happened anyway? Why?

3. After reading Charles I's speech, discuss the following questions: Why did Charles choose not to hold his peace? What, according to Charles, was the right course for his accusers to take? What in Charles's speech suggests that he had not changed his ideas about absolutism?

4. Divide the class into groups of three or four. Explain that each group will be assigned a topic on which it will write a newspaper article. Students must imagine that they are living during this time period of Charles I in order to write a realistic article. The following article topics might include: Charles I's execution (including quotations by the king), a brief overview of the events that led up to his execution, editorials from the point of view of members of Parliament and supporters of Charles I, political cartoons, and a World section summarizing events in other areas. Students should also include photographs and/or drawings to insert throughout the newspaper.

5. Before students submit their final articles, have them engage in peer editing. Have at least one other student read the article and edit for spelling, grammar, sentence structure, style, flow, and clarity. Also have the peer editor suggest three areas that need revision. The editor should make sure that the article conforms to the guidelines of newspaper writing *(who, what, where, when, and how in first paragraph; clear and concise language, etc.)*

6. Combine articles to create the newspaper dated January 31, 1649. The job of layout may be assigned to a few student volunteers as extra credit.

7. Conclude by having students present their contributions to the newspaper.

ASSESSMENT

1. To assess students' work, use Rubrics 14, 27, and/or 37.

2. Additional grades can be based on students' performance in class discussion and presentations to the class.

Paris, 1789

Have students examine the map on page 515. What is the subject of the map? Where were Louis XVI and his family imprisoned? In which direction is the prison from the Tuileries?

Lesson 1

(For use with Sections 1 and 2, pp. 508–516)

OBJECTIVES

1. Describe how the Old Regime was structured.

2. Analyze why discontent began to grow in the mid-1700s.

3. Explain why Louis XVI wanted to call the Estates General.

4. Describe how the meeting of the Estates General pushed France toward revolution.

5. Explain why and how the French Revolution spread.

6. Analyze how a constitution changed French government.

7. Explain why the monarchy and the Legislative Assembly came to an end.

BELLRINGER

Present students with the following scenario: You're a hard worker, but you barely earn enough money to survive. You earn 15 monetary unites for a 12- to 16-hour workday, but a loaf of bread costs 1 monetary unit, a pound of meat costs 3 monetary units, and a dozen eggs cost 10 monetary units. You also pay high rent to your landlord and give one tenth of your income to the church. Although you pay the heaviest taxes, you have no voice in the government. Discuss with students how they would feel about this situation. Tell them that, in Section 1, they will learn about conditions in France prior to the Revolution.

TEACH OBJECTIVE 1

All Levels: Have students create a pie chart that shows the percentage of the population in each of the three estates and the types of people who belong to each estate. *(First Estate, less than 1%, clergy; Second Estate, less than 2%, nobility; Third Estate, 97%, bourgeoisie, city workers, artisans, and rural peasants)*
[English Language Learners, Cooperative Learning]

TEACH OBJECTIVE 2

All Levels: Have students create a chart with two columns and four rows. Title the rows using the following terms: *First Estate, Second Estate, Bourgeoisie,* and *Third Estate (except bourgeoisie).* In the second column, have students list factors that caused each estate to feel discontent.
[English Language Learners]

TEACH OBJECTIVE 3

Level 1: Ask students to create a flow chart showing how Louis XIV, Louis XV, and Louis XVI all contributed to financial crisis in France. Close by asking students how Louis XVI attempted to resolve the situation in 1789.
[English Language Learners]

Levels 2 and 3: Ask each student to imagine that he or she is Louis XVI. Have them write a short explanation from this point of view that explains what has prompted them to seek a meeting of the Estates General. Be sure that students include a summary of the events leading up to the decision.

TEACH OBJECTIVE 4

Levels 1 and 2: Ask students to explain why the Third Estate refused to follow the tradition of each estate having one vote. How did this decision push France toward revolution?
[English Language Learners]

Level 3: Have students read the statement of Sieyès, "What is the Third Estate?" on page 510 and write brief essay providing evidence to support it. Have students write a statement that a member of each of the estates and King Louis XVI might have made at the meeting of the Estates General and indicate how these differing viewpoints pushed France toward revolution.

TEACH OBJECTIVE 5

Levels 1 and 2: Ask students to create a flow chart illustrating the spread of the French Revolution. Why did the Revolution spread? How did the events of July 14, 1789, change France?
[English Language Learners]

Level 3: Have students work in small groups using a problem-solving process to determine whether the people of France were justified in using violence. Encourage students to consider the king's action, the people's fears and beliefs, and the National Assembly's response to the violence. Have each group make a list of reasons for and against the issue and report their solutions to the class.
[Cooperative Learning]

TEACH OBJECTIVE 6

All Levels: Have students read the paragraphs under "The Constitution of 1791" on page 514. Create a two-column graphic organizer titled "Constitution of 1791" on the chalkboard. Rows should be titled *type of government, division of powers, legislature,* and *voters.* Have volunteers fill in the chart. Then discuss how the constitutional monarchy established by the Constitution of 1791 differed from France's previous government under the king. (*Students should note that the monarch was not limited in powers; the powers rested in the king and his advisors, not branches of government; there was no voting.*)
[English Language Learners]

TEACH OBJECTIVE 7

All Levels: Have students construct a flow chart indicating events that led up to the end of the monarchy.

REVIEW AND ASSESS

Have students complete the **Review Sections 1 and 2.** Have students complete **Daily Quizzes 21.1 and 21.2.** As Alternative Assessment, you may want to use the graphic organizer of the Constitution of 1791 or the homework assignment in this section's lessons.

RETEACH

Have students complete **Main Idea Activities 21.1 and 21.2.** Then create a time line on the chalkboard extending from 1789 to 1792. Have volunteers add significant events from the time period and explain why each was important.
[English Language Learners]

CHALLENGE AND EXTEND

Have students conduct research on the storming of the Bastille on July 14, 1789. Then have them imagine they are part of the Paris crowd that stormed the Bastille. Have them write diary entries describing their part in the event and how they felt about it.

Lesson 2

(For use with Sections 3 and 4, pp. 517–528)

OBJECTIVES

1. Explain how the National Convention ruled France. Describe how the Reign of Terror affected France.

2. Identify the Directory and explain how it ruled.

3. Analyze why Napoléon was able to come to power.

4. Identify the ways in which Napoléon's government was successful.

5. Explain how France became an empire.

6. Describe how Napoléon reorganized Europe.

7. Analyze the events that led to Napoléon's final defeat at Waterloo.

BELLRINGER

Ask students to write responses to the following questions: What happened after the U.S. Constitution was written? How did the government function? Did any one person or small group of persons attempt to take control of the government? Remind students that France's National Assembly wrote a Constitution similar to that of the United States. Then tell students that, in the next section, they will learn how France took a very different turn after its new Constitution.

TEACH OBJECTIVE 1

All Levels: Have students form small groups to discuss the establishment and work of the National Convention. Have each group develop a list of ways in which the National Convention supported democracy.
[**English Language Learners, Cooperative Learning**]

TEACH OBJECTIVE 2

All Levels: Tell students that it has been estimated that more than 10,000 people were killed during the Reign of Terror. Then read the following quotation by Madame Roland, the wife of the Girondist leader, uttered moments before her death on the guillotine: "O Liberty, O Liberty, what crimes are committed in thy name!" Have students write an opinion piece explaining why the Reign of Terror has gone too far, works against the Declaration for the Rights of Man and of the Citizen, and is counterproductive to the goals of the Revolution.
[**English Language Learners**]

TEACH OBJECTIVE 3

All Levels: Ask students to create a compare/contrast graphic organizer of two columns and four rows. Columns should be titled with the following: *National Convention, Directory.* Row headings should read as the following: *Voters, Executive Branch, Length of Rule, Use of Terror.* Have students fill in the chart to describe how the Directory ruled France.
[**English Language Learners**]

TEACH OBJECTIVE 4

All Levels: Have students list Napoléon Bonaparte's important achievements prior to 1799. Then have students explain how they think Napoléon's military victories helped him come to power.

TEACH OBJECTIVE 5

Levels 1 and 2: Have students create a web diagram around the words *Napoléon's Government.* Have students focus on the accomplishments of Napoléon's government.
[**English Language Learners**]

Level 3: Have students list the accomplishments of Napoléon. Who might agree that his accomplishments were successful? Who might disagree?

TEACH OBJECTIVE 6

All Levels: Have students work in pairs to list the steps that Napoléon took to establish and enlarge the French Empire. *(crowned himself emperor; blockaded the British Isles; crushed Russian and Austrian forces and destroyed their coalition; forced Austria and Prussia to sign peace treaties; ruled the Netherlands and Spain directly; and formed alliance with Denmark and the Papal States)*
[**Cooperative Learning**]

TEACH OBJECTIVE 7

All Levels: Have students study the map on page 525 and describe their general impression of Europe in the early 1800s. (*France controlled or influenced much of the continent.*) Then have them compile a list of the positive and negative aspects of Napoléon's conquests in Europe.
[**English Language Learners**]

TEACH OBJECTIVE 8

All Levels: Remind students that Napoléon's defeat in Russia was one of the worst military catastrophes in history. Tell students that less than half of Napoléon's Grand Army was composed of French soldiers. The other soldiers were from conquered countries or countries that he had forced into an alliance. Encourage students to think about what this defeat meant for Napoléon and his empire. Have students write an essay explaining how they think Napoléon's defeat in Russia contributed to his final defeats at Leipzig and at Waterloo.

REVIEW AND ASSESS

Have students complete **Review Sections 3 and 4**. Have students complete **Daily Quizzes 21.3 and 21.4**. As Alternative Assessment, you may want to use the comic strip activity or the flow-chart activity in the section's lessons.

RETEACH

Have students complete **Main Idea Activities 21.3 and 21.4**. Then have students outline the chapter.
[**English Language Learners**]

CHALLENGE AND EXTEND

Have students imagine they are soldiers in the Grand Army, retreating from Russia during that cold winter. Have them write a letter to a loved one at home describing their experiences.

Lesson 3
(For use with Section 5, pp. 529–533)

OBJECTIVES

1. Describe how the Congress of Vienna attempted to restore stability to Europe.
2. Explain why politicians practiced conservative policies.
3. Analyze how Metternich influenced conservative politics and stopped revolution.

TEACH OBJECTIVE 1

All Levels: Ask students to list the guiding principles of the Congress of Vienna. Then have students explain the ways in which the leaders at the Congress of Vienna upheld the three principles.
[**English Language Learners**]

TEACH OBJECTIVE 2

All Levels: Have students create a chart with the following column headings: *Main Purpose, Members,* and *Organization.* The row headings should read as the following: *Quadruple/ Quintuple Alliance, Holy Alliance,* and *Concert of Europe.* Have students fill in the chart. Then lead a discussion about why politicians of Europe wanted to form these alliances.
[**English Language Learners**]

TEACH OBJECTIVE 3

All Levels: Ask students to suggest some effects that Metternich's system of suppression and the ideas of liberalism had on Europe. Then lead a discussion about which of these systems prevailed at first.
[**English Language Learners**]

REVIEW AND ASSESS

Have students complete **Review Section 5**. Have students complete **Daily Quiz 21.5**. As Alternative Assessment, you may want to use the graphic organizer in this section's lessons.

RETEACH

Have students complete **Main Idea Activity 21.5**. Then have students create a chart showing the three principles of the Congress of Vienna and how each was implemented by the Congress.
[**English Language Learners**]

CHALLENGE AND EXTEND

Assign students one of the following leaders: Metternich, Czar Alexander I, or Talleyrand. Tell students to use primary and secondary sources such as computer software to find out more about these individuals. Then have students write a newspaper article based on an imaginary interview with their leader.

CHAPTER 21

Modern Chapter **12**

Time Traveling

GOAL

In this activity, students will use their knowledge of the changing French governments from the Revolution and Republic to the Napoléonic Era to create displays and determine which time period is most appealing to them. Students will use this information to prepare them for writing a short story.

PLANNING

- **Purpose** This activity may be used in combination with teacher-directed lessons, as an enrichment activity, or as a performance-based assessment of content mastery.

- **Suggested Time** Plan to spend two lesson blocks and one homework assignment on this activity.

- **Teaching Team** At least one social studies teacher and one language arts teacher should take part in teaching this activity.

- **Group Size** This activity works best by organizing the class into five groups for the first activity. You may wish to assign the activity as an extra credit option for individual students.

- **Materials and Resources** Provide students with copies of Rubrics 22 and 37. Have students use their textbooks to help them find information about the changing French governments.

IMPLEMENTATION

1. Give students an overview of the activity by explaining that they will first create a display illustrating the changing French governments from the Revolution and Republic to the Napoléonic Era. They will then write a short story from the point of view of an individual living during the general time period.

2. Organize the class into five groups. Assign each group one of the following governmental time periods in French history: (1)

1789-1972 beginning when the National Assembly assumed power to the end of the Legislative Assembly when the monarchy was suspended; (2) 1792–1795 beginning with the end of the monarchy and ending when the National Convention drafted another new constitution creating the Directory; (3) 1795–1799 beginning with the creation of the Directory and ending with Napoléon Bonaparte's coup d'état; (4) 1799–1805 beginning with the establishment of the Consulate under Napoléon's leadership and ending with Napoléon's defeat of Austria and Prussia; and (5) 1805–1815 beginning with Napoléon gaining domination over Europe and ending with his final defeat. Each group is to create a display on its time period which gives details of any governments France established during this time, including organization of each government, powers exercised by it, reforms or changes brought about by the government, and major events which occurred during the government's time in power. These displays can take the form of illustrated time lines, charts, posters, or any other form the group decides to use.

3. When finished, have each group present its display. Emphasize that all these changes took place in 26 years. Then engage the class in a discussion of which time period they would choose if they could "time travel" back in history and why they would select that time. Ask them to consider this choice in the light of whom they might be when they traveled back in time (a noble, a peasant, a soldier, the King, Napoléon, or another leader or politician).

4. Ask each student to write a short story in which his or her new identity is the main character. Remind students that their characters should conform to that which was appropriate during the time period. For example, a peasant would engage in activities that differ greatly from those experienced by Napoléon. Students may base their stories on actual historical events or create fictional accounts.

5. Once students are finished, ask them to engage in peer editing. At least two students should read one piece, editing for spelling, grammar, punctuation, sentence structure, flow, and clarity. The authors should then make revisions based upon their peer editors' comments.

6. If time allows, have students share their pieces with the class. They may either read them aloud or compile them into a class book.

ASSESSMENT

1. To assess students' displays, use Rubric 22. To assess short stories, use Rubric 37.

2. Additional grades can be based on students' participation in the discussions.

The Industrial Revolution in Great Britain

Have students examine the map on page 545. Ask students to identify which industries dominated the surrounding areas of Glasgow.

Lesson 1

(For use with Sections 1 and 2, pp. 544–554)

OBJECTIVES

1. Explain why the Industrial Revolution began in Great Britain.

2. Describe how inventions in the textile industry led to other new inventions.

3. Analyze the effects that developments in transportation and communication had on the spread of the Industrial Revolution.

4. Explain how the increased use of machinery affected workers and working conditions.

5. Identify the differences between the middle class and the working class.

6. Analyze how the lives of women changed during the Industrial Revolution.

BELLRINGER

Discuss with students the meaning of the word *revolution*. Tell students that the one thing all revolutions have in common is change. Ask students to list the types of long-term and short-term changes that revolution can bring about. Ask students why the Industrial Revolution is classed a revolution. Tell students that, in Section 1, they will learn about changes in the textile, transportation, and communication industries that occurred during the Industrial Revolution.

TEACH OBJECTIVE 1

All Levels: Have students list the factors of production as you write them on the chalkboard. Have students explain what physical and human geographic factors during the Agricultural Revolution gave Great Britain each of its factors

of production. *(for example: natural resources— enclosure movement created wealth and large labor force in centralized area)* Ask students to identify some parts of the world that remain nonindustrialized and to explain why this is so. *(Students should identify missing factors of production.)* [**English Language Learners**]

TEACH OBJECTIVE 2

All Levels: Have students work in pairs to create an illustrated and captioned time line of the major technological advancements and events that contributed to the development of the textile industry. [**English Language Learners, Cooperative Learning**]

TEACH OBJECTIVE 3

All Levels: Discuss the impact of new transportation technologies on society of the 1700s and 1800s. Have students write a paragraph in which they analyze the effects of these technologies on society. To help students generate ideas and understand the bewildering rate of change during the 1700s and 1800s, ask them to name five areas of modern technology that are undergoing rapid change, such as computers, communications, and aeronautics. Discuss with the class the level of technology in these areas ten years ago and today. Then ask students to project advancements in ten more years. [**English Language Learners**]

TEACH OBJECTIVE 4

All Levels: Tell students to imagine that they and their families have just moved from the country to a big city during the Industrial Revolution. Tell them to describe a typical day in the factory system. [**English Language Learners, Cooperative Learning**]

TEACH OBJECTIVE 5

All Levels: Ask students to create two web diagrams. One should revolve around *Working*

Class and the other should be centered around *Middle Class*. Ask students to complete the diagrams by identifying the characteristics of each class in England.
[English Language Learners, Cooperative Learning]

TEACH OBJECTIVE 6

Level 1: Ask students to create a chart that illustrates women's work before and after the Industrial Revolution.
[English Language Learners]

Levels 2 and 3: Discuss with the class their impressions of what women's lives were like and what political, economic, and social influence women had during the Industrial Revolution.
[English Language Learners]

REVIEW AND ASSESS

Have students complete **Review Sections 1 and 2**. Then have students complete **Daily Quizzes 22.1 and 22.2**. As Alternative Assessment, you may want to use the "Young People in History" feature in this section's lessons.

RETEACH

Have students complete **Main Idea Activities 22.1 and 22.2**. Then ask each student to create a web diagram that shows the effects of the factory system on women, the working class, the middle class, and children.
[English Language Learners]

CHALLENGE AND EXTEND

Have students do research to identify primary sources that describe or discuss topics covered in the section.

Lesson 2

(For use with Sections 3 and 4, pp. 555–563)

OBJECTIVES

1. Explain how and why the methods of production changed during the Industrial Revolution.

2. Identify what caused corporations to emerge and the effects they had on business.

3. Define the business cycle and explain how it affected society.

4. Identify Adam Smith's ideas and explain how they affected people's views of industrialism.

5. Explain the causes of reform movements.

6. Analyze how workers tried to improve their lives.

BELLRINGER

Ask students to write down what they know about assembly lines and corporations. Have volunteers share their responses with the class. Then ask students to name other production methods and business organizations with which they are familiar. Tell students that, in the next section, they will learn about new methods of production and business organizations that arose during the Industrial Revolution.

TEACH OBJECTIVE 1

Level 1: Divide the class into three groups and have each group create a picture that illustrates the effects of the three methods of production.
[English Language Learners, Cooperative Learning]

Levels 2 and 3: Have students identify the new methods of production during the Industrial Revolution. Then write a paragraph on the board consisting of the same number of words as students in the classroom. Ask each student to copy the paragraph into his or her notebook. Time the activity. Then assign each student one word from the paragraph. Tell students that they will write their word on a piece of paper and then pass it on to the next person who will write their word, and so on. The order of students' seats should correspond to the order of the words in the paragraph. Time this activity as well. Explain that the students have just used an assembly line. Discuss which activity was easier, faster, etc.

TEACH OBJECTIVE 2

Levels 1 and 2: Have students explain how a corporation functions. Ask them to identify the positive and negative aspects of a corporation. [**English Language Learners**]

Level 3: Ensure that students understand the terms sole proprietorship, partnership, and corporation. Then have students apply this knowledge by identifying one or more businesses in their community for each category. Finally, have them write two or three paragraphs about why corporations have been so important to the U.S. economy since the Industrial Revolution.

TEACH OBJECTIVE 3

All Levels: Direct students' attention to the chain of causes and effects described in the second paragraph on page 558. Provide students with a copy of the circular flow chart on page 557 of the Teacher's Edition and tell them to fill in the empty boxes to complete the business cycle chain of events. [**English Language Learners**]

TEACH OBJECTIVE 4

All Levels: Organize students into five groups and assign each group one of the following economists or philosophers: Adam Smith, Thomas Malthus, David Ricardo, Jeremy Bentham, or John Stuart Mill. Have each group use the process of historical inquiry to create a multimedia presentation focusing on the economic theories of its assigned individual. Have students make their presentations in front of the class and tell the other students to take notes. [**English Language Learners, Cooperative Learning**]

TEACH OBJECTIVE 5

Levels 1 and 2: Ask students what motivated humanitarians to try to reform the workplace. Ask students to suggest their own ideas for reform of specific, current working conditions.

Level 3: Have students take on the roles of reform activists in the 1800s to create handbills urging the government to pass laws regulating labor and the workplace. Encourage students to use their textbooks, the library, the Internet, and other sources to come up with statistics, meaningful images, and other persuasive items to include in their handbills.

TEACH OBJECTIVE 6

Levels 1 and 2: Ask students why the first labor unions were formed. What impediments were there to the formation of unions throughout much of Europe? What changed this situation in Great Britain? [**English Language Learners**]

Level 3: Mention to students that strikes and collective bargaining are still very much a part of the management/union relationship in the United States today. Tell students to write a one-page report that answers the following question: Are unions as necessary today as they were during the Industrial Revolution? Students should support their answers with specific reasons and details and provide a bibliography.

REVIEW AND ASSESS

Have students complete **Review Sections 3 and 4**. Then have students complete **Daily Quizzes 22.3 and 22.4**. As Alternative Assessment, you may want to use the Economist/Philosophers chart activity in Section 4.

RETEACH

Have students complete **Main Idea Activities 22.3 and 22.4**. Then ask each student to create an outline of the information provided in this section. [**English Language Learners**]

CHALLENGE AND EXTEND

Have students create collages that highlight the reality of life in London during the Industrial Revolution.

Lesson 3

(For use with Section 5, pp. 564–567)

OBJECTIVES

1. Describe the type of society that early socialists wanted to establish.

2. Explain how Robert Owen put his socialist beliefs into action.

3. Explain what Karl Marx believed would happen to the capitalist world of the 1880s.

4. Identify some of the competing ideas that arose out of Marxism.

BELLRINGER

Ask students to write down what they know about how the Industrial Revolution affected both employers and their workers. What conflicts arose between the two classes? Have volunteers share their responses with the class. Tell students that, in Section 5, they will learn how the ideas of social reform emerged as a result of the uneven distribution of wealth caused by the Industrial Revolution.

TEACH OBJECTIVE 1

Level 1: Ask students what the means of production are and why socialists believed government should control it.
[English Language Learners]

Levels 2 and 3: Ask students to list both the positive and negative aspects of socialism. What future problems could socialists theoretically face?

TEACH OBJECTIVE 2

Levels 1 and 2: Have students define and give their opinions of *utopian socialism*. How did Robert Owen put his beliefs into action? What were the results?
[English Language Learners, Cooperative Learning]

Level 3: Have students apply different methods that historians use to interpret the past

(such as point of view and frame of reference) to create a summary plan for a planned community similar to those proposed by Robert Owen. Students should consider how many people would live in the community, how it might be governed, and who would do what types of work.
[Cooperative Learning]

TEACH OBJECTIVE 3

All Levels: Have students write papers expressing their opinions about communism. Tell them to justify their opinions with facts, examples, and evidence.
[English Language Learners]

TEACH OBJECTIVE 4

All Levels: Ask students to create a web diagram centered around *Ideas that arose out of Marxism* by identifying the competing ideas that arose out of Marxism and their characteristics. Diagrams should include information that identifies the roles of both people and government.
[English Language Learners]

REVIEW AND ASSESS

Have students complete **Review Section 5**. Then have students complete **Daily Quiz 22.5**. As Alternative Assessment, you may want to use the web diagram for "Ideas that Arose out of Marxism" in this section's lesson.

RETEACH

Have students complete **Main Idea Activity 22.5**. Then ask students to create a compare-and-contrast chart on capitalism, democratic socialism, and communism.
[English Language Learners]

CHALLENGE AND EXTEND

Have students create a visual that illustrates a topic covered in this lesson. Visuals can include charts, diagrams, maps, collages, etc., and can be computer-generated.

Working Towards Reform

GOAL

In this activity, students will enrich their understanding of workers' lives during the Industrial Revolution. They will also assume the identities of various individuals who aimed to reform living and working conditions.

PLANNING

- **Purpose** This activity may be used in combination with teacher-directed lessons, as an enrichment activity, or as a performance-based assessment of content mastery.

- **Suggested Time** Plan to spend two lesson blocks and one homework assignment on this activity. Provide time for students to present their writing pieces.

- **Teaching Team** At least one social studies teacher and one language arts teacher should take part in teaching this activity.

- **Group Size** This activity works best by organizing students into seven groups.

- **Materials and Resources** Provide students with copies of "A Working Day in a Manchester Cotton Mill" and "A Visit to New Lanark" on pages 154 and 158, respectively, in *Readings in World History*. Also provide students with copies of Rubric 3: Artwork and Rubric 37: Writing Assignments. Encourage students to use their textbooks to review information.

IMPLEMENTATION

1. Give students an overview of the activity by explaining that they will first read "A Working Day in a Manchester Cotton Mill" and "A Visit to New Lanark" to enrich their understanding of workers' lives during the Industrial Revolution. Students will then create handbills from different points of view keeping the readings in mind.

2. Have students read "A Working Day in a Manchester Cotton Mill" noting the hard-

ships with which the workers lived. Discuss the following questions: How were workers punished for being late? What similarities and differences are there between the life of the Manchester mill workers and the life of workers in a modern factory in the United States? Do the students sympathize with the workers? Why or why not?

3. Then have students read "A Visit to New Lanark." Discuss what Robert Owen envisioned for his utopian society and which parts of this vision actually came into being. What contradictions does Southey observe in Owen's system of social organization? Do students agree with Southey? Why or why not? How do students feel overall about Owen's ideas? Would they work in today's world?

4. Organize the class into groups to represent the following individuals and groups of people living during the Industrial Revolution: workers, socialists, Robert Owen, Karl Marx, Jeremy Bentham, Charles Dickens, John Stuart Mill. Students should review their individuals with the assistance of their textbooks.

5. Have each group take on the role of its assigned individual or group as nineteenth-century reform activists who are to create handbills urging the government to pass laws regulating labor and the workplace. Remind groups that their handbills should reflect their beliefs and sentiments based on which group or individual they are assigned to represent. Their handbills are to be persuasive in nature and should include specific language that addresses related issues such as how workers themselves have attempted to improve their situations and what type of society early socialists wanted to establish. Encourage students to use the library, the Internet, and other sources, in addition to the textbook, to obtain statistics, meaningful images, and other persuasive items to include in their handbills.

6. Allow students to present their handbills to the class. Encourage classmates to ask questions and contribute comments. Which handbills were most persuasive? Why?

ASSESSMENT

1. To assess students' handbills, use Rubrics 3 and 37.

2. Additional grades can be based on students' participation in the initial discussion.

The Spread of Electricity in the United States

As students enter the classroom, ask them to consult the map of the United States on page 573. Ask them which regions of the United States were among the first to receive electricity? How do they think this affected the economies of those regions? What about the middle section of the map? How do they think that these regions suffered from not having electricity?

Lesson 1

(For use with Sections 1, 2, and 3 pp. 572–585)

OBJECTIVES

1. Examine how the development of electricity led to other technological advances.

2. Identify the inventions that improved communication.

3. Analyze the importance of the internal combustion engine.

4. Explain how cell theory changed over time.

5. Investigate why Darwin's theory was so significant and controversial.

6. Describe how scientific discoveries changed the nature of medicine and surgery.

7. Identify the advances made in the field of physics.

8. Explore how science influenced the study of politics, economics, and history.

9. Examine how archaeology, anthropology, and sociology explored cultures.

10. Investigate how the study of the human mind developed.

BELLRINGER

As students enter the classroom, ask each one to write on the board a significant discovery, invention, or event that occurred during the Industrial Age. When all students have listed their choices, hold a class discussion on which the class thinks was the most significant, and why.

TEACH OBJECTIVE 1

Level 1: Ask students what important scientific discovery Michael Faraday made in the early 1800s. *(He found that magnetism could be used to generate electricity.)* Then ask students to briefly chronicle the sequence of events that followed in the history of electricity. Close by asking students what this sequence of events show about the discovery of new power sources. *(Just one new source of power can lead to many important developments.)*

TEACH OBJECTIVE 2

Level 3: Ask students what advances were made in the field of communications in the late 1800s. *(the development of the telephone and wireless telegraph)* Then ask students to imagine they are average Americans who are witnessing one of these developments being used for the first time. How do they regard it? How will it affect their lives? What do they think such development might foreshadow for the future? Then have students write a letter in which they describe the development and their thoughts about it.
[English Language Learners, Cooperative Learning]

TEACH OBJECTIVE 3

Levels 1, 2, 3: Have students explain how the internal combustion engine differed from the electric motor and to what inventions the internal combustion engine led. Then have students create a before-and-after chart, describing changes that resulted from the invention of the internal combustion engine.
[English Language Learners]

TEACH OBJECTIVE 4

Level 3: Have students create and complete a chart with the following four column headings:

Cell Theory, Theory of Inheritance, Theory of Evolution, and Genetics. They should use the following row headings: Who? When? Basic Outline of Theory, and How it Was Received. (Cell theory—Rudolf Virchow, 1850s: cell is the basic unit of living matter; by late 1800s, scientists generally accepted theory. Theory of inheritance—Jean-Baptiste Lamarack, early 1800s: living things changed form in response to their environment; theory was disproved. Theory of evolution—Charles Darwin, mid-1800s: creatures that are best adapted to their environments will survive to reproduce and pass on their advantageous traits to their offspring; theory was controversial because it stated that human beings developed from other animals and it contradicted the Bible. Genetics—Gregor Mendel, mid-to-late 1800s: inborn characteristics are inherited as if they were separate particles; other scientists did not learn about genetics until later.)
[English Language Learners, Cooperative Learning]

Level 2 and 3: Ask students to choose one of the discoveries above and to write a newspaper article for the year of the discovery. The paper can support and oppose the theory, but must articulate the theory and its importance to the scientific world. Share essays with the class.
[English Language Learners, Cooperative Learning]

TEACH OBJECTIVE 5

Level 1: Ask students to compare and contrast the theory of inheritance and the theory of evolution. (The theory of inheritance stated that living forms change in response to their environments, but the theory of evolution stated that creatures are born with different characteristics and those that are best adapted to their environments survive to reproduce offspring that share their characteristics.)
[English Language Learners, Cooperative Learning]

TEACH OBJECTIVE 6

Level 1: Ask students to provide information about the major medical advances of the 1800s, what triggered these advances, and the effect they had on society. (Major Medical Advance: Edward Jenner developed a vaccine for smallpox. What Triggered the Advance: Jenner learned that people who had once had cowpox, a disease similar to smallpox, did not contract smallpox. Effect on society: Fewer people contracted and died of smallpox.)
[Cooperative Learning]

TEACH OBJECTIVE 7

Level 2: Have students define each of the following scientists with his or her findings: J.J. Thomson (discovered electrons); Dmitry Mendeleyev (produced the first periodic table); Pierre and Marie Curie (discovered process of radioactivity); Albert Einstein (concluded that no particles of matter move faster than the speed of light); Wilhelm K. Röntgen (discovered X-rays); Max Planck (developed quantum theory); Ernest Rutherford (found that an atom's nucleus contained protons); John Dalton (outlined a method of "weighing" atoms)
[Cooperative Learning]

TEACH OBJECTIVE 8

Levels 2 and 3: Ask students to explain how science influenced the study of politics, economics, and history in the 1800s. (Scholars attempted to study law and politics with the same scientific manner that physicists and biologists used.) Ask them to write a short essay describing the influence.
[English Language Learners, Cooperative Learning]

TEACH OJECTIVE 9

All Levels: Ask students which social sciences focus on human behavior. (anthropology, sociology, psychology) Have students write a statement about the new theories that each of these produced. (Different societies share certain beliefs and behaviors. Human society evolved from lower to higher forms through natural selection. All habits constitute a series of conditioned reflexes. The unconscious is a determining factor in behavior.)
[English Language Learners, Cooperative Learning]

TEACH OBJECTIVE 10

Levels 2 and 3: Ask students to research the life of Sigmund Freud (1856–1939) and write a short essay on his contribution to the field of psychology.

REVIEW AND ASSESS

Have students complete **Review Sections 1 and 2**. Have students complete **Daily Quiz 23.1 and 23.2**. As Alternative Assessment, you may want to create a chart of the medical advances or a matching exercise of scientist/discoveries.

RETEACH

Have students complete **Main Idea Activities 23.1 and 23.2**. Then tell them to think about the achievements of the Industrial Age. Have students write down three important advances and describe why each was important.
[**English Language Learners**]

CHALLENGE AND EXTEND

Have students conduct additional research into one aspect of the work of Albert Einstein, such as how it has been studied, received, and expanded upon by later scientists. Have students conduct research to find out how the work of social scientists of the 1800s and 1900s is viewed today. Students should write an essay about their discoveries.

Lesson 2

(For use with Sections 4 and 5 pp. 586–597)

OBJECTIVES

1. Explain why people immigrated.
2. Analyze why cities grew and how they changed as they grew.
3. Identify the ways in which public education changed society.
4. Describe how the leisure activities we know today began to develop.
5. Explore the ideas that drove the romantic movement.

6. Identify the artists, writers, and musicians of the romantic movement.
7. Explain how realism differs from romanticism.
8. Explore the other artistic movements that emerged during this time.

BELLRINGER

As students enter the classroom, ask them to list some of the reasons that people from other countries immigrate to the United States today. *(Students responses will vary, but may include education, economic prosperity, and jobs.)* Tell students that, in Section 4, they will learn about large groups of people who came to the United States from their native lands in the late 1800s and early 1900s.

TEACH OBJECTIVE 1

Level 1: Ask students to list the reasons why people immigrated to the United States and Europe. List their responses on the chalkboard. *(fled from countries with poor economic conditions, fled oppression and discrimination)*
[**English Language Learners**]

Levels 2 and 3: Ask students to consult go.hrw.com to listen to the firsthand accounts of immigrants to the United States. Ask them to write a brief summary of what they heard. Then ask the students to imagine they are immigrants to this country. Ask them to write a first-person narrative explaining the immigration process and their first several days in their new country. Share the essays with the class.
[**English Language Learners, Cooperative Learning**]

TEACH OBJECTIVE 2

Level 2: Have students read the introductory paragraph to the section on page 586. Then have them list the factors that led to the rapid growth of population in the 1800s. Ask students what demands this enormous growth in population would place on society.
[**English Language Learners**]

TEACH OBJECTIVE 3

Level 1: Ask students what positive effects the spread of education had. *(People became better informed about current issues. They took an active interest in government activities. More people could read. More newspapers, magazines, and books were published.)* Then create the following headings on the chalkboard and have students list the effects: *Changes in newspapers:* expanded their coverage to include politics, foreign affairs, and art and science. *Effects of new technology:* linotype allowed newspapers to be set by machine. *Ways of expanding circulation:* lower prices.
[English Language Learners]

TEACH OBJECTIVE 4

Level 3: After students have read the section under "Leisure and Cultural Activities," have them list ways in which people in the 1800s spent their spare time. *(playing and watching sports, going to concert halls, museums, and libraries, going to public parks)* Close by asking students to speculate on how the activities in the 1800s differed from the same activities in the 2000s.

TEACH OBJECTIVE 5

Level 1: Ask students to list characteristics of romantic art including artistic ideals and visual principles. Have them give specific examples.
[English Language Learners, Cooperative Learning]

TEACH OBJECTIVE 6

All Levels: Write the following headings on the board: *Artist, Type of Art/Example,* and *Why is it considered romantic? (Artists: William Wordsworth, Percy Bysshe Shelley, John Keats, Lord Byron, Samuel Taylor Coleridge; Type of Art/Example: poetry; Why is it considered romantic?: Poems are filled with emotions and a strong love for beauty and nature)*
[English Language Learners, Cooperative Learning]

TEACH OBJECTIVE 7

Level 2: Write the headings *Romanticism* and *Realism* on the chalkboard. Then have students list characteristics of each artistic movement. Then lead students in a discussion about which artistic movement is more beneficial to society.
[English Language Learners, Cooperative Learning]

TEACH OBJECTIVE 8

Level 3: Write the following headings on the chalkboard: *Naturalism, Impressionism, Post-impressionism.* Then organize students into three groups and assign to each group one heading. Have groups write a paragraph in which they explain where the name for each school of art was derived from and give a description of the artistic technique and aims of each of the schools.
[English Language Learners, Cooperative Learning]

REVIEW AND ASSESS

Have students complete **Review Sections 4 and 5**. Have students complete **Daily Quiz 23.4 and 23.5**. As Alternative Assessment, you may want to use the *Romanticism* and *Realism* exercise in this section's lessons.

RETEACH

Have students complete **Main Idea Activities for English Language Learners and Special Needs Students 23.4 and 23.5**. Then ask each student to write a paragraph that briefly summarizes each of the artistic movements discussed in the chapter.
[English Language Learners, Cooperative Learning]

CHALLENGE AND EXTEND

Organize students into small groups to create bulletin board displays comparing leisure and cultural activities that people enjoyed in the 1800s and in the 2000s. Use the displays to discuss the similarities and differences between activities of the two time periods.

Romanticism

GOAL

In this activity, students will learn more about the Romantic Period and its literary ideals.

PLANNING

- **Purpose** This activity incorporates teacher-directed lessons and individual and group assignments. It should be used as a concurrent or culminating activity.

- **Suggested Time** Plan to spend two lesson blocks and one homework assignment on this activity. Provide time for students to share and discuss their projects.

- **Teaching Team** At least one social studies teacher and one language arts teacher should take part in teaching this activity.

- **Group Size** This activity will work as a small group activity or for individual students.

- **Materials and Resources** *The Lyrical Ballads*, William Wordsworth and Samuel Taylor Coleridge

IMPLEMENTATION

1. Give students an overview of the Romantic Period in literature. Explain that Wordsworth believed that poetry was the "spontaneous overflow of powerful feelings." He thus located the source of a poem not in the outer world, but within the individual poet. Explain that the Romantics valued emotion, imagination over reason, the individual over the community, the glorification of the commonplace and nature, and the supernatural.

2. Give them the background of the *Lyrical Ballads*. (*Wordsworth and Coleridge were friends who went to Cambridge as undergraduates and who traveled the countryside together. They published, anonymously, the Lyrical Ballads in 1798, which marks the beginning of the Romantic Period. The collection of poems opens with*

Coleridge's Ancient Mariner and closes with Wordsworth's Tintern Abbey.)

3. Ask students to read the *Ancient Mariner* and *Tintern Abbey*. Ask them to identify the Romantic ideals in each poem. (*Students should note that in the first poem, the Mariner sins against nature by killing the Albatross. He must wear it around his neck for punishment. It isn't until he blesses the snakes that the Albatross falls from his neck. Nature is the central theme in the poem. There are elements of the supernatural in the poem as well—the ship of death, the curse the Mariner brings upon himself, etc. In Tintern Abbey, Wordsworth ponders a ruin—a commonplace site in England. Nature is his teacher and guide in the poem. His creed is the natural world. He writes, "A lover of the meadows and the woods, /And mountains; and of all that we behold/From this green earth; of all the might world/Of eye, and ear, —both what they half create/And what perceive; well pleased to recognise/In nature and the language of the sense,/The anchor of my purest thoughts, the nurse/The guide, the guardian of my heart, and soul/Of all my moral being." Again, nature is the central teacher, guide, and anchor in life. It is not through books the two learn, but through the experience of nature.*)

4. After students have identified the Romantic elements in the poem, ask them to write a poem about a meaningful moment they have had in nature. Begin by asking them to write a paragraph about being in a park, the woods, or the seashore. Ask them to describe the setting and the feelings the setting produces in their mind.

5. From their rough drafts, ask the students to compose a poem. Remind them that poems can be rhymed or unrhymed, have formal meter, or not. Review some of the elements of poetry. (*rhyme scheme, meter, stanzas, metaphors, similes, alliteration*) Ask them to make a conscious decision about the voice the poem will be told in. What tone would they like in the poem? Serious,

ironic, funny? Ask them to use several of the poetic elements in their poems.

6. Have students share their poems with the class.

ASSESSMENT

1. Assess students' work by their understanding of the Romantic period and their use of those ideals in their own work.

2. Additional grades can be based on students' participation in the presentation.

The Growth of Canada, 1791-1912

Have students examine the map on page 606. What is the subject of the map? Ask students to identify the national and provincial capitals.

Lesson 1

(For use with Sections 1 and 2, pp. 602–614)

OBJECTIVES

1. Describe ways the British government and social welfare changed in the 1800s.

2. Explain the policies that Disraeli and Gladstone followed.

3. Describe changes in British government and social welfare in the early 1900s.

4. Identify changes that occurred in other areas of the British Empire during the 1800s and 1900s.

5. Specify how the United States expanded westward.

6. Explain why the United States fought a civil war.

7. Describe ways the United States changed after the Civil War.

BELLRINGER

Invite students to imagine they have been transported in a time machine to Great Britain in the 1800s. Ask them to predict how demo-cratic a society, by today's standards, they would expect to find. Have volunteers share their responses with the class. Tell students that, in Section 1, they will learn how democracy grew in Great Britain and its empire.

TEACH OBJECTIVE 1

Level 1: On the chalkboard, create a three-column chart titled *Social and Political Reforms of the 1800s.* Column headings should read *Inequalities, How Remedied,* and *Results of Change.* Ask students to complete the chart. **[English Language Learners]**

TEACH OBJECTIVE 2

All Levels: Organize students into groups to discuss whether Disraeli or Gladstone made the more important contribution to British history. Have each group report its conclusions and rea-soning to the class. Then ask students how Gladstone's emphasis might have differed if he had been a leader of the Conservative Party. How might being a Liberal leader have changed Disraeli's focus? **[Cooperative Learning]**

TEACH OBJECTIVES 1 AND 2

Level 3: Have students choose two of the fol-lowing questions to answer in a short essay: Why did Gladstone and the Liberals do more to reform education in England than Disraeli and the Conservatives? Why did the expansion of public education accompany the expansion of suffrage in Great Britain? How did the reforms in education broaden educational opportunities in Great Britain? Do you think a well-educated populace is essential to the long-term success of a democratic government?

TEACH OBJECTIVE 3

All Levels: Have pairs of students imagine a dialogue between a suffragette and a member of Parliament in 1919. The suffragette should make arguments to convince the member to vote for universal women's suffrage. The mem-ber of Parliament should respond as a Conservative would have. Select pairs to recre-ate their dialogues for the class. Then ask stu-dents to suggest how the response might have differed if the member belonged to the Liberal Party or the Labour Party. **[English Language Learners, Cooperative Learning]**

TEACH OBJECTIVE 4

Level 1: Remind students that, despite a strong commitment to democracy today, there have been times in Australia's and New Zealand's history when some of their people acted in ways that suggested this commitment was limited. Organize the class into small groups. Have half the groups create posters that illustrate limits on Australia's commitment to democracy in the 1800s. Have the other groups design posters that show limits on democracy in New Zealand during the same period.
[English Language Learners, Cooperative Learning]

Levels 2 and 3: Draw a time line on the board running from 1830 to 1900. Have the class fill in the time line with dates and events in Canada's expansion and movement toward self-rule. Then highlight events that are related to self-government. Ask students why there were such strong efforts by Parliament to make home rule successful in Canada. *(Regional suspicions made Canadian unity difficult; Parliament determined to avoid repeating mistakes it made with American colonies.)*
[English Language Learners]

TEACH OBJECTIVE 5

All Levels: On the chalkboard, create a three-column chart titled *The Expansion of the United States.* Column headings should read *Territory, How/When Obtained,* and *States Created.* Ask students to copy and complete the chart. Tell them to include the following: the name of each new territory added after 1800; when, how, and from whom each territory was obtained; and the states that eventually were wholly or partly created from each new territory. Have students exchange and review one another's completed charts for accuracy.
[English Language Learners]

TEACH OBJECTIVE 6

All Levels: Organize the class into groups to discuss whether sectionalism, slavery, or Lincoln's election was the most important cause of the Civil War. Ask spokespersons from each group to report its conclusion to the class. If no agreement exists among the groups, lead a discussion that explores the reasons for each group's evaluation of the causes and arrive at a class consensus about which was most important.
[Cooperative Learning]

TEACH OBJECTIVE 7

Levels 1 and 2: Ask students to identify the ways the United States changed after the Civil War. List their responses on the chalkboard.
[English Language Learners]

Level 3: Ask students to identify the three major social changes that resulted from the Civil War. *(end of slavery, citizenship and equal protection for African Americans, African American voting rights)* Then ask if these changes would have affected the women's rights movement, and why or why not. *(Have students review the mention of the Fifteenth Amendment on page 611 and note that it does not prohibit denying the right to vote on the basis of gender.)*

REVIEW AND ASSESS

Have students complete **Review Sections 1 and 2.** Then have students complete **Daily Quizzes 24.1 and 24.2.** As Alternative Assessment, you may want to use the territorial expansion chart in this section's lessons.

RETEACH

Have students complete **Main Idea Activities 24.1 and 24.2.** Then pair students and direct them to pick three events from each of the section's major headings and write two or three sentences explaining the importance of each event.
[English Language Learners, Cooperative Learning]

CHALLENGE AND EXTEND

Have students create posters or political cartoons that could have been used at the time to support or oppose one of the land acquisitions or social or political reforms they have read about in this section.

Lesson 2

(For use with Sections 3 and 4, pp. 615–627)

OBJECTIVES

1. Explain why the rule of Louis Philippe led to a revolution in 1848.

2. Describe how Louis-Napoléon started a second empire in France.

3. Summarize France's relations with Germany and other countries.

4. Explain how the Third Republic maintained political stability in France.

5. Describe what life was like in the Spanish and Portuguese colonies of Latin America.

6. Explain why Latin Americans began to oppose colonial rule.

7. Explain how Latin American colonies won their independence.

8. Summarize how the new Latin American nations fared after independence.

BELLRINGER

Invite students to assume the role of French citizens during the mid-1800s. Ask them to write a paragraph in support of or opposition to the following statement: *It is acceptable for the government to limit civil liberties if more jobs and a stronger France are the result.* After some students have shared their paragraphs, ask if their position would be the same if "United States" were substituted for "France" in the statement. Tell students that, in Section 3, they will learn about the clashes of values that characterized the Age of Reform in France.

TEACH OBJECTIVE 1

Level 1: Ask students to list grievances that various French groups had with Louis Philippe, identifying the source of each grievance. Then ask them to explain how the king responded in each situation and why he took those measures. Conclude by problem-solving with students about what they would have done if they had been ruler of France during this period.
[**English Language Learners**]

Levels 2 and 3: Have students write a letter to Louis Philippe from the point of view of a lower class French citizen of the 1840s. Ask them to identify specific policies with which they disagree. They may even offer suggestions to improve the situation.

TEACH OBJECTIVE 2

All Levels: Form the class into four groups to present five-minute "live radio news broadcasts" covering the abdication of Louis Philippe, the coronation of Napoléon III, the Paris Commune, and the Dreyfus trial. Broadcasts should include background information for listeners about the event, delivered by the news anchor or reporter on the scene. In addition, the broadcasts should contain interviews with even participants, descriptions of the event in progress, and sound effects as the event takes place.
[**Cooperative Learning**]

TEACH OBJECTIVE 3

All Levels: Have students work pairs to prepare a memo to Louis-Napoléon about whether France should or should not go to war with Russia or with Germany. After pairs representing both positions on each issue have presented their memos, have the class act as the National Assembly and debate Louis-Napoléon's decision in each instance. Conclude by discussing with students what Louis-Napoléon and France each had to gain by involvement in these conflicts.
[**Cooperative Learning**]

TEACH OBJECTIVE 4

Levels 1 and 2: Ask students to list the problems the Third Republic faced. Record answers on the chalkboard.
[**English Language Learners**]

Level 3: Call on volunteers to define the following terms: *monarchists, republicans, socialists, factions,* and *coalition.* Ask students if monarchists, republicans, and socialists are examples of factions. Ask students why factionalism necessitated coalition governments in France during the Third republic. Ask if coalition government is a better form of government than majority government. *(Coalitions may establish temporary stability by sharing power, but they are unstable in the long term because they can easily fall apart.)*

TEACH OBJECTIVE 5

Level 1: List the following items on the board: *hacienda, peninsulare, Creole, mestizo, mulatto,* and *missionary.* Call on students to define each term and ask another class member to use it correctly in a sentence. Then conduct a class discussion about the role that each item of the list played in the society that developed in colonial Latin America.
[**English Language Learners, Cooperative Learning**]

Levels 2 and 3: Have students take the roles of peninsulare, Creole, mestizo, mulatto, Indian, or African men or women and write a journal entry reflecting on the life they lead in their colony. Entries should indicate why they are content with their lot in life or why they wish it were different.

TEACH OBJECTIVE 6

All Levels: Organize the class into several groups. Ask students to imagine they are Creoles. Each group should determine how Creoles would feel about one of the following policies of their home country's government: (1) the hacienda system; (2) the labor system; (3) the class system; (4) peninsulares in top colonial jobs; (5) trade restrictions. After groups have reported on their opinions, have the class summarize Sapins' early policy toward its colonies and how policy changed in the mid-1700s.
[**Cooperative Learning**]

TEACH OBJECTIVE 7

Level 1: Have students create a flow chart that illustrates how Brazil gained independence from Portugal. Then discuss with the class the similarities and differences between the way Brazil and Spain's colonies gained independence.
[**English Language Learners**]

TEACH OBJECTIVES 6 AND 7

Level 3: Have students speculate about why revolution originated with the creoles and not among the lower classes. Then have them write a short paragraph explaining how the revolutionary experience in Mexico was both similar to and different from other Latin American countries.

TEACH OBJECTIVE 8

All Levels: Have students compare the map on page 626 with modern maps of Central and South America. Ask what the differences between the 1830 map and the modern maps suggest about Latin America in the years following independence. Discuss why Latin America's internal situation might have encouraged European intervention, and how that possibility was avoided.
[**English Language Learners**]

REVIEW AND ASSESS

Have students complete **Review Sections 3 and 4**. Then have students complete **Daily Quizzes 24.3 and 24.4**. As Alternative Assessment, you may want to use one of the homework assignments in this section's lessons.

RETEACH

Have students complete **Main Idea Activities 24.3 and 24.4**. Then have pairs of students write sentences that summarize the main idea of each heading in the section.
[**English Language Learners, Cooperative Learning**]

CHALLENGE AND EXTEND

Ask students to create short stories about a fictional teenager living in South America sometime during or shortly after the wars for independence. Have students choose to be Indians, peninsulares, or any class in between.

Women's Suffrage

GOAL

In this activity, students will learn more about women's suffrage and Emmeline Pankhurst's role in the fight for equality. They will reflect upon their own feelings about suffrage and create an editorial expressing their views.

PLANNING

- **Purpose** This activity may be used in combination with teacher-directed lessons, as an enrichment activity, or as a performance-based assessment of content mastery.

- **Suggested Time** Plan to spend two lesson blocks and one homework assignment on this activity. Provide time for students to share their writing with one another.

- **Teaching Team** At least one social studies teacher and one language arts teacher should take part in teaching this activity.

- **Group Size** This activity is meant for individual students. You may wish to assign the activity as an extra credit option for students.

- **Materials and Resources** Provide students with copies of Emmeline Pankhurst's "A Suffragette Goes to Prison" on page 170 of *Readings in World History*. Also provide students with a copy of Rubric 37: Writing. Students will need their textbooks to review information about women's suffrage.

IMPLEMENTATION

1. Give students an overview of the activity by explaining that they will read an account by Emmeline Pankhurst, a leader of the suffrage movement. Students will then use this information to write an editorial addressing the issue of women's suffrage.

2. Have students review the text beneath the heading "A Changing Nation" in their textbooks. Ask them the following questions: Who helped to found women's suffrage? What did these individuals do? What other group's recent acquisition of rights triggered the movement?

3. Ask students to find the text of the Civil War Amendments (*the Thirteenth, Fourteenth, and Fifteenth Amendments*). Have them summarize what rights each amendment provides and discuss to whom these rights apply. Ask students if it is clear if women ought to enjoy the right to vote.

4. Have students read "A Suffragette Goes to Prison" on page 170 of *Readings in World History*. Explain that the piece is Emmeline Pankhurst's account of her trial resulting from the destruction of David Lloyd George's home. Ask students the following questions: Why did Mrs. Pankhurst plead not guilty to the charge of inciting to commit a felony? What did Mrs. Pankhurst say she would do if she was found guilty and sent to prison? Do you agree with her actions? Do you think the statement "The end justifies the means" is true with reference to the militant suffragettes' actions? Are violent actions justified if they are committed in the name of a good cause? Why or why not?

5. Have each student write an editorial that is in support of or in opposition to extending the right to vote to women. Tell students that their editorial will be published on April 3, 1913, the day after Emmeline Pankhurst was found guilty in her trial. Students may include their opinions on the trial, evidence in the form of the Civil War Amendments, opinions on acceptable and/or unacceptable ways to achieve women's rights, including the use of violence and the connection between the rights of African Americans and women.

6. Once students are finished drafting their editorials, have them engage in peer editing. At least two students should read one editorial, editing for grammar, spelling, punctuation, sentence structure, flow, and clarity. Students should spend time revising their pieces based upon peer editors' corrections. Have volunteers share their editorials with the class.

ASSESSMENT

1. To assess students' editorials, use Rubric 37: Writing.

2. Additional grades can be based on students' participation in the initial discussion as well as their performance as peer editors.

Unification of Italy

As students enter the classroom, have them work in pairs to draw a sketch of Italy, based on the map on page 636, and identify various independent states.

Lesson 1
(For use with Sections 1,2, and 3, pp. 630–646)

OBJECTIVES

1. Describe the events that led to nationalistic movements for unification in Italy.

2. Identify the important leaders in the fight for the unification of Italy.

3. Explain the problems Italy faced after unification.

4. Explain how Prussia replaced Austria as the leading German state in Europe.

5. Identify the ways in which German unification differed from Italian unification.

6. Describe the changes in German government that occurred as a result of unification.

7. Explain the problems Bismarck faced as chancellor of the German Empire.

8. Describe how Germany became industrialized under Bismarck's leadership.

9. Identify the factors that led to the decline of Bismarck's power as chancellor.

BELLRINGER

Tell students that in the early 1800s Italy was divided into several separate states. Ask what factors might contribute to or detract from a desire for national unification. *(contribute: common culture, common resistance to external or internal forces; detract: differing economic interests, e.g., southern agriculture vs. northern industry)* Tell students that, in Section 1, they will lean how factors related to culture, government, and global relations led to Italy's unification.

TEACH OBJECTIVE 1

Level 1: Have students work in pairs to make visual representations of the events leading to Italian unification. Encourage students to use visual symbolism such as stair steps up to or highways converging toward unification. *(young Italy movement, 1831; Cavour enlists Napoleon III, 1858; war with Austria, 1859; Garibaldi's rise, 1860; final unification, 1860)*
[English Language Learners]

TEACH OBJECTIVE 2

Level 1: Ask students to prepare for and give an oral presentation on one of the following individuals and his role in the Italian unification: Cavour, Garibaldi, Mazzini, or Victor Emmanuel II.
[English Language Learners, Cooperative Learning]

Level 3: Have students define the Problem and Options, Advantages, and Disadvantages for the following topic: Garibaldi could take power from Cavour. *(Option 1: attack Garibaldi; advantage: reasserts the leadership of Sardinia; disadvantage: decreases likelihood of capturing northern Italy. Option 2: allow Garibaldi to take power; advantage: increases likelihood of taking northern Italy from Austria; disadvantage: gives Emmanuel II's power to Garibaldi)*
[Cooperative Learning]

TEACH OBJECTIVE 3

Level 2: Have students list the problems Italy faced after unification. *(little experience with self-government, regions divided by cultural traditions, tensions between industrialized north and agricultural south, low standard of living, labor problems, disagreements about colonial war)*
[English Language Learners, Cooperative Learning]

TEACH OBJECTIVE 4

Level 1: Ask students to tell how Prussia became the leading German state in Europe. (*Prussia trained a large army and defeated the French, becoming one of the four great powers at the Congress of Vienna.*)
[**English Language Learners, Cooperative Learning**]

Levels 2 and 3: Copy the following headings on the board, omitting the italicized answers. Have students work in groups to complete the chart and then lead a class discussion about the unification of Germany.

State within Germany that led unification process: *Prussia;* Means by which unification was achieved: *Bismarck built strong Prussian military machine, defeated Austria and her hold over Bavaria by fighting three successful wars;* Acquisition of land in unification process: *Schleswig, Holstein, the North German Confederation, independent states of southern Germany, Alsace, and Lorraine;* Major factors leading to unification: *German nationalism, Zollverein, Bismarck's Prussian army.*
[**English Language Learners**]

TEACH OBJECTIVE 5

All Levels: Have students create a chart to compare and contrast nationalism and unification in Germany and Italy. (*Italian states: shared history, economic oppression, common enemies, led by Cavour and Garibaldi, kingdom under Victor Emmanuel II; German states: shared history and language, economic unity, common enemy, led by Bismarck, empire under William I*)

TEACH OBJECTIVE 6

Level 2: Ask students to compare and contrast the German Empire's government with that of the United States today. (*German Empire: upper branch appointed, lower branch elected by male landowners, elected branch couldn't create laws, kaiser and chancellor could ignore legislature; U.S. today: upper branch elected, lower branch elected by all citizens, elected branches can create laws, executive branch cannot ignore legislature*)

Level 3: Have students make a two-column chart showing the positions and branches of government in the German Empire and the powers of each position or branch. (*kaiser: emperor, head of government, commanded military in war, could declare defensive war without approval, appointed chancellor and Bundesrat; chancellor: under kiaser, over legislature; Bundesrat: federal council, approved or vetoed budgets; Reichstag: legislative assembly, approved military budgets every seven years after Bundesrat*)

TEACH OBJECTIVE 7

Level 1: Have students write the following headings on their paper: **Bismarck's problems** (*liberal and democratic ideas, non-Prussian politicians, Social Democratic Party Catholics/ Centre Party, new kaiser*) **Bismarck's solutions** (*help industry, repress socialism, social reforms, Kulturkamf, threaten to resign*) **Outcome** (*resignation accepted*).
[**English Language Learners**]

TEACH OBJECTIVE 8

Level 1: Have students read the subsection "Industrial Development under Bismarck." Then ask them to name factors that led to rapid industrialization for Germany. (*rich iron and coal deposits, good transportation, standardized money laws, centralized postal and telegraph, cartels to control prices, high tariffs to protect industries*)

REVIEW AND ASSESS

Have students complete **Review Sections 1, 2, and 3** on pages 636, 642, and 646. Have students complete **Daily Quiz 25.1, 25.2, and 25.3.** As Alternative Assessment, you may want to use the compare-and-contrast chart or the branches of government exercise in this section's lessons.

RETEACH

Have students complete **Main Idea Activities 25.1, 25.2 and 25.3.** Assign each student a

Reading Check question from **Section 1, 2, or 3**. Then have students write the section headings and subheadings on a sheet of paper, leaving a space between each. Ask students to list the main ideas of each heading and subheading in the appropriate space.
[English Language Learners]

CHALLENGE AND EXTEND

Have students imagine they are farmers in southern Italy. Tell students to use their textbooks, biographies, the Internet, and any other available resources to find out about daily life for Italian farmers in the early 1800s. Then have them write a dialogue between a farmer and his wife about their problems and their hopes. Next, have students imagine they are Red Cross volunteers accompanying Bismarck's soldiers to war. Tell students to use their textbooks, biographies, the Internet, and any other available resources to find out about wartime medicine in the 1860s and 1870s. Then have them write journal entries.

Lesson 2

(For use with Sections 4 and 5, pp. 647–659)

OBJECTIVES

1. Explain the geographical and cultural factors that made Russia different from the rest of Europe.

2. Describe the characteristics of Russian domestic and foreign policies.

3. Identify the reform movements that occurred in Russia and their results.

4. Explain what led to the formation of the Dual Monarch and what problems it faced.

5. Describe how the decline of the Ottoman Empire affected European politics.

6. Discuss how ethnic clashes in southern Europe set the stage for a showdown among the major powers.

BELLRINGER

As students enter the classroom, tell them that they are the czar or czarina of Russia. Ask them

what they can do to improve economic and social conditions. *(develop resources and technology, expand borders toward east, introduce land and labor reforms and free serfs)* Tell students that, in Section 4, they will learn how conflicts between the conservative Russian monarchy and radical liberals led to revolution.

TEACH OBJECTIVE 1

Level 1: Have students read "The Russian Empire" and locate the map on page 651. Have them list reasons why Russia, though the largest in land and population of any European nation, remained weak. *(lagging industrial development, undeveloped natural resources, lack of access to the seas and oceans, conflict with other nations, lack of unity)*

Levels 2 and 3: Have students evaluate Russian's problems by using the text to complete the following headings: ***Problem*** *(lagging industry, underdeveloped natural resources, lack of ports, external and internal conflict)* ***Option 1*** *(expand military force)* ***Advantage*** *(adds resources and ports, unifies populace)* ***Disadvantage*** *(risk, loss of ports and resources, popular opposition)* ***Option 2*** *(develop resources)* ***Advantage*** *(avoids external conflict, supports economy)* ***Disadvantage*** *(requires unavailable technology, labor and capital)*
[Cooperative Learning]

TEACH OBJECTIVE 2

Level 1: Have a group of students design a visual, such as a collage, that shows the characteristics of the domestic and foreign policies of Russia. They could also write a song/rap, or produce a skit to present their information. *(Responses will vary but should indicate that domestic policy was repressive and foreign policy was expansive)*
[English Language Learners, Cooperative Learning]

TEACH OBJECTIVE 3

Level 1: Ask students what event finally triggered a revolution in Russia. *(defeat in war with*

Japan) Now ask students for the outcome of the revolution. (*The czar yielded to the revolutionaries' demands and issued the October Manifesto, which guaranteed individual liberties and provided for the election of the Duma.*) Then ask students how the czar got around these concessions. (*increased representation of large landowners to create a conservative Duma*) Finally, have students write a paragraph or two summarizing why the Revolution of 1905 failed. (*The army remained loyal, French lent money to government, and revolutionary groups were divided in their goals.*)

TEACH OBJECTIVE 6

Level 3: Have students write encyclopedia entries about the dual monarchy of Austria-Hungary. Students should complete the following outline to structure their entries.

I. Structure

A. Francis Joseph I (*emperor of Austria, king of Hungary*)

B. Ministries (*war, finance, and foreign affairs*)

C. Parliament of Austria (*Vienna*) and Hungary (*Budapest*)

II. Problems

A. Economy (*Austria wanted high tariffs*)

B. Ethnic Minorities (*did not benefit from unification*)

C. Balkans/Ottoman Empire (*Balkan nationalists wanted to break up the Ottoman Empire*)

TEACH OBJECTIVE 7

Level 1: On the chalkboard or overhead projector, draw the beginning of a cause-and-effect model covering the events that led to the decline of the Ottoman Empire. Have students complete second and third boxes.

Religious differences and unfair tax system in Ottoman Empire (*rise of nationalism in the*

Balkans—Greece won independence; Serbia won same self-rule)

TEACH OBJECTIVE 8

All Levels: Organize the class into four groups. Have each group present to the class a press conference that explains how the ethnic clashes in Southern Europe set the stage for a showdown among major powers. (*Presentations will vary but should creatively indicate the impact of ethnic clashes.*)

REVIEW AND ASSESS

Have students complete **Review Sections 4 and 5.** Then have groups of students construct a crossword puzzle using all of the terms and individuals mentioned in the Section Reviews. Have students complete **Daily Quiz 25.4 and 25.5.**

RETEACH

Have students complete **Main Idea Activities 25.4 and 25.5.** Then pair students to answer the **Reading Check** questions in **Sections 4 and 5.** **[English Language Learners, Cooperative Learning]**

CHALLENGE AND EXTEND

Tell students they are resource economists and engineers who must write a plan for developing the energy resources and expanding the transportation/communication system in the Russian Empire. They may use the library, computer software, or any other available resources to formulate their plans. Remind them to use correct terminology and standard English. Tell students they are Muslim Turks in the Ottoman Empire. Have them explain their religious beliefs and give a rationale for not allowing Christians equality. Have them use correct terminology and standard English.

Mary Shelley's Frankenstein

GOAL

In this activity, students will learn more about the significant themes in Mary Shelley's *Frankenstein* and how they reflect the historical time in which the book was written.

PLANNING

- **Purpose** This activity may be used in combination with teacher-directed lessons, as an enrichment activity, or as a performance-based assessment of content mastery.

- **Suggested Time** Plan to spend two lesson blocks and one homework assignment on this activity. Provide time for the presentation of the narratives at the end of the lesson.

- **Teaching Team** At least one social studies teacher and one language arts teacher should take part in teaching this activity.

- **Group Size** This activity will work as a small group activity or for individual students.

- **Materials and Resources**

Mary Shelley's *Frankenstein*

IMPLEMENTATION

1. Give students an overview of the activity by explaining that they will first hear the accounts of the life of Mary Shelley. They will then be asked to read excerpts of *Frankenstein* and be asked to define the major themes of the work and how those themes connect with the historical time in which the book was written. Finally, they will be asked to write a paper on the role of science, technology, and religion in Mary Shelley's work.

2. Give a brief overview of the life of Mary Shelley and the impetus for her writing the book. (*She was the daughter of the influential feminist Mary Wollstonecraft who*

authored A Vindication of the Rights of Women. *Her father was William Godwin, a philosophical anarchist, who believed in the possibility of utopia where such institutions as governments, churches, and marriage would be unnecessary. She met and married Percy Bysshe Shelley, who was a poet and anarchist. The famous tale of Frankenstein began as a parlor game. One evening Percy Shelley, Lord Byron, and Mary Shelley sat by the fireside telling ghost stories, and Byron suggested they have a contest to see who could write the scariest story. The result: the novel* Frankenstein.)

3. Ask students to read Victor Frankenstein's account of his creation and then the "monster's" account of his creation. Have students discuss what is ironic about this creation story? (*Life is created from death. Dr. Frankenstein abandons his creation after he has spent so much effort creating it. He calls it an "evil fiend" before the creation has done nothing but come to life.*) Have students read the monster's encounter with the blind man. How is this encounter different from all other human encounters? (*The blind man is kind to him, whereas the rest of humankind wants to kill the "monster."*) Ask students to discuss who is truly the monster in this story? (*humanity, not the deformed creature*)

4. Ask students to review the scientific and technological advances of the 1800s. What sorts of advances were made in Mary Shelley's time? (*electricity, the Industrial Revolution, advances in medicine, etc.*) How does this story reflect the darker side of scientific triumph?

5. Discuss the theme of the creator's responsibility to the created. What is Shelley's comment on this dynamic? How is she doubting the fundamentals of religion? Ask students to research the religious and philosophical movements that were part of Mary Shelley's life.

6. Ask students to write a theme paper on Mary Shelley's work and discuss how the work reflects the 1800s. Ask students to create a thesis statement and supporting paragraphs with topic sentences. Remind them to quote the text for support of their ideas.

ASSESSMENT

1. Assess students' work by their use of historical information, combined with their ability to fulfill the writing components.

2. Additional grades can be based on students' participation in class discussions.

African Boundaries

Have students examine the map on page 671. What is the subject of the map? What native African state had direct access to the Red Sea coastal trade in 1883?

Lesson 1

(For use with Sections 1 and 2, pp. 662–669)

OBJECTIVES

1. Explain what imperialism is and how imperialists sought to control other peoples.

2. Identify the economic causes of Western imperialism.

3. Explore the ways in which Western imperialism was a product of cultural differences.

4. Explain why the French wanted to gain control of North Africa.

5. Identify the events and aims that promoted British expansion in North and East Africa.

BELLRINGER

Write the following quotation from Winston Churchill on the chalkboard: "What enterprise is more noble and more profitable than the reclamation from barbarism of fertile regions and large populations?" Ask students what this quotation can tell them about Europeans' attitudes toward foreign nations that have not become westernized. Tell students that in Section 1, they will learn more about Western attitudes toward foreign nations.

TEACH OBJECTIVE 1

Level 1: Ask students to define imperialism. Then have students list and describe the different types of imperial control.
[English Language Learners]

Levels 2 and 3: Ask students to express their opinions concerning imperialism. Do they approve? Disapprove? Are their views more

complicated? Have students name and explain the types of imperial control. Which types seem fairer to the natives?

TEACH OBJECTIVE 2

Levels 1 and 2: Ask students to list the motives for Western imperialism. To what ideas did some extreme imperialists subscribe? What factors accompanied industrialism?
[English Language Learners]

Level 3: Ask students why European leaders and industrial leaders began to worry about the future of their industries in the 1800s. *(They got raw materials from other countries. Western countries would not be able to buy all goods they could produce.)* Ask students how imperialism solved these problems. *(If Europeans controlled countries that had the raw materials, they knew they would always have access to materials. If Europeans controlled foreign markets, they could encourage local inhabitants to buy their goods.)*

TEACH OBJECTIVE 3

All Levels: Have students create a chart with the column headings *Cultural Reasons, Political Reasons,* and *Economic Reasons.* Then have students fill in the chart with the different reasons that Europeans established colonies in foreign empires.
[English Language Learners]

TEACH OBJECTIVE 4

All Levels: Tell students that France expanded its influence in North Africa by taking control of Algiers, Tunis, and Morocco. Have students create a Venn diagram to include characteristics of each region.
[English Language Learners]

Level 1: Have students list various regions in North Africa that European nations claimed. *(Algiers, Tunis, Morocco, Egypt, the Sudan)* Ask students why Europeans wanted these regions.

Then ask students which of the regions studied in this section they find most valuable and why. [**English Language Learners**]

TEACH OBJECTIVE 5

Levels 1 and 2: Ask students to identify and define the Suez Canal. How did the British gain control of it? Why did the British want this control? How did these events lead to a violent confrontation?
[**English Language Learners**]

Level 3: Have students look at the map of Africa on page 672 and point out the location of the Suez Canal. Ask students to write down hypotheses about why Britain would want control of the Suez Canal. Then have students return to the map and locate the Sudan. Again, ask students to hypothesize why Britain would want control of this area. Finally, have students read the text under "The British in North Africa" on page 668 and ask why Britain wanted control of the Suez Canal.

REVIEW AND ASSESS

Have students complete **Review Sections 1 and 2**. Then have students complete **Daily Quizzes 26.1 and 26.2**. As Alternative Assessment, you may want to use the Venn diagram or Suez Canal exercises in this section's lessons.

RETEACH

Have students complete **Main Idea Activities 26.1 and 26.2**. Ask students in groups representing Britain and France to prepare outlines of their country's claims in North Africa.
[**English Language Learners, Cooperative Learning**]

CHALLENGE AND EXTEND

Have students research the ways in which European political dominance affected the daily life of Africans in a particular colony.

Lesson 2

(For use with Sections 3 and 4, pp. 670–681)

OBJECTIVES

1. Describe what patterns of colonization Europeans followed in West Africa.

2. Identify what Europeans gained by colonizing central and East Africa.

3. Explain why South Africa was so important to the colonial powers.

4. Examine the effect imperialism had on all of Africa.

5. Describe the role Great Britain played in the development of India.

6. Explain how Japan changed its ancient and tradition-based culture in response to Western imperialism.

7. Explain how Western imperialism affected the peoples of Southeast Asia.

8. Explain why European and American imperialists were interested in the Pacific islands.

BELLRINGER

Ask students what features of a region are attractive to colonizers. *(Students should mention raw materials and markets for goods.)* Tell students that, in Section 3, they will learn about what made sub-Saharan Africa attractive to European colonizers.

TEACH OBJECTIVE 1

All Levels: Ask students to explain the claims in West Africa by the early 1900s. *(European nations claimed all of it except Liberia.)*
[**English Language Learners**]

TEACH OBJECTIVE 2

Level 1: Ask students to explain European interest in colonizing central and East Africa.
[**English Language Learners**]

Levels 2 and 3: Ask students to imagine that they are critics of Henry Stanley. Ask each student to compose a letter to Stanley explaining why his actions are unacceptable.

TEACH OBJECTIVE 3

All Levels: Ask half the students to create a flow chart of events in southern Africa beginning with the British seizure of Cape Colony and ending with the competition among Western nations for land in South Africa. Ask the other half of the students to create a flow chart beginning with this competition and ending with the creation of the Union of South Africa. Have one student from each group write the flow chart on the chalkboard.

TEACH OBJECTIVE 4

All Levels: Create a chart that lists the costs and benefits of European imperialism in Africa. Encourage students to use specific examples from Section 3 to fill in the chart. Ask students to judge whether imperialism had an overall positive or negative effect on Africa.

TEACH OBJECTIVE 5

Level 1: Ask students to identify British motivations and methods used to achieve rule over India. What were the results?
[English Language Learners]

Levels 2 and 3: On the chalkboard create a chart showing the positive and negative effects of British rule in India. After students have completed the chart, ask them if they can see why the Indians began to develop nationalistic feelings while under British rule. Then have them read the text under "The rise of Indian nationalism." Ask students to write a few sentences explaining how British rule led to Indian nationalism.

TEACH OBJECTIVE 6

Levels 1 and 2: Ask students to list the ways in which Japan changed in response to imperialism.
[English Language Learners]

Level 3: Ask students to identify the main factor that encouraged Japan to embark on a course of imperialist expansion. Then present to students the following statements about Japan's imperialist attempts in Asia: (1) A rebellion broke out in Korea that called for freedom from Chinese control; and (2) Japan won the Sino-Japanese War. Have students write a result that stemmed from the action expressed in each statement.

TEACH OBJECTIVE 7

All Levels: Have students look at the map on page 678 and list the imperialist countries and their territory in Southeast Asia. Write *Britain, France, Netherlands,* and *Siam* on the chalkboard. Then have students match each of the following statements to the correct country:

a. gained several small nations and combined them into one territory *(France)*

b. built the city of Singapore; created an important naval base in the region *(Britain)*

c. revolts caused gradual changes and reforms in colonial policies *(Netherlands)*

d. had a more stable government than other parts of Southeast Asia; operated as a buffer zone for other countries *(Siam)*
[English Language Learners]

TEACH OBJECTIVE 8

Levels 1 and 2: Ask students to list the primary and secondary reasons that Western countries were interested in the Pacific islands. Then ask students to detail the problems that developed as Western nations expanded in the Pacific islands.
[English Language Learners]

Level 3: Divide the class into three groups. Assign each group one of the following topics: the Samoa Islands; the Hawaiian Islands; and the Philippines, Guam, and Wake Island. Ask each group to describe in detail what occurred when major powers such as the United States tried to gain power of the islands.
[Cooperative Learning]

REVIEW AND ASSESS

Have students complete **Review Sections 3 and 4**. Then have students complete **Daily Quizzes 26.3 and 26.4**. As Alternative Assessment, you may want to use the map or Pacific islands exercises in this section's lessons.

RETEACH

Have students complete **Main Idea Activities 26.3 and 26.4**. Then have students create an annotated time line of imperialism in India and Southeast Asia.
[English Language Learners]

CHALLENGE AND EXTEND

Have students conduct research to find out what effects of colonization are still evident in Indian society today.

Lesson 3

(For use with Section 5, pp. 682–687)

OBJECTIVES

1. Explain how economic pressure was used by imperialist powers to control Latin America.

2. Identify the causes and outcomes of the Spanish-American War of 1898.

3. Explain why the Panama Canal was important.

4. Compare the "Roosevelt Corollary" to the Monroe Doctrine.

BELLRINGER

Have students think about how a country with a strong economy can assert power over a country with a weaker economy. Ask them to list policies that might make this possible. Tell students that in Section 5 they will learn how the United States and Europe asserted economic control over the countries of Latin America.

TEACH OBJECTIVE 1

All Levels: Have students read the opening paragraphs of Section 5. Then ask them how imperialism in Latin America differed from imperialism in Africa, Asia, and the Pacific.

TEACH OBJECTIVE 2

All Levels: Ask students to list the causes and outcomes of the Spanish-American War of 1898. Then have students create a time line of the Spanish-American War.
[English Language Learners]

TEACH OBJECTIVE 3

All Levels: Ask students to describe why the Panama Canal was important to the United States. What factors hindered the building of the canal?
[English Language Learners]

TEACH OBJECTIVE 4

All Levels: Write the words *Roosevelt Corollary* on the chalkboard. Underneath write *who? what? where? when? why?* and *how?* Tell students that these are the questions that reporters often ask themselves when writing a story. Then have students write a short news report about the Roosevelt Corollary that answers all of the questions.

REVIEW AND ASSESS

Have students complete **Review Section 5**. Then have students complete **Daily Quiz 26.5**. As Alternative Assessment, you may want to use the Spanish-American War or Panama Canal exercises in this section's lessons.

RETEACH

Have students complete **Main Idea Activity 26.5**. Then ask students to list the main ideas of each heading.
[English Language Learners]

CHALLENGE AND EXTEND

Have two groups prepare a debate discussing if imperialism practiced in Latin America was less harmful or equally harmful to its inhabitants than that practiced in Africa and Asia.

African Proverbs

GOAL

In this activity, students will learn the impact of Imperialism on African cultures by studying African proverbs before imperialism and then by composing new proverbs for colonial Africa.

PLANNING

- **Purpose** This activity incorporates teacher-directed lessons and individual and group assignments. It should be used as a culminating activity for a study of imperialism in Africa.

- **Suggested Time** Plan to spend two lesson blocks and one homework assignment on this activity. Provide time for students to share and discuss their original proverbs.

- **Teaching Team** At least one social studies teacher and one language arts teacher should take part in teaching this activity.

- **Group Size** This activity can be adapted for either individuals or groups.

- **Materials and Resources** Provide students with the following: examples of African proverbs, such as those found in *World Literature* (Holt, Rinehart, Winston, Inc.) or library resources; *Things Fall Apart* by Chinua Achebe; Video: Program 6—*The Magnificent African Cake* from the series *Africa: A Voyage of Discovery with Basil Davidson* (distributed by RM Arts, 1984) or any other video about colonial Africa; and student copies of Rubric 41: Writing to Express.

IMPLEMENTATION

1. Give students an overview of this activity by explaining that they will read a chapter from a Nigerian novel about tribal life before imperialism. They will pick out its proverbs and determine what the sayings reveal about the culture and values of the Ibo tribe. They will then write new proverbs reflecting the culture of the people after imperialism.

2. Review Chapter 8 with students to reexamine traditional Africa. Consider the following questions: What was the African oral tradition? What was the role of kinship in African society? What is a matrilineal society? Then discuss the meaning of a proverb, perhaps asking students to brainstorm English proverbs they know, such as the following: "An apple a day keeps the doctor away," "The early bird catches the worm," etc. According to the *World Literature* text, proverbs are short sayings that express a common truth or experience, usually about human failings and the ways that people interact with one another. They frequently incorporate such literary elements as metaphor ("An ounce of prevention is worth a pound of cure"), alliteration ("He who laughs last laughs best"), parallelism ("Where there's a will, there's a way"), and rhyme ("When the cat's away, the mice will play"). In African culture, proverbs are more than quaint sayings; instead, they represent a poetic form that uses few words but achieves great depth of meaning. Before written literature, proverbs functioned as the distilled essence of a people's values and knowledge. They were used to settle legal disputes, resolve ethical problems, and teach children the philosophy of their people. They also provided entertainment.

3. Read Chapter 8 of *Things Fall Apart* and identify the proverbs. For each proverb, explain what it reveals about the culture, values, or beliefs of the Ibo people and restate it in American cultural terms. Proverbs found in this chapter are the following: "A chick that will grow into a cock can be spotted the very day it hatches," "A child's fingers are not scalded by a piece of hot yam which its mother put into its palm," "When mother cow is chewing grass, its young ones watch its mouth," "If I fall down for you and you fall down for me, it is play." Have students look at the other African proverbs taken out of context and see if students can determine what they

reveal about African culture, values, or beliefs.

4. Focusing on Sections 1 and 2 of Chapter 26, review the causes of imperialism. Consider questions such as the following: What types of people promoted imperialism? What did they hope to gain? What was the impact of imperialism on Africa?

5. View a video describing the impact of imperialism on Africa. As they watch, have students identify changes in African culture and African reactions to Europeans. Consider the following: By what methods did Europeans control Africa? By what means did Europeans force Africans to work for them? How did Europeans change the African economy?

6. Using proverbs studied as models, have students alone or in groups write original proverbs reflecting conditions in colonial Africa. Topics might include new economic conditions, attitudes toward Europeans, ruling tactics used by Europeans, and European attitudes toward Africans. As students share their proverbs, have other students identify the values, beliefs, or cultural elements reflected in them.

ASSESSMENT

1. To assess students' proverbs, use Rubric 41: Writing to Express.

2. Additional grades could be based on student participation in class discussion or on written analysis of proverbs.

Europe and the Middle East on the Eve of World War I, 1914

Have students examine the map on page 700. Ask the following questions: Which military alliance was split by the territory of the other? Which alliance gained the most land?

Lesson 1

(For use with Sections 1 and 2, pp. 698–710)

OBJECTIVES

1. Explain why rivalries increased among European nations.

2. Identify the military alliances that existed at the beginning of World War I and explain how they changed by late 1915.

3. Explain why the Balkans were a "powder keg."

4. Identify the advantages that each side had in World War I.

5. Explain how new technology affected the way in which World War I was fought.

6. Explain what led the United States to join the Allied Powers.

BELLRINGER

Ask students to discuss the meaning of the term *world war. (a military conflict between many nations)* Ask them to list conditions that might turn a small, local conflict between two countries into a world war. Tell students that, in Section 1, they will learn how conflict between Austria-Hungary and Serbia led to World War I.

TEACH OBJECTIVE 1

All Levels: Draw a word web on the board with *World War I* at the center and the terms *Rivalries, Alliances, Nationalism,* and *Militarism* around it. Form the class into four groups and assign one of the board terms to each group. Tell the groups to define their term and determine how it was a

factor in the events that led to World War I. Have each group report its conclusions to the class. **[English Language Learners, Cooperative Learning]**

TEACH OBJECTIVE 2

All Levels: Help students to create a graphic organizer that illustrates the countries and dates of alliances that existed in Europe at the outbreak of World War I. Then have students explain how the alliances had changed by late 1915. *(Germany and Austria-Hungary allied with the Ottoman Empire and Bulgaria; Great Britain and France allied with Japan and Italy; Germany opposed Russia; Russia supported Serbia)* **[English Language Learners]**

TEACH OBJECTIVE 3

Levels 1 and 2: Have students list the events that led up to the ignition of the Balkan "powder keg." Then discuss the results. Record answers on the chalkboard. **[English Language Learners]**

Level 3: Ask pairs of students to develop a paragraph explaining why the Balkans could be considered a "powder keg" in 1914. *(rivalries between Great Britain, Russia, Austria-Hungary, and Germany in the Balkans; the alliance system; and Austria-Hungary's ultimatum)* **[Cooperative Learning]**

TEACH OBJECTIVE 4

All Levels: Have students create a two-column chart labeled *Advantages of the Central Powers* and *Advantages of the Allied Powers.* Students should list the advantages of each side in the appropriate columns. **[English Language Learners]**

TEACH OBJECTIVE 5

All Levels: Ask students to identify new weapons and tactics that were introduced during World War I and list them on the board. *(weapons: U-boats, poison gas, machine guns,*

long-range artillery, airplanes, and tanks; tactics: trenches, drafted civilians, propaganda) Then form students into groups and assign each group one item from the list. Tell each group to imagine that they are a strategic task force in the British War Office. Their task is to analyze how the enemy is likely to use the innovation and to suggest strategies for combating its anticipated effects. Have each group report its conclusions and suggestions.
[English Language Learners, Cooperative Learning]

Level 3: Have students write an explanation of how they think the two sides would have fought World War I without airplanes and tanks. Tell students to base their writing on a thinking process similar to the following problem-solving process: (1) Identify a situation that requires a decision; (2)Gather information; (3) List and consider options; (4) Consider advantages and disadvantages; (5) Choose a solution; (6) Evaluate the effectiveness of the solution.

TEACH OBJECTIVE 6

Level 1: Have students create a research outline for the information on page 710. Then discuss with students what led the United States to join the Allied Powers.
[English Language Learners]

Levels 2 and 3: Have students work in pairs to determine what factors influenced American opinion about World War I. *(sinking of the Lusitania, effect of German blockade on American trade, British propaganda, Zimmermann telegram, Germany's unrestricted submarine warfare)* Tell pairs to summarize these factors and then state why they would or would not support the decision of the United States to enter the war.
[Cooperative Learning]

REVIEW AND ASSESS

Have students complete **Review Sections 1 and 2**. Then have students complete **Daily Quizzes 27.1 and 27.2**. As Alternative Assessment, you may want to use the diagram or the time line in this section's lessons.

RETEACH

Have students complete **Main Idea Activities 27.1 and 27.2**. Then ask each student to create a research outline of the sections' main ideas and supporting details.
[English Language Learners]

CHALLENGE AND EXTEND

Organize the class into two groups representing the Central Powers and the Allied Powers. Have the groups research the position that their side took in the war. Then have the groups support their point of view in a class debate.
[Cooperative Learning]

Lesson 2

(For use with Sections 3 and 4, pp. 711–717)

OBJECTIVES

1. Identify the events that led to the Russian Revolution.

2. Explain how the Communists came to power.

3. Explain how Russia's revolution affected its participation in World War I.

4. Define the Fourteen Points.

5. Explain how the war ended.

6. Identify the disagreements that the peacemakers faced.

BELLRINGER

Ask students to write down what they know about Russia during the war up to 1917. *(was originally part of the Triple Alliance; supported Serbia; Germany declared war on Russia in 1914, which led to Russia's alliance with the Allied Powers; lost half its army and was defeated at the Battle of Tannenberg; army lacked guns and ammunition)* Tell students that, in the next section, they will learn why the Russian Revolution occurred and how it affected Russia's future.

TEACH OBJECTIVES 1 AND 2

All Levels: Work with students to create a diagram that shows the events leading to the

Russian Revolution and the creation of the Communist Party.
[**English Language Learners**]

TEACH OBJECTIVE 3

Level 1: Help students to identify the main idea of the subsection "Peace and the Civil War." (*treaty with Central Powers and civil war ended Russia's participation in World War I*)
[**English Language Learners**]

Levels 2 and 3: Have students create a cause-and-effect chart that shows the relationship among the events that ended Russia's participation in World War I.

TEACH OBJECTIVE 4

Level 1: Have students identify the six general points within the Fourteen Points. List responses on the board. Discuss how each point would contribute to Wilson's goals of making the world "safe for democracy" and securing a "just peace." Ask students to identify points that seem to be a basis for American foreign policy today. (*arms reduction, free trade, and a world organization*)
[**English Language Learners**]

Levels 2 and 3: Have students list the six general points within the Fourteen Points. Ask students to identify the positive and/or negative aspects of each of the points. Can they foresee problems with any of them?

TEACH OBJECTIVE 5

Ail Levels: Have students create a time line to show the events of 1918 that brought World War I to a close.
[**English Language Learners, Cooperative Learning**]

TEACH OBJECTIVE 6

Level 1 and 2: Have students create a list of the disagreements the peacemakers faced. With whom do students agree most? Why?
[**English Language Learners**]

Level 3: Have groups of students role-play radio interviews with representatives of the Big Four. The program's host should ask the guests their opinions of the Fourteen Points, what they hope to gain for their countries, and how the Central Powers should be punished. (There should be clear differences of opinion among the guests.) Select one group to recreate its role-play for the class.
[**Cooperative Learning**]

REVIEW AND ASSESS

Have students complete **Review Sections 3 and 4**. Then have students complete **Daily Quizzes 27.3 and 27.4**. As Alternative Assessment, you may want to use the chart in this section's lessons.

RETEACH

Have students complete **Main Idea Activities 27.3** and **27.4**. Then have students write a main idea question and answer for each subheading in the section.
[**English Language Learners**]

CHALLENGE AND EXTEND

Have students use the process of historical inquiry to research the effect the armistice had on Germany. Ask students to write short reports of their findings.

Lesson 3
(For use with Section 5, pp. 718–723)

OBJECTIVES

1. Identify the terms of the Treaty of Versailles.

2. Explain how territories were redivided after the war.

3. Explain how the League of Nations was structured.

BELLRINGER

Ask students to list the countries that lost World War I. (*Germany, Austria-Hungary, Bulgaria, and Russia*) Ask students what they think happened to these countries after the war. *(Students might suggest that the countries lost territory, as well as military, economic, and political power.)* Tell students that, in Section 5, they will learn what happened to the nations involved in World War I.

TEACH OBJECTIVE 1

All Levels: Have students work in groups to create a newspaper page about the Treaty of Versailles. Assign the groups different countries or regions to represent, such as France, Germany, Serbia, Syria, or Africa. Each group's page should contain at least two columns expressing how the terms of the treaty affected its country or region.
[English Language Learners, Cooperative Learning]

TEACH OBJECTIVE 2

Levels 1 and 2: Have pairs of students take turns asking and answering questions about the geographic distribution of nations and territory as it is shown on the maps on pages 719 and 720. *(example: Which country lost the area now known as Czechoslovakia? answer: Austria-Hungary)* Have students record their questions and answers in a two-column chart with the columns labeled *Questions* and *Answers*.
[English Language Learners, Cooperative Learning]

Level 3: Distribute two copies of an outline map of Europe to each student. On one map, students should show the countries of Europe before World War I. On the other map, they should show Europe after World War I. Tell students to label each map, and on a separate sheet of paper write a paragraph explaining how and why their maps differ. Students should use standard grammar, spelling, sentence structure, and punctuation to write their paragraphs.

TEACH OBJECTIVE 3

Level 1: Call on volunteers to state the League of Nation's two main goals. *(to promote international cooperation; to maintain peace)* Have students identify methods the League used to accomplish these goals. *(such as arms reductions)* Ask how the mandate process related to the League's goals. *(protected nations until ready for independence)*
[English Language Learners]

All Levels: Create an organization chart that illustrates the structure of the League of Nations and its relationship to the World Court.

REVIEW AND ASSESS

Have students complete **Review Section 5.** Then have students complete **Daily Quiz 27.5.** As Alternative Assessment, you may want to use the *Interpreting Maps* feature in the section's lessons.

RETEACH

Have students complete **Main Idea Activity 27.5.** Then have students write a two-paragraph summary of the section.
[English Language Learners]

CHALLENGE AND EXTEND

Have students write a short paper explaining why they agree or disagree with the opinion that the settlement of World War I made another major war in Europe almost inevitable.

Wartime Letters

GOAL

In this activity, students will understand various points of view about World War I and create an alter ego from whose point of view they will react to the war.

PLANNING

- **Purpose** This activity incorporates teacher-directed lessons and individual assignments. It should be used as a culminating activity for a study of World War I.

- **Suggested Time** Plan to spend two lesson blocks and one homework assignment on this activity. Provide time for students to share and discuss their letters.

- **Teaching Team** At least one social studies teacher and one language arts teacher should take part in teaching this activity.

- **Group Size** This activity is best suited for individuals.

- **Materials and Resources** Students will need the following: *All Quiet on the Western Front* by Erich Maria Remarque; *The Great War* series video produced by Ken Burns for PBS, or any other video that describes living conditions for soldiers during World War I; encyclopedias of costumes such as *What People Wore* (Viking Press, 1969), and *The Chronicle of Western Fashion* by John Peacock (Thames and Hudson Ltd, 1991), Student copies of Rubric 25: Personal Letters from *Portfolio and Performance Assessment for Social Studies*.

IMPLEMENTATION

1. Give students an overview of the activity by explaining that, after studying literature of World War I, they will create an alter ego through whose eyes they will react to the events of the war. From this point of view, they will compose two original letters about the war and its effects.

2. Review with students Section 2 of Chapter 27 about the facts of World War I and the people involved. Consider questions such as the following: Where were the fighting fronts? What new weapons were used in World War I? What was the role of women in the war?

3. View segments of *The Great War* or another video. Discuss daily living conditions for these soldiers. With what problems were they confronted? How did they attempt to solve these problems? How did they relate to each other? How did they feel about the enemy? How did they entertain themselves?

4. Read the portion of *All Quiet on the Western Front*, Chapter 7, describing the main character Paul's return home on leave from the front. Discuss the points of view of the characters involved. Consider the following questions: How does Paul feel about his visit home? How does his sister react to him? How does his mother relate to him? What is his father's chief concern? How does Paul feel about his encounter with the Major? With his German master? With the men in the tavern? How do Paul and Frau Kemmerich react to each other? How does Paul feel about his old clothes and books? How do these various characters reveal widely differing values and beliefs?

5. Now have each student create his own alter ego of a person from the World War I time period. Students might choose a soldier, a political leader, a friend or family member of a soldier, a wartime volunteer, etc. To avoid stereotypical characters, have students describe fully who this person is, including age and date of birth, nationality, marital status, occupation, family members, educational background, work history, and a brief description of past friends or relationships that may have had an impact on him or her, hobbies and friends, and problems and highlights.

6. From the alter ego's point of view, the student should compose two letters, each to a different person such as a character in the book, a friend, a co-worker, or a family member. Within the letters, there must be at least three specific references to historical details of the war. When writing, the student should take into consideration the type of paper or stationary the alter ego might use and the writing implement, the style of handwriting, and the diction that person would use. When sharing their letters with the class, you might require students to come to class dressed as their alter ego after consulting reference books for historical accuracy.

ASSESSMENT

1. To assess students' proverbs, use Rubric 25: Personal Letters in *Portfolio and Performance Assessment for Social Studies*.

2. Additional grades could be based on student participation in class discussion or on written analysis of the video, the novel, and the alter ego profile.

Influenza Pandemic of 1918: the Second Wave

Have students examine the map on page 729. What continent suffered the most deaths from the influenza pandemic? Why might estimates of the number of deaths from the influenza pandemic vary so much?

Lesson 1

(For use with Sections 1 and 2, pp. 728–737)

OBJECTIVES

1. Explain how scientific theories affected thinking in other areas of life.

2. Identify ways in which writers, musicians, painters, and architects experimented with new forms.

3. Describe how popular culture and consumerism affected societies.

4. Identify the weaknesses that appeared in the global economy during the postwar era.

5. Describe how nations initially responded to the Great Depression.

6. Explain how the New Deal marked a shift in the U.S. government's relationship with its citizens and the economy.

BELLRINGER

Ask students to write a list of ways recent wars or international conflicts have influenced life in the United States. Have volunteers share their responses with the class. Tell students that, in Section 1, they will learn how World War I changed society in Europe and the United States.

TEACH OBJECTIVE 1

Level 1: Ask students what new developments in science occurred during the 1920s and how they affected people's understanding of their world.
[**English Language Learners, Cooperative Learning**]

TEACH OBJECTIVE 2

All Levels: Read aloud brief selections from Charles Dickens and Mark Twain. Ask students to describe these writings. Then read brief selections from James Joyce and Franz Kafka and ask students how they differ from the earlier literature.
[**English Language Learners, Cooperative Learning**]

Level 3: Organize students into groups of five. Tell them that each group will complete a multimedia presentation covering the literature, art, music, popular culture, and architecture of the 1920s. Suggest that each member of the group specialize in one topic. Have students use their textbooks, the library, computer software, and interviews of senior citizens, if possible. Encourage students to include audio and video clips, images of artwork and buildings, and other images of popular culture.
[**Cooperative Learning**]

TEACH OBJECTIVES 1 AND 2

Level 3: Have students create a graphic organizer titled *Science and Art in the Postwar Era.* One column should read *Cause* and the other should be labeled *Effect.* Ask students to complete the chart.

TEACH OBJECTIVE 3

All Levels: Have students select some aspect of the popular culture of the 1920s and 1930s to study in more depth. They might investigate the rise of the motion picture industry, sports, popular music, the Temperance Movement, radio entertainment, and so on. Ask each student to find out something interesting about his or her chosen topic and share it with the class in a three- to five-minute presentation.
[**English Language Learners, Cooperative Learning**]

TEACH OBJECTIVES 4 AND 5

All Levels: Have students complete a flow chart showing how economic weaknesses led to the Great Depression.
[**English Language Learners, Cooperative Learning**]

TEACH OBJECTIVE 6

Level 1: Have students define the New Deal. How did it affect the citizens of the United States and the economy? What was the Social Security Act?
[**English Language Learners**]

Levels 2 and 3: Have students use the library or computer software to make a chart identifying the main provisions of each of these New Deal programs: Civilian Conservation Corps (CCC), Federal Emergency Relief Administration (FERA), Agricultural Adjustment Act of 1933, Tennessee Valley Authority (TVA), Federal Deposit Insurance Company (FDIC), Works Progress Administration (WPA), National Labor Relations Act (Wagner-Connery Act), Social Security Act.

REVIEW AND ASSESS

Have students complete **Review Sections 1 and 2**. Then have students complete **Daily Quizzes 28.1 and 28.2**. As Alternative Assessment, have students make a cause-and-effect chart like the chalkboard chart in this section's lessons.

RETEACH

Have students complete **Main Idea Activities 28.1 and 28.2**. Then ask students to write three lists about the Great Depression: *causes, effects,* and *government responses.*
[**English Language Learners**]

CHALLENGE AND EXTEND

Have students search the Internet through the HRW Go site for information about the Great Depression. Then write several journal entries as if they were teenagers living then.

Lesson 2

(For use with Sections 3 and 4, pp. 738–748)

OBJECTIVES

1. Describe the difficulties that France faced during the postwar years.
2. Explain how the British government dealt with its domestic problems.
3. Identify the problems that weakened eastern European governments.
4. Describe how Benito Mussolini transformed Italy into a fascist state.
5. Explain why the Weimar Republic failed.
6. Trace how Adolf Hitler became an important figure in Germany.
7. Describe how the Nazis used power in Germany.

BELLRINGER

Ask students to list problems that usually follow a war. *(need to rebuild, pay war debts, return soldiers to civilian life, change wartime to peacetime economy)* Lead a discussion on how the nations of Europe should have solved these problems. Tell students that, in Section 3, they will learn how the nations of Europe attempted to cope with these problems.

TEACH OBJECTIVE 1

All Levels: After students read about postwar France, have them list France's main problems while you record them on the chalkboard. *(land in ruins, technology destroyed, young men killed in war, inflation, war debt, cost of Maginot Line, political unrest)* Group students into pairs or triads to brainstorm ways French leaders might have tried to solve these problems. Have groups compare suggested solutions.
[**English Language Learners, Cooperative Learning**]

TEACH OBJECTIVE 2

Levels 1 and 2: After students read about postwar Great Britain, have them write letters to the editor of a fictional 1920s British newspaper expressing an opinion about an issue covered in their textbook, such as labor troubles or the Irish independence movement. Encourage students to edit one another's letters before they submit their final drafts.
[English Language Learners, Cooperative Learning]

Level 3: Tell students to imagine that they are members of Sinn Fein, fighting for Irish nationhood. Have them write speeches giving reasons why Ireland should be free from British rule, and exhorting others to join the cause. Some students may also wish to write speeches giving the opposing point of view.

TEACH OBJECTIVE 3

All Levels: Have students review challenges facing Austria, Hungary, and Poland after World War I. (*Austria: weak economy, private armies; Hungary: succession of weak governments, new boundaries interrupted trade; Poland: political conflicts, high German tariffs*) Then have them create a series of three political cartoons about the postwar political situations in Austria, Hungary, and Poland. Encourage students to share their finished cartoons with the class.

TEACH OBJECTIVE 4

Level 2: Ask students what personal characteristics would help a person gain power in postwar Italy. Lead a class discussion about how events might have been different if Mussolini had not lived.

TEACH OBJECTIVES 4 AND 5

Level 1: Have students write a list of the problems that faced Italy and Germany after World War I. Have students brainstorm ways that Italy and Germany might have addressed these common conditions. Tell students that they will find out as they study this section that both

countries seemed unable to respond effectively to these problems.
[English Language Learners, Cooperative Learning]

TEACH OBJECTIVES 4 AND 6

All Levels: Assign half the class to study Mussolini and the other half to study Hitler. Tell the two large groups to organize themselves into subgroups of two, three, or four students to do research. Have subgroups organize their findings onto a time line of events illustrating when their assigned leader achieved dominance and established totalitarian rule. Encourage students to include even minor events and to add illustrations.
[English Language Learners, Cooperative Learning]

TEACH OBJECTIVES 4, 5, AND 6

Level 3: Have students create a graphic organizer titled *Reasons People Embraced Totalitarianism*. The first column should read *Italy* and the second *Germany*. Have each student complete the chart.

TEACH OBJECTIVE 7

All Levels: Tell students that, in November of 1938, more than 7,500 Jewish-owned businesses and more than 250 synagogues were set on fire in a single night: *Kristallnacht,* or "night of broken glass." Have students take on the roles of people who witnessed the horrors of *Kristallnacht* and write personal letters to friends or relatives in the United States describing the event and their feelings.

REVIEW AND ASSESS

Have students complete **Review Sections 3 and 4**. Then have students complete **Daily Quizzes 28.3 and 28.4**. As Alternative Assessment, you may want to use the graphic organizer chart or time line exercise in this section's lesson.

RETEACH

Have students complete **Main Idea Activities 28.3 and 28.4**. Then have students prepare outlines of how Mussolini and Hitler came to power. **[English Language Learners, Cooperative Learning]**

CHALLENGE AND EXTEND

Have students imagine that they are living in the United States when Hitler and Mussolini rise to power. Ask them to write letters to the editor of a local newspaper suggesting how the U.S. government should respond to Hitler and Mussolini. Encourage them to consider what the results of the two leaders' policies will be.

Lesson 3

(For use with Section 5, pp. 749–753)

OBJECTIVES

1. Identify the terms of the New Economic Policy.

2. Describe how Stalin shaped the Soviet economy.

3. Explain why Stalin imprisoned and executed millions of Soviet people.

BELLRINGER

Ask students what they think the phrase "command economy" might mean. *(government controls all means of production)* Tell students that, in 1928, Stalin initiated the first Five-Year Plan, returning the Soviet economy to a command economy with government control of all industry and agriculture. Tell students that, in Section 5, they will learn how Joseph Stalin shaped the Soviet economy and took control of the nation.

TEACH OBJECTIVES 1 AND 2

All Levels: Ask students to make a graphic organizer titled *Problems of the New Soviet Union.* Three columns should be labeled as the following: *Problem, Attempted Solution,* and *Results.* Have students fill in the chart with at least five problems.
[English Language Learners]

TEACH OBJECTIVE 3

All Levels: Have students imagine living in a society where they might be imprisoned or executed at any time for even the slightest infraction. Ask them to write a diary entry describing the situation and why they think the government leaders created the situation. Remind students that, depending on what they write, their diary could lead to serious consequences if found by government officials.

REVIEW AND ASSESS

Have students complete **Review Section 5**. Then have students complete **Daily Quiz 28.5**. As Alternative Assessment, you may want to use the *Problems of the New Soviet Union* chart exercise in this section's lessons.

RETEACH

Have students complete **Main Idea Activity 28.5**. Then have them write *Lenin, Trotsky,* and *Stalin* with space between the names and use their textbooks to list as many facts as they can about each.
[English Language Learners]

CHALLENGE AND EXTEND

Have students review the time period from 1919 to 1936. Have students research the time period, recording events in the Soviet Union on one side of a time line and important world events on the other side. Invite students to illustrate their time lines with drawings or other art. Display the completed time lines in the classroom.

A Different United States

GOAL

In this activity, students will learn more about the specific programs of the New Deal and evaluate them. Students will determine the importance of programs still in place today.

PLANNING

- **Purpose** This activity may be used in combination with teacher-directed lessons, or as an enrichment activity.

- **Suggested Time** Plan to spend two lesson blocks and one homework assignment on this activity.

- **Teaching Team** At least one social studies teacher and one language arts teacher should take part in teaching this activity.

- **Group Size** This activity works best if students work individually. However, students may work in smaller groups to undertake research. You may wish to assign the activity as an extra credit option for individual students.

- **Materials and Resources** Provide students with sources other than their textbooks to research information on New Deal programs. Also provide students with copies of Rubrics 11 and 40.

IMPLEMENTATION

1. Give students an overview of the activity by explaining that they will look at the New Deal programs in detail. They will then write a piece describing a United States that is very different from the country in which they live now.

2. List the following causes of the Great Depression on the chalkboard or overhead projector and have students volunteer some effects of these causes: increased farm production *(demand did not match supply, so farm prices fell)*, easy credit *(more buying on credit, buying stock on margin, stock spec-*

ulation, *Great Bull Market*), panic selling of stocks *(stock market crash of 1929, run on the banks, bank closures, financial ruin for many)*, stock market crash *(defensive international trading practices, worldwide bank failures, global depression)*. Discuss student responses.

3. Create a two-column chart on the chalkboard or overhead projector. The column headings should read as follows: *New Deal Programs* and *Provisions*. In the first column under *New Deal Programs*, list the following:

- Civilian Conservation Corps (CCC)

- Federal Emergency Relief Administration (FERA)

- Agricultural Adjustment Act of 1933, Tennessee Valley Authority (TVA)

- Federal Deposit Insurance Corporation (FDIC)

- National Recovery Administration (NRA)

- Works Progress Administration (WPA)

- National Labor Relations Act (Wagner-Connery Act)

- Social Security Act

Have students use their textbooks and other sources that you may provide to fill in the second column of the chart. Tell students that the chart represents a sampling of New Deal programs.

4. After students have completed their charts and the class has discussed the programs of the New Deal, have students conduct a panel discussion about the pros and cons of the New Deal. Questions to investigate include the following: How do relief programs like those of the New Deal affect people's incentive to work? How would too much government regulation of business affect the economy? How would too little regulation affect it? What New Deal programs are still in place today? Are they still

necessary to the well-being of the United States and its people?

5. Have students choose one or two programs that are still in place today. Ask them to write a description of a United States that does not have the program(s) students have chosen. What would everyday life be like? What would the United States be like in times of economic disaster? How would the lack of the program(s) affect young children? Adults? The elderly? Have students share their writing with the class.

ASSESSMENT

1. To assess students' writing, use Rubrics 11 and 40.

2. Additional grades can be based on students' completion of the New Deal chart.

New Nations in the Middle East

Have students examine the map on page 763. What is the subject of the map? What two countries controlled the land surrounding the Strait of Hormuz? Why would the Strait of Hormuz be important?

Lesson 1

(For use with Sections 1 and 2, pp. 758–764)

OBJECTIVES

1. Identify what caused the end of British rule in Egypt and the Middle East.

2. Describe how the people of India pursued independence.

3. Explain the British response to calls for change in other parts of the empire.

4. Explain Turkey's development into a modern republic.

5. Identify the ideas regarding modern nationalism adopted by Persia.

6. Describe the effect of World War I on African attitudes toward colonialism.

BELLRINGER

Ask students to write down reasons why Americans were dissatisfied with British rule in the 1700s and predict how and why other British colonies might react to long-term British authority. *(Students might note taxation and lack of representation. Other British colonies may revolt as a result of the same concerns.)* Ask volunteers to share their thoughts with the class. Tell students that in Section 1 they will learn about the independence movements of several colonies under British rule.

TEACH OBJECTIVE 1

Level 1: Write the words Egypt, Transjordan, Iraq, and Palestine on the chalkboard. Ask stu-

dents what these places had in common in the early 1900s and how they differed. *(all under British control after World War I; Egypt, Transjordan, and Iraq gained independence though Britain kept military presence; Palestine was retained due to its location)*
[**English Language Learners**]

Levels 2 and 3: Ask students to create a flow chart that illustrates how Egypt and the Middle East became independent from British rule.

TEACH OBJECTIVE 2

All Levels: Have students create a graphic organizer that explores the effects of passive resistance on India's independence from Britain. Column headings should be titled *Passive Resistance* and *British Reaction*. Ask students to fill in the chart.
[**English Language Learners**]

TEACH OBJECTIVE 3

Levels 1 and 2: Have students review the information under the heading "The Statute of Westminster" on page 761. Ask students the following questions: Which areas also called for complete self-government? Once Great Britain granted them autonomy, how did these countries change in terms of government and control?
[**English Language Learners**]

Level 3: Have students conduct further research on the Statute of Westminster.

TEACH OBJECTIVE 4

Level 1: Have students list Kemal's reforms. Then ask them what effect his reforms had on Turkey.
[**English Language Learners, Cooperative Learning**]

Levels 2 and 3: Have students list the various things Mustafa Kemal brought to the Turks. Discuss which changes students view as positive and/or negative.

TEACH OBJECTIVE 5

Level 1: Have students identify those things Reza Shah Pahlavi enacted to modernize Persia. Record students' answers on the chalkboard. **[English Language Learners]**

Levels 2 and 3: Have students write an essay that compares and contrasts the nationalist reforms of Mustafa Kemal and Reza Shah and evaluates qualities of each leader.

TEACH OBJECTIVE 6

All Levels: In this activity, students will examine the changes in African attitudes towards colonialism. Have students create a two-column chart with the headings *Experience* and *Result*. In the rows beneath *Experience*, have students write the following: World War I, colonial education, racism and political repression. Ask students to fill in the *Result* column. **[English Language Learners]**

REVIEW AND ASSESS

Have students complete the **Review Sections 1 and 2**. Then have students complete **Daily Quizzes 29.1 and 29.2**. As Alternative Assessment, you may want to use the African Attitudes graphic organizer or the essay exercise in this section's lessons.

RETEACH

Have students complete **Main Idea Activities 29.1 and 29.2**. Then ask students to create, trade, and solve riddles, using words in Sections 1 and 2.

CHALLENGE AND EXTEND

Have students research a leader and write a one- to two-page scene relating to the leader's nationalist ideas.

Lesson 2

(For use with Sections 3 and 4, pp. 765–773)

OBJECTIVES

1. Describe how resentment of foreign interests led to the downfall of the Qing dynasty.

2. Identify the ways the nationalist movement in China changed under the leadership of Sun Yixian and Chiang Kai-shek.

3. Explain the development of communism in China.

4. Explain the Japanese pursuit of expansion that began in the late 1800s.

5. Describe the changes in Japanese life during rapid modernization.

6. Identify the effects of the military on Japan during the 1920s and the 1930s.

BELLRINGER

Ask students to write two lists—one describing Western influence on China and the other identifying problems with the Qing rule. *(opium, astronomy, religion, free trade ideas; corruption, high taxes)* Then ask students how their listed items affected the Qing dynasty. *(government felt threatened, opium addiction, loss of money to finance opium trade, rebellions)* Tell students that, in Section 3, they will learn about the fate of the Qing dynasty and about Chinese nationalism.

TEACH OBJECTIVE 1

All Levels: Have students create a graphic organizer to help them list the steps that led to the downfall of the Qing dynasty. **[English Language Learners]**

TEACH OBJECTIVE 2

Levels 1 and 2: Ask students to describe Sun Yixian and Chiang Kai-shek's backgrounds before leading the Nationalists. Discuss with students how a person's background affects their point of view and ask them how these leaders' points of view affected the nationalist

movement in China. (*Sun Yixian supported modernization and republican government. Chiang Kai-shek strengthened the army and supported the conservatives.*)
[**English Language Learners**]

Level 3: Have students prepare and enact a court trial with the Qing dynasty as defendant and the Kuomintang as witnesses for the prosecution.

TEACH OBJECTIVE 3

Level 2: Have students work in pairs to create a storyboard with captions underneath representing the key events that led to the rise of communism in China.
[**Cooperative Learning**]

All Levels: Ask students to imagine they are supporters of Chiang Kai-shek, Henry P'u-i, or Mao Zedong. Ask them to write a letter to a Chinese student outside of the country describing the development of communism in China.
[**English Language Learners**]

TEACH OBJECTIVE 4

All Levels: Have students create a two-column chart titled *Japanese Expansion*. Label one column *How* and the other *Why*. Have students fill in the columns with the methods and reasons for Japanese expansion.

TEACH OBJECTIVE 5

Level 1: Write *increased population, economic trouble,* and *social tensions* on the chalkboard. Have students write one-sentence summaries describing each problem with Japan's rapid modernization.

Levels 2 and 3: Ask students to write a radio news segment discussing the positive and negative effects of modernization in Japan following the period of the Meiji Restoration. Have them personalize their stories with short fictional interviews from different people in Japanese society.

TEACH OBJECTIVE 6

Level 1: Ask students to define militarism. Why did Japan become increasingly influenced by militarism? What were the results of this preoccupation?
[**English Language Learners**]

Levels 2 and 3: Ask students to write a persuasive speech from the point of view of a top ranking Japanese military official. In the speech, students should explain the changes the military wants in Japan and include reasons for those changes.

REVIEW AND ASSESS

Have students complete the **Review Sections 3 and 4**. Then have students complete **Daily Quizzes 29.3 and 29.4**. As Alternative Assessment, you may want to use the Japanese Expansion chart or the speech exercise from this section's lessons.

RETEACH

Have students complete **Main Idea Activities 29.3 and 29.4**. Then have students write review questions and exchange them with a partner to answer.

CHALLENGE AND EXTEND

Have students find and read a translated literary work from a Japanese author of the early 1900s, such as Akutagawa Ryūnosuke or Tanizaki Junichiro. Ask students to give brief presentations, discussing the plot of each work. Encourage them to take notice of Western and traditional Japanese influences that appear in the work.

Lesson 3

(*For use with Section 5, pp. 774–777*)

OBJECTIVES

1. Describe the significant changes in Latin American nations after World War I.

2. Explain why authoritarian regimes gained power in many Latin American nations.

3. Describe the relationship between Latin America and the United States.

BELLRINGER

Ask students to name the major change that took place in Latin American countries just prior to World War I. (*gained their independence from European nations*) Ask students how the United States reacted and what the nature of its interest in these countries was. (*began asserting influence; economic*)

TEACH OBJECTIVE 1

Level 1: Have students work in pairs to list the changes that took place in Latin America after World War I. (*growth in industries and populations, foreign investments, labor union activity, professional jobs, education, middle class power, attempts at stability, reforms*) Have students explain whether the changes were positive or negative.
[English Language Learners, Cooperative Learning]

Levels 2 and 3: Have students imagine that they are living in Latin America during the 1920s and 1930s. Ask them to write a description of how life has changed economically, socially, and politically since World War I.

TEACH OBJECTIVE 2

All Levels: Ask students to fill in a web diagram showing major factors that led to the rise of authoritarian regimes in Latin America in the 1930s.

TEACH OBJECTIVE 3

Levels 1 and 2: Ask students to identify the following: Good Neighbor Policy, Pan-American Conference, Fulgencio Batista, Lazaro Cardenas. How did Latin American countries generally view the United States and Europe?
[English Language Learners]

Level 3: Have students conduct research on one Latin American country's relationship with the United States. Ask them to focus on changes in the relationship from the early 1900s to today. Have students create a chart that displays the changes they uncover in their research.

REVIEW AND ASSESS

Have students complete the **Review Section 5**. Then have students complete **Daily Quiz 29.5**. As Alternative Assessment, you may want to use the U.S.-Latin America relations graphic organizer or the diary exercise in this section's lessons.

RETEACH

Have students complete **Main Idea Activity 29.5**. Then have students create a detailed flow chart showing the chain of events following World War I in Latin America.
[English Language Learners]

CHALLENGE AND EXTEND

Have students locate pictures and descriptions of works by Latin American artists of the early 1900s that demonstrate an artistic ideal such as social realism.

Documenting Change

GOAL

In this activity, students will learn more about the political forces on Africa, Asia, and Latin America in the 1920s and 1930s.

PLANNING

- **Purpose** This activity may be used in combination with teacher-directed lessons or as an enrichment activity.

- **Suggested Time** Plan to spend two lesson blocks and one homework assignment on this activity.

- **Teaching Team** At least one social studies teacher and one language arts teacher should take part in teaching this activity.

- **Group Size** This activity works best by organizing students into six groups.

- **Materials and Resources** Provide students with copies of Rubrics 37 and 14. Have students use their textbooks and other resources to help them find information about Africa, Asia, and Latin America in the 1920s and 1930s.

IMPLEMENTATION

1. Give students an overview of the activity by explaining that they will learn more about the political forces on Africa, Asia, and Latin America in the 1920s and 1930s. They will then create a documentary based upon the information.

2. Draw students' attention to a wall map of the Middle East, Africa, and India. Ask students if they can think of commonalities that existed among these regions in the 1920s. *(Students should suggest that these regions were all colonized, many by Britain.)* Then draw students' attention to Latin America, China, and Japan. Again, ask students if they can think of commonalities as well as differences among these regions in the 1920s. *(Students should suggest that foreign powers exerted influence in China and*

Latin America, but that Japan was already on the road to industrialization.) Then ask students to tell what they know about the political situation in these countries or regions and the changes that took place in the 1920s and 1930s.

3. Organize students into six cooperative learning groups, and assign to each group one of the following: India; China; Japan; Turkey & Persia; Africa & the Middle East; or Latin America. Tell the groups to imagine that they are filmmakers assigned the project of creating a documentary about the changes their country or region underwent in the 1920s and 1930s. Students should begin with information from their textbooks and do additional research in order to create an outline for their documentary film. This outline should include such information as where the documentary would be taped, people to be interviewed, any archival footage or still photographs that would be used, and an outline of the narration to be followed. Students should also prepare at least two pages of a sample script for the documentary. Outlines should be written on poster board or large sheets of butcher paper, and the outlines and sample scripts should be presented to the class by each group.

4. In addition to the general instructions stated above, individual groups should adhere to the following guidelines in preparing the outlines for their documentary:

- India group: documentary outline and sample script should focus on why British rule in Egypt came to an end, how the people of India pursued their desire for self-rule, and how the British responded to calls for change in other parts of their empire.

- China group: documentary outline and sample script should discuss how resentment of foreign interest led to the downfall of the Qing dynasty, describe how the nationalism movement grew and changed under the leadership of Sun

Yixiam and Chiang Kai-shek, and explain how communism developed in China.

- Japan group: documentary outline and sample script should explain how and why Japan pursued a policy of expansionism in the 1800s, summarize the causes and results of the Russo-Japanese War, and describe the changes in Japanese life that were caused by rapid modernization.

- Turkey and Persia group: documentary and outline sample script should explain how ideas about modern nationalism manifested themselves in Turkey and Persia.

- Africa and the Middle East group: documentary outline and sample script should explain why British rule in the Middle East came to an end, how Britain responded to calls for change in other parts of the empire, and how World War I changed the attitude of Africans toward colonial government.

- Latin American group: documentary outline and sample script should describe how the economies of Latin American nations changed after World War I, explain why authoritarian regimes came to power in many Latin American nations, and describe the relationship between Latin America and the United States.

ASSESSMENT

1. To assess students' documentaries, use Rubrics 37 and 14.

2. Additional grades can be based on students' participation in the initial discussion.

The Expansion of Japan

Have students examine the map on page 783. Through what two cities in Manchuria did the Japanese advance? Why did Japan choose Manchuria as its first site of expansion?

Lesson 1

(For use with Sections 1 and 2, pp. 782–790)

OBJECTIVES

1. Analyze why Japan and Italy were able to carry out aggressive territorial policies in the 1930s.

2. Explain why the League of Nations was unable to stop international aggression.

3. Describe how Spain's civil war led to a fascist dictatorship there.

4. Explain how Hitler took over Austria and Czechoslovakia.

5. Discuss how and why Great Britain and France attempted to avoid another war.

6. Describe how Great Britain and France prepared for war.

7. Discuss why Hitler and Stalin created the Nazi-Soviet Pact, and how Western nations responded to Hitler's invasion of Poland.

BELLRINGER

Ask students to think of a bully they have known and how they responded. Lead class discussion of ways to deal with bullies and the advantages and disadvantages of each. Tell students that in Section 1 they will learn how some nations in the 1930s acted as bullies and how other nations reacted.

TEACH OBJECTIVE 1

Levels 1 and 2: Tell students that Japan had critical shortages of raw materials. Explain that Italy had economic problems and resented

not getting more territory after World War I. Ask what the military leaders of Japan and Mussolini in Italy did to solve their problems. **[English Language Learners]**

Level 3: Have students write a brief essay comparing and contrasting aggression by Italy and Japan in the 1930s.

TEACH OBJECTIVE 2

All Levels: Have small groups of students, acting as Chinese and Japanese officials, present their side in the Asian crisis to the League of Nations. Then have the rest of the class, as the League, debate what to do. As the debate nears resolution, announce that Japan has withdrawn from the League and ask how that changes the options. **[English Language Learners, Cooperative Learning]**

TEACH OBJECTIVE 3

All Levels: Have students work in pairs to chart the opposing sides in the Spanish Civil War. Then ask students to deduce from their charts why the Nationalists won. **[English Language Learners, Cooperative Learning]**

TEACH OBJECTIVE 4

All Levels: Have students work in pairs to create chain-of-events charts of Hitler's aggression against Czechoslovakia. Lead a discussion of how the Munich Conference affected events. **[English Language Learners, Cooperative Learning]**

TEACH OBJECTIVE 5

All Levels: Have students work in groups to create editorial pages that might have appeared in French or British newspapers after the Munich Conference. Each group's page should

include views for and against appeasement, a feature article providing background, letters to the editor, and a political cartoon. Post the finished pages around the room.
[English Language Learners, Cooperative Learning]

TEACH OBJECTIVE 6

Levels 1 and 2: Tell students to imagine they are British or French leaders who have decided to prepare for war. Ask students how they would prepare.
[English Language Learners]

TEACH OBJECTIVE 7

All Levels: Organize the class into four groups to represent the military high commands of Germany, France, Great Britain, and Poland. Have the groups discuss what course a war in Europe might take and how the Soviet Union might be a factor. Then have each group draft a memorandum to its national leaders on the importance of the Soviet position. Discuss each group's memo.
[English Language Learners, Cooperative Learning]

REVIEW AND ASSESS

Have students complete **Review Sections 1 and 2**. Then have students complete **Daily Quizzes 30.1 and 30.2**. As Alternative Assessment, you may want to use the newspaper pages exercise in this section's lessons.

RETEACH

Have students complete **Main Idea Activities 30.1 and 30.2**. Then have students make a chart of events in this section.
[English Language Learners]

CHALLENGE AND EXTEND

Have students research the history of Gdánsk. Ask them to write a dialogue between imaginary advocates of German and Polish ownership of the Polish Corridor.

Lesson 2

(For use with Sections 3 and 4, pp. 791–800)

OBJECTIVES

1. Explain how German control of Norway, Denmark, and the Low Countries benefited Hitler.

2. Describe the success German forces experienced in France.

3. Identify the Battle of Britain and the reasons that Germans could not win it.

4. Describe the United States' role at the beginning of the war and how it changed.

5. Identify the steps the Axis Powers took to gain control of eastern Europe, the Middle East, and North Africa.

6. Describe how Germany planned to gain control of the Soviet Union, and evaluate the success of the Soviets' defense.

7. Explain how Japan's goals in the Pacific led to war with Britain and the United States.

BELLRINGER

Ask students to consider ways warfare might have changed between 1918 and 1939. Ask students how these changes might affect soldiers.

TEACH OBJECTIVE 1

All Levels: Have students draw and illustrate maps showing the pattern of German invasions in western Europe and why Germany wanted to control Norway, Denmark, and the Low Countries. Maps should show how occupation of the Low Countries let Germany bypass the Maginot Line to attack France, and how occupying those countries, plus the Atlantic coast of France, gave Germany control of all the Atlantic seaports and bases for attacking Britain.

TEACH OBJECTIVE 2

All Levels: Have students work in pairs to create Venn diagrams that compare and contrast Vichy France and occupied France.
[English Language Learners, Cooperative Learning]

TEACH OBJECTIVE 3

All Levels: Form students into groups to discuss whether the Battle of Britain should be considered a turning point of World War II. Ask a spokesperson for each group to explain its determination to the class. Then have students work individually to create poems, song lyrics, raps, political cartoons, or posters about the RAF's saving of Great Britain. Select students to present their creations to the class.
[English Language Learners, Cooperative Learning]

TEACH OBJECTIVE 4

All Levels: Ask students how the Neutrality Acts were intended to prevent a recurrence of the circumstances that drew the United States into World War I. Ask how and why American policy changed toward the war in Europe. Then draw a horizontal continuum line on the chalkboard and work with students to plot changes in U.S. foreign policy along it, from the Neutrality Acts at one end to undeclared naval warfare at the other.
[English Language Learners]

TEACH OBJECTIVE 5

All Levels: On the chalkboard, create a table of countries under Axis or Allied control in eastern Europe and the Mediterranean from 1940 though 1942. Call on students to add a country to the chalkboard table. Discuss the steps Axis Powers took to gain control of each area.
[English Language Learners]

TEACH OBJECTIVE 6

All Levels: Split the class into two groups representing German and Soviet perspectives. Ask the German group to discuss why Hitler invaded the Soviet Union and how the invasion progressed. Ask the Soviet group to discuss how the Soviets defended themselves. Have the groups compare perspectives.
[Cooperative Learning]

TEACH OBJECTIVE 7

Level 1: Remind students what they learned in Section 1 about Japanese militarism and expansion in China in the 1930s. Tell them that Japan continued to bully its neighbors in 1940, moving troops into French Indochina. Ask why Japan bombed Pearl Harbor and how Americans responded. Then have students write two newspaper headlines that might have appeared after the bombing of Pearl Harbor.
[English Language Learners]

REVIEW AND ASSESS

Have students complete **Review Sections 3 and 4**. Then have students complete **Daily Quizzes 30.3 and 30.4**. As Alternative Assessment, you may want to use the table of Allied- and Axis-controlled countries exercise in this section's lessons.

RETEACH

Have students complete **Main Idea Activities 30.3 and 30.4**. Then have students make a list of the major headings within Sections 4 and 5 and the important details under each heading.
[English Language Learners]

CHALLENGE AND EXTEND

Have students interview older family members or members of the community about their memories of the attack on Pearl Harbor. Then have students write a short article using their interviews and other information they can find about Pearl Harbor.

Lesson 3

(For use with Sections 5 and 6, pp. 801–809)

OBJECTIVES

1. Explain how the Final Solution developed.

2. Describe concentration camp conditions.

3. Identify ways people resisted the Holocaust.

4. Identify the outcomes of Allied military actions in the Soviet Union, North Africa, Italy, and the Atlantic.

5. Describe how the Allies were able to achieve victory in Europe.

6. List the steps the Allies took to end the war with Japan.

BELLRINGER

Send those students with blond hair to the back of the room. Say that a new policy declares that blond students are inferior and may not interact with other students. Ask all students how they would feel about such a policy. Tell students that in Section 5 they will learn what happened when the Nazis treated Jews and other people as inferior.

TEACH OBJECTIVE 1

All Levels: Tell students that Hitler's wish for "living space" for his "pure Aryan race" led him to kill Jews and others he considered inferior. Have students make a cause-and-effect chart of the Final Solution.
[English Language Learners]

TEACH OBJECTIVE 2

All Levels: Have students read a description of concentration camp life by a survivor, such as Elie Wiesel or Primo Levi. Have them write an essay and report to the class.

TEACH OBJECTIVE 3

All Levels: Ask students to consider why people might not act to help those who are being threatened and killed. Ask how those who did help showed courage.

TEACH OBJECTIVE 4

All Levels: Ask students why the Soviets wanted Britain and the United States to attack the Germans from the west or south. Ask where the Allies attacked the Germans in 1942 and 1943. Ask why they moved into Europe from the south instead of the west.
[English Language Learners]

TEACH OBJECTIVE 5

All Levels: Form students into four groups to conduct military press briefings on Operation Overlord, the surrender of Italy, the piercing of the Siegfried Line, and the Battle of the Bulge. Each briefing will need a press officer to coordinate it; officers to brief the press on tactics, locations, and other geographic aspects; and troops to recount their experiences.
[English Language Learners, Cooperative Learning]

TEACH OBJECTIVE 6

All Levels: Draw students' attention to the map on page 807 of their textbooks and have them find the two principal lines of Allied advance. Have them work in pairs to draw a graphic organizer showing each line of advance.
[English Language Learners, Cooperative Learning]

REVIEW AND ASSESS

Have students complete **Review Sections 5 and 6.** Then have students complete **Daily Quizzes 30.5 and 30.6.**

RETEACH

Have students complete **Main Idea Activities 30.5 and 30.6.** Then have students divide a piece of paper into five columns, headed: *North Africa, Southern Europe, Eastern Europe, Western Europe,* and *Pacific.* Under each heading have them list the major war events in sequence.
[English Language Learners]

CHALLENGE AND EXTEND

Have students assume the role of a soldier or a citizen during the war. Have them write five diary entries for dates at different phases during the war, telling what is happening and describing their feelings about it.

A Horrific Discovery

GOAL

In this activity, students will relate more deeply to the nature of Hitler's "New Order" and "Final Solution." They will also assume the point of view of Anne Frank in order to write a journal entry.

PLANNING

- **Purpose** This activity may be used in combination with teacher-directed lessons, or as an enrichment activity.

- **Suggested Time** Plan to spend two lesson blocks and one homework assignment on this activity. Provide time for students to share their writing.

- **Teaching Team** At least one social studies teacher and one language arts teacher should take part in teaching this activity.

- **Group Size** Students must work individually in this activity.

- **Materials and Resources** Provide students with copies of "The Discovery of Anne Frank's Hiding Place" on page 227 of *Readings in World History* and Rubrics 11 and 37.

IMPLEMENTATION

1. Give students an overview of the activity by explaining that they will investigate the nature of Hitler's "New Order" and "Final Solution." Students will then read about Anne Frank and create a journal entry from her point of view.

2. In order to focus on the motives behind Hitler's aggression, start by polling the class to determine which students are left-handed. Propose a hypothetical situation for conducting the class: the left-handed students will run the class and decide everyone's grade, while all non-left-handed students (or similar differences such as those students whose hair is longer than two inches, or who wear earrings, etc.) will automatically fail. Encourage students to express their viewpoints or feelings about this proposal. Have students who were singled out for failure, in particular, share their thoughts and opinions. Ask these students if they would do something to alter their distinguishing physical trait to avoid automatic failure. Ask other students, including the left-handers who were not in leadership positions if they would risk failing the class themselves to protest the fate of those who were destined for failure. Ask what is wrong with giving left-handed students control of the class.

3. After students have discussed and vented their feelings about this new "system," ask them to compare it to Hitler's "New Order" and "Final Solution" policies that were implemented across German-occupied Europe. Have students identify the "left-handers" and "non-left-handers" in Hitler's system. *(Answers should include those in position of power who enacted Hitler's policies were the left-handers, and Slavs, Jews, Gypsies, homosexuals, and others who did not fit the perfect "Ayran mold" were non-left-handers.)* Ask students why the "left-handers," who were in the majority in Germany, did nothing to stop Hitler. *(Answers should indicate that the majority of Germans were not in positions of power. Even those who disagreed with Hitler's policies were passive and allowed the minority, under Hitler's leadership, to control them.)*

4. Then have students read "The Discovery of Anne Frank's Hiding Place" on page 227 of *Readings in World History.* Discuss the following questions: How does Miep indicate that life in the attic was difficult? How did Miep dispose of the Franks' illegal ration cards? What feelings did Miep have for the Austrian officer?

5. The piece is from the point of view of those who hid Anne Frank and her family. Have students imagine that they are Anne Frank. Ask them to write a journal entry from her point of view that discusses what happened when she and her family were discovered.

In addition to the actual discovery, have students write about the emotional aspects involved. Ask volunteers to share their writing with the class.

ASSESSMENT

1. To assess students' writing, use Rubric 37.

2. Additional grades can be based on students' participation in the preceding discussion. Rubric 11 may be used.

Occupied Germany

Have students consult the map on page 821. Ask them to note how Germany was divided after World War II.

Lesson 1

(For use with Sections 1 and 2, pp. 820–830)

OBJECTIVES

1. Describe the origins of the postwar settlement for Europe.

2. Explain why Germany was divided into four occupation zones and what developed as a result.

3. Explore how the United Nations is organized.

4. Identify the problems the Allies faced in keeping the peace.

5. Examine how and why the alliance between the Western Allies and Soviet Union ended.

6. Investigate how the United States attempted to stop the spread of communism and aid Europe.

7. Describe how Germany became two separate countries.

8. Identify Cold War alliances in Europe.

BELLRINGER

Ask students what the Allies' policies were regarding Germany after World War I. *(disarmament, territorial losses, enormous reparations, little economic aid)* Ask students how this treatment affected Germany. *(inflation, resentment toward Allies, disenchantment with Weimar government, and ultimately, the rise of the Nazi government)* Tell students that, in Section 1, they will learn about the Allies' post–World War II policies toward Germany.

TEACH OBJECTIVE 1

Level 3: Copy the following chart onto the board or overhead projector, leaving out the italicized answers. Have student complete the chart.

Yalta Conference: Purpose: *to ensure lasting peace, to decide how to deal with defeated nations;* Result: *establishment of United Nations and partitioning of Germany*

Allied Control Council: Purpose: *to oversee temporary German government;* Result: *members deadlocked on decisions; each ended up governing in its own zone*

United Nations: Purpose: *to prevent another war;* Result: *41 nations drafted charter; members worked together to avoid conflict*
[English Language Learners, Cooperative Learning]

TEACH OBJECTIVE 2

Level 2: Ask students to explain why Germany was divided into four occupation zones. *(to defeat Germany)* Then have students list the decisions made at Potsdam. *(Germany should remain a single country, although for the time being it would be divided. Germany must be demilitarized. The Nazi Party must be outlawed. German political structure should be rebuilt on a democratic basis. Individuals responsible for war crimes should be brought to trial.)*
[English Language Learners, Cooperative Learning]

TEACH OBJECTIVE 3

Level 1: Direct students' attention to the "Organization of the United Nations" chart on page 823. Have students list the six main bodies of the UN. *(General Assembly, Security Council, Trusteeship Council, International Court of Justice, Economic and Social Council, Secretariat)* Then ask students to list and explain the purposes of the United Nations. *(maintain international peace and security; foster international cooperation to solve cultural, economic, and social problems)*
[English Language Learners]

TEACH OBJECTIVE 4

All Levels: Ask students why the Western Allies disagreed with Soviet plans for the future of Europe. *(Soviets wanted to establish communist governments, unlike the Allies who wanted free elections and representative governments.)* Have students explain under what condition Austria was restored as an independent, sovereign republic. *(It had to agree to remain neutral.)* Then ask students what happened to the division of Germany into eastern and western parts. *(It became a formal division into two countries.)*
[English Language Learners]

TEACH OBJECTIVE 5

All Levels: Organize students into groups of three and have each triad develop an illustrated time line of the events that contributed to the development of the Cold War. Time lines should cover the years 1945 through 1968, though you might wish to encourage students to go back as far as the Russian Revolution and as far forward as the fall of the Iron Curtain.
[English Language Learners, Cooperative Learning]

TEACH OBJECTIVE 6

Level 3: Have students read the subsection, "The Truman Doctrine," on pages 826–827. Ask students to define *containment. (policy of restricting the spread of communism wherever possible)* Then ask them what they think might have been different if the United States had not instituted the Truman Doctrine. *(Answers will vary but most will probably say the countries like Turkey and Greece would have fallen quickly under communist aggression, and the Iron Curtain would have continued to expand across a weakened Europe.)* Have students create two political cartoons commenting on the Truman Doctrine from opposing points of view.

TEACH OBJECTIVE 7

Level 1: Ask students to describe the Berlin airlift. *(provided food and supplies to the inhabitants of the western part of the city)* Ask them what consequence resulted from the Berlin blockade. *(the division of Germany)* Have student explain why the division of Germany was symbolic of the Cold War in general. *(It symbolized the division between communism in the East and democratic government in the West.)*
[English Language Learners]

TEACH OBJECTIVE 8

Level 2: Draw the following Venn diagram on the board or overhead projector, leaving out the italicized sample answers. Ask student to help you fill in the similarities and differences between the NATO and the Warsaw Pact.

NATO: *members relied heavily on U.S. nuclear weapons as a deterrent to aggression*

BOTH: *meant to provide protection for member nations in case of attack*

WARSAW PACT: *members pledged to supply troops in proportion to their population in case of attack*
[English Language Learners, Cooperative Learning]

REVIEW AND ASSESS

Have students complete the **Review Section 1** on page 824. Have students complete **Daily Quiz 31.1 and 31.2** on page 830. As Alternative Assessment, you may want to use one of the chart activities, the time line or Venn diagram exercises in this sections lesson.

Lesson 2

(For use with Sections 3 and 4, pp. 831–841)

OBJECTIVES

1. Describe the West German "miracle."

2. Explain why the British met with mixed success in stimulating economic growth.

3. Explore how France maintained an independent position in European affairs.

4. Analyze how the Soviet Union changed under new leadership.

5. Identify the problems Eastern European nations faced.

6. Examine the major domestic problems the United States faced in the postwar era.

7. Investigate how the policy of containment led to foreign conflicts.

8. Identify the challenges the Canadian people responded to in the postwar era.

BELLRINGER

As students enter the classroom, ask them to recall the primary economic policy adopted worldwide after World War I. *(economic nationalism—high protective tariffs and trade restrictions)* Then ask them to discuss the results of this policy. *(failure and global depression—nearly every country that practiced it was hurt by it)* Tell students that, in Section 3, they will examine how countries around the world tried to avoid a similar economic catastrophe after the World War II. Then ask students to make a list of words they associate with the United States in the 1950s and then the 1960s. *(1950s: students might list words such as prosperity, consumerism, suburban sprawl, racial prejudice, beatniks, Korean War, McCarthyism, and so on; 1960s: civil rights, protests, Vietnam War, hippies, and so on)* Ask them if they think their lists of words present an accurate and complete picture of these two decades. *(Students should realize that, although they are probably somewhat accurate, such lists create a picture that is far from complete.)* Tell students that in Section 4 they will learn about problems the United States faced in the postwar years.

TEACH OBJECTIVES 1 AND 2

Level 3: Organize students into groups and assign each group one of the following topics: West Germany, Great Britain, France, or Other Western European Nations. Have students work in their groups to fill in the following chart with answers such as the italicized examples. Then have each group evaluate the effectiveness of each policy or program and summarize their opinions for the class. If students think a nation's policies were lacking, encourage them to offer alternative ideas.

West Germany: Economic policies: *free-market economy* Result: *"miracle" recovery*

Great Britain: Economic policies: *welfare state* Result: *slow economic growth, low productivity*

France: Economic policies: *help from Marshall Plan* Result: *slow recovery, political instability*
[**Cooperative Learning**]

TEACH OBJECTIVE 3

Level 1: Ask students to describe France's position in European affairs after the war. *(remained independent)* Have them list steps France took to maintain this position. *(withdrew French forces from NATO command; opposed U.S. and British influence in Europe)*
[**English Language Learners**]

TEACH OBJECTIVE 4

All Levels: Ask students the following questions: Who succeeded Stalin as the Soviet leader? *(Khrushchev)* What was the policy of "destalinization?" *(condemned Stalin for crimes against the Soviet people; lifted restrictions on intellectuals and artists; freed many political prisoners; ended some of the terrorism of the secret policy)* What was Khrushchev's primary economic goal? *(to make more consumer goods available to the Soviet people)* What were the results of his economic policies? *(economy expanded; living conditions improved; became a modern industrialized society)*
[**English Language Learners**]

TEACH OBJECTIVE 5

Level 2: Have students prepare a compare-and-contrast chart. One column should be labeled *Western Europe* and the other column labeled *Eastern Europe*. Have each student list aspects of postwar reconstruction in the appropriate columns. After students have completed their charts, use the lists as a class to determine categories for the aspects of postwar reconstruction. *(e.g., Western Europe established market economies; Eastern Europe had government-controlled economies; category for these aspects of postwar reconstruction is economic systems)*

TEACH OBJECTIVE 6

All Levels: Have students work individually or in small groups to create collages that represent the people, issues, and events that shaped the United States between 1945 and 1968. Students should include images that represent aspects of domestic policy, the economy, McCarthyism, and the civil rights movement. [**English Language Learner, Cooperative Learning, Block Scheduling**]

TEACH OBJECTIVE 7

Level 1: Have students fill in the following chart to illustrate the results of the policy of containment. [**English Language Learners**]

TEACH OBJECTIVE 8

Level 3: Ask students to list the major changes that took place in Canada during the postwar years. (*Canada experienced tremendous economic growth and enjoyed a close relationship with the United States. The two countries cooperated to build the Distant Early Warning Line and the St. Lawrence Seaway. Postwar problems included the risk of separatism in Quebec.*) Then have students work in pairs to write personal letters as if they were American and Canadian pen pals who enjoy writing to each other about their respective countries. They should exchange four letters (two each) that discuss events during a particular decade or year in their countries. For example, a pair might discuss events during the Cuban missile crisis. [**Cooperative Learning, Block Scheduling**]

REVIEW AND ASSESS

Have students complete the **Review Section 3** on page 836. Have students complete **Daily Quiz 31.3**. As Alternative Assessment, you may

want to use the chart activity in the section's lessons. Have students complete the **Review Section 4** on page 841. Have students complete **Daily Quiz 31.4**. As Alternative Assessment, you may want to use the collage exercise in the section's lessons.

RETEACH

Have students complete **Main Idea Activity for English Language Learners and Special-Needs Students 31.3**. Then ask students to write a question and answer that covers the main idea for each subsection in the section. Have students complete **Main Idea Activity for English Language Learners and Special-Needs Student 31.4**. Then have students create a chart with the headings *U.S. Domestic Challenges, U.S. Foreign Policy Challenges,* and *Canada's Challenges* that summarizes each of those categories. [**English Language Learners**]

CHALLENGE AND EXTEND

Ask students to imagine what kinds of stories the Berlin Wall could tell if it could speak. What kinds of suffering and turmoil did it see before it was brought down in 1989 and 1990? How might it have felt about the events it witnessed? Have students write creative stories from the point of view of the wall. They should base their stories on historical facts and actual events. Have students find out more information about the civil rights movement for one of the following groups in the United States: African Americans, American Indians, women, disabled individuals, or Hispanics. Ask them to write a paragraph summarizing the postwar goals and activities of the movement they choose. [**Block Scheduling**]

Famous Persuasive Speeches

GOAL

In this activity, students will learn the elements of a persuasive speech, as well as learn about the political situations that the speeches were written to address.

PLANNING

- **Purpose** This activity may be used in combination with teacher-directed lessons, as an enrichment activity, or as a performance-based assessment.

- **Suggested Time** Plan to spend two lesson blocks and one homework assignment on this activity. Provide time for the presentation of student speeches.

- **Teaching Team** At least one social studies teacher and one language arts teacher should take part in teaching this activity.

- **Group Size** This activity will work as a small group activity or for individual students.

- **Materials and Resources**

  Student copies of the texts of persuasive speeches of the postwar world, such as John F. Kennedy's Inaugural Address, Winston Churchill's "Iron Curtain" speech, or Dr. Martin Luther King's "I Have a Dream" speech

  Recordings of these persuasive speeches

  For teacher reference, examples of persuasive techniques found in any student writing handbook, such as *The Power to Persuade: A Rhetoric and Reader for Argumentative Writing*, by Sally DeWitt Spurgin, Prentice-Hall, Englewood Cliffs, New Jersey, 1985

  Student copies of Rubric 43: Writing to Persuade, Rubric 24: Oral Presentations, and Rubric 36: Time Lines from *Portfolio Performance Assessment for Social Studies*

IMPLEMENTATION

1. Give students an overview of this activity by explaining that they will listen to and read famous persuasive speeches, identifying the persuasive techniques and rhetorical strategies used. Then they will compose original persuasive speeches concerning postwar issues.

2. Students should choose events, such as the Berlin Blockade, the Cuban Missile Crisis, the Vietnam War, the civil war in Angola, the Suez Crisis, the Communist takeover of China, the partition of India, political instability in Mexico, civil war in Nicaragua, control of the Panama Canal Zone, the Bay of Pigs, etc.

3. With the students, define persuasion and provide examples of emotional appeals such as glittering generalities, plain folks appeal, bandwagon, snob appeal, transfer, and nationalism. Also provide examples of appeals to reason, such as card stacking, faulty logic, and two extremes.

4. While silently reading the persuasive speeches, students should mark examples of the persuasive techniques as they see them. As individual students read their examples aloud, have the class categorize the techniques used as emotional or logical appeals. Then listen to the recordings of the speeches as the students follow along. Discuss the ways in which the oral presentations enhance the persuasive messages. With the students, identify such rhetorical strategies as repetition, parallelism, metaphor, and allusion, as well as delivery techniques, such as emphasis and pauses.

5. Each student or group of students should choose one event from their time line. They will then write a speech in which they try to influence world opinion about this event. They should speak from the point of view of one of the original participants in the issue and include accurate historical references.

6. Each speech must include at least one emotional appeal, one logical appeal, two rhetorical devices, and one delivery technique. Have students present their speeches to a mock United Nations General

Assembly with their classmates serving as delegates to the assembly.

ASSESSMENT

1. Assess students' work by their use of historical information, combined with their ability to fulfill the persuasive components. Consult Rubric 43: Writing to Persuade.

2. Additional grades can be based on students' participation in the presentation of their speeches.

Religious Divisions in India

Ask students to refer to the map on page 848. Have them note the major religions of the area (*Muslim, Hindu, Sikh, Buddhist and Christian*) Ask them to create a list of reasons why neighbors might not get along. (*feuds over property, lifestyle or personality differences*)

Lesson 1

(For use with Sections 1, 2, and 3, pp. 846–862)

OBJECTIVES

1. Explain how differences between Hindus and Muslims led to a divided India.

2. Identify problems that India faced after independence.

3. Describe how Pakistan and Bangladesh developed after the partition of India.

4. Describe how Mao Zedong's government tried to rebuild China after World War II.

5. Identify what happened at Tiananmen Square and what the consequences were for China.

6. Explain why Korea was divided and how the two Koreas have developed since 1953.

7. Explain why China and Taiwan have been in conflict.

8. Identify the factors that allowed Japan to recover effectively after World War II.

9. Describe the economic and social changes that occurred in Japan from the 1950s onward.

10. Explain how the relationship between Japan and the United States changed in the years since World War II.

BELLRINGER

Have students use their lists of major religions and reasons why neighbors might not get along to create a class list on the chalkboard. Then ask volunteers to explain how the items on the list

might apply to relations between neighboring nations. Tell students that, in Section 1, they will learn how some of the reasons on the list have shaped the history of South Asia since the mid-1900s. For Section 2, have them refer to the map on 853. What do they notice about the political differences in China? Tell them they will learn about revolution in China and changes that occurred in Japan after World War II.

TEACH OBJECTIVE 1

Level 1: Copy the following chart on the chalkboard, omitting the italicized answers. Work with the class to fill in the chart. Ask students whether the British solution was a good one.
[English Language Learners]

Independence Movements in India		
GROUP	**HINDUS**	**MUSLIMS**
Leader	*Mohandas Gandhi*	*Muhammad Ali Jinnah*
Organization/ Motivation	*"Quit India"*	*Muslim League*
Goal for India	*Independence for India*	*Partition of India*
Outcome	*Creation of India*	*Creation of Pakistan*

TEACH OBJECTIVE 2

All Levels: Write the following four headings on the chalkboard: *Social Problems, Economic Problems, Political Problems,* and *Foreign Relations Problems.* Call on students to identify problems India has faced since independence and list them under the appropriate headings. Then have students work in pairs to decide which category of problem presents the most serious challenge for India.

Level 3: Organize students into small groups to assume the roles of economic advisers to

India's prime minister. Each group should decide whether India should pursue a socialist, free market (capitalist), or mixed economy. Each group should draft a memo for the prime minister stating its recommendation and explaining why the group thinks it is the best course for India to follow.
[Cooperative Learning]

TEACH OBJECTIVE 3

Level 1: Ask students to create flow charts showing the sequence of events that led to Pakistan becoming two nations. After students have completed their flow charts ask them what challenges Bangladesh faces today.
[English Language Learners]

TEACH OBJECTIVE 4

Level 1: Call on students to identify the three major programs undertaken by Mao Zedong to change China in the 1950s and 1960s. Then put the chart on the chalkboard, including one italicized example in each column as shown. Have students add to each column to complete the chart. Then have them decide which program was the most beneficial to China and which the most harmful.
[English Language Learners]

How Mao's Programs Affected China:

First Five-Year Plan:	Great Leap Forward:	Cultural Revolution:
(1) transferred farmland from landlords to peasants	(1) threatened Mao's leadership	(1) had a disastrous effect on China's economy

TEACH OBJECTIVE 5

All Levels: Organize students into groups to decide whether the events at Tiananmen Square in 1989 were good or bad for China. Have each group explain its reasoning.
[Cooperative Learning]

TEACH OBJECTIVE 6

Level 1: Have students construct a Venn diagram comparing the characteristics of North Korea and South Korea from the 1960s to the 1990s.
[English Language Learners]

TEACH OBJECTIVE 7

All Levels: Have two panels of students take the roles of Chinese and Taiwanese diplomats to debate the status of Taiwan. One panel should represent the position of the Chinese government regarding Taiwan and the other the Chinese Nationalist position. Have the rest of the class act as observers and direct questions to each panel about its position. Have students vote on whether Taiwan should be part of China or remain independent.
[Cooperative Learning]

TEACH OBJECTIVES 8 AND 9

Level 1: Write the following on the chalkboard: *Japan's recovery after World War II was a result of change in its (1) government, (2) economy, and (3) society.* Divide students into pairs. Assign each pair one of the three categories listed. Have pairs use their texts to find examples that belong in their assigned categories.
[English Language Learners, Cooperative Learning]

TEACH OBJECTIVE 9

All Levels: Copy the graphic organizer on the chalkboard, omitting the italicized worlds. Have students complete the diagram, Social Changes in Japan after World War II.

TEACH OBJECTIVE 10

Level 3: Divide students into groups of four or five. Have each group decide whether or not the United States is still the dominant partner in the Japanese-U.S. relationship. When all groups have reached a consensus, have a class discussion about their conclusions.
[Cooperative Learning]

REVIEW AND ASSESS

Have students complete **Review Sections 1, 2, and 3**. Have students complete **Daily Quiz 32.1**. As Alternative Assessment, you may want to use the homework assignment or the graphic organizers in this section's lesson.

RETEACH

Have students complete **Main Idea Activity for English Language Learners and Special-Needs Students 32.1, 32.2, and 32.3**. Then have them use the section's headings and sub-headings to create an outline.
[English Language Learners, Cooperative Learning]

CHALLENGE AND EXTEND

Organize two groups of students, one representing colonial India's Hindus and the other its Muslims. Have each group prepare a written proposal, including maps or diagrams, for how India could function as a single nation if granted independence from Great Britain.
[Block Scheduling, Cooperative Learning]

Lesson 2

(For use with Sections 4 and 5, pp. 863–873)

OBJECTIVES

1. Describe the causes and effects of dictatorships in the Philippines and Indonesia.

2. Explain how the Vietnam War affected Vietnam, Laos, and Cambodia.

3. Identify the problems that the nations of Southeast Asia faced as they struggled to create stable governments.

4. Explain what led Asian governments to impose tight controls in their countries.

5. Describe the problems Asian countries faced as they tried to develop their economies, and how they solved those problems.

6. Explain how economic success in Asian countries affected the West.

BELLRINGER

As students enter the classroom, ask them to write a paragraph explaining how economic conditions might cause unrest in a nation. Call on volunteers to read their explanations to the class. Then ask students if a government has a right to limit citizens' freedoms in order to achieve a peaceful and stable society. Ask those who say "no" if their opinions would be different if Communists were behind the unrest. Tell students that in Section 4 they will learn how concern about communism has shaped the history of Southeast Asia since World War II. Then ask students to compile lists of items they can buy in the United States that are produced in Asian countries. Then begin a master list on the chalkboard, calling on students to add to it from the lists that they have prepared. Tell students that, in Section 5, they will learn about the tremendous economic growth and development that has occurred in Asia in recent years.

TEACH OBJECTIVE 1

Level 1: Ask students to describe the relationship between government, power, and the people in the Marcos/Sukarno regimes. Then ask them to describe these relationships in a democracy. Have them write these relationships in graphic form on the board.
[English Language Learners, Cooperative Learning]

TEACH OBJECTIVES 1 AND 3

Level 2: Tell students that both the Philippines and Indonesia underwent a period of authoritarian rule after they achieved self-rule. Have half the class create *Before, During,* and *After* charts for the Philippines and the other half for Indonesia. Charts should list the factors that led to authoritarian rule; the country's key problems during authoritarian rule; how this rule was overthrown, and the country's subsequent progress.

TEACH OBJECTIVE 2

Level 3: Ask students why the neutral countries of Cambodia and Laos were drawn into the Vietnam War. Then organize students into three groups: one to represent American interest, one to represent Cambodian interest, and the third to represent Laotian interest. Have the groups hold a debate responding to the following statement: The United States acted justly in bombing countries that were neutral in the Vietnam War.

TEACH OBJECTIVES 2 AND 3

All Levels: Ask students to list ways that the Vietnam War affected the people of North and South Vietnam. Write responses in two columns on the chalkboard. Then ask students which country suffered more as a result of the war, North Vietnam or South Vietnam. Ask students to justify their opinions. Conclude by asking the class whether the people of the former South Vietnam are better off today under a communist government than they were during the war, when South Vietnam was fighting a communist takeover.

TEACH OBJECTIVE 3

All Levels: Ask students to identify problems that the nations of Southeast Asia had in common. List responses on the chalkboard. Then ask which country, since World War II, has the most unusual history and why.

TEACH OBJECTIVES 4 AND 5

Level 1: Copy the chart on the chalkboard, omitting the check marks. Have students copy and complete the chart by checking the reasons that apply for each country.
[English Language Learners]

Why Governments Limited Civil Rights

	Ethnic/Religious Conflicts	Oppose or Protect Communism	Promote Economic Developments
Burma	✓	✓	
Cambodia		✓	
China		✓	✓
Indonesia		✓	
Laos		✓	
Malaysia	✓		
Philippines	✓	✓	✓
Singapore			✓
South Korea		✓	✓
South Vietnam		✓	

TEACH OBJECTIVE 5

All Levels: Ask students to cite obstacles that stood in the way of economic development in many Asian countries. As students respond, make a list on the chalkboard. Then discuss why each was an obstacle. Conclude by having students identify which obstacles might encourage foreign investment and which might discourage it.

TEACH OBJECTIVE 6

Level 3: Provide students with the following quotation from turn-of-the-century British writer and poet Rudyard Kipling (1865–1936): "East is East and West is West and never the twain shall meet." Ask students to what extent Kipling's observation applies to today's world.

REVIEW AND ASSESS

Have students complete the **Review Sections 4 and 5**. Have students complete **Daily Quiz 32.4 and 32.5**. As Alternative Assessment, you may want to use the chart or the homework assignment or the graphic organizer in this section's lessons.

RETEACH

Have students complete **Main Idea Activity for English Language Learners and Special-Needs Students 32.4 and 32.5**. Then have them write a sentence summarizing each of the section's major subdivisions and relating the information to the section's main idea. Then have them list the main idea of each heading and subheading of the section.
[English Language Learners]

CHALLENGE AND EXTEND

Have students work in groups to compare and contrast the Korean War and the Vietnam War. Allow each group to choose its own method for making its comparison, such as charts, maps, poems, or first-person accounts in the roles of participants. Have groups present their work to the class.
[Block Scheduling, Cooperative Learning]

Yasunari Kawabata

GOAL

In this activity, students will learn about the life and work of the Japanese writer, Yasunari Kawabata who won the Nobel Peace Prize for literature in 1968. They will also learn about ancient Japanese writers and their use of nature, tea-ceremonies, and gardens in their art.

PLANNING

- **Purpose** This activity may be used in combination with teacher-directed lessons, as an enrichment activity, or as a performance-based assessment of content mastery.

- **Suggested Time** Plan to spend two lesson blocks and one homework assignment on this activity.

- **Teaching Team** At least one social studies teacher and one language arts teacher should take part in teaching this activity.

- **Group Size** This activity will work as a small group activity or for individual students.

- **Materials and Resources**

  Yasunari Kawabata's, "The Silver Fify-Sen Pieces" in Elements of Literature, 5th course

  Internet and library sources for the Japanese tea ceremony

  Nobel Lecture of Yasunari Kawabata's, December 12, 1968, found on www.nobel.se/ literature/laureates

  Photographs of Japanese art and gardens

IMPLEMENTATION

1. Give students an overview of the activity by explaining that they will first read Yasunari Kawabata's acceptance speech of the Nobel Peace Prize for literature. They will be asked to note the historical significance poetry has played in Japanese history. They will also be asked to research Japanese art, tea ceremonies, and gardens. Then they will read some of Kawabata's works and see how these elements appear in the historical Japanese poetry. Finally, ask students to make a collection of Japanese art, poetry, and gardens.

2. Ask students to read Kawabata's Nobel Lecture. Write this quote on the board about Japanese art, "'The time of the snows, of the moon, of the blossoms—then more than ever we think of our comrades.' When we see the beauty of the snow, when we see the beauty of the full moon, when we see the beauty of the cherries in bloom, when in short we brush against and are awakened by the beauty of the four seasons, it is then we think most of those close to us, and want them to share the pleasure."

3. Ask students to note some of the examples Kawabata gives in his speech about the importance of nature in Japanese poetry. Then ask them to note what he writes about the tea ceremony and the arrangement of Japanese gardens (*"A rock garden gives expression to mountains and rivers that are not present, and even suggests the waves of the great ocean breaking in upon cliffs."*)

4. Ask students to research the tea ceremony, Japanese gardens, and art on their own. Ask them to bring photos of the gardens, of the natural landscape of Japan, and the art that they have found. Ask them to write about the characteristics they all share. (*beautiful, but sparse*)

5. Have students read Kawabata's work and make specific notes about his use of nature. Ask students to write about what he has said in his speech and the way he uses nature in his art. How does he "become" nature? How is he one with it? Why is the following quote important? "Winter moon, going behind the clouds and coming forth again, making bright my footsteps as I go to the meditation hall and descend again, making me unafraid of the wolf: does not the wind sink into you, does not the snow, are you not cold?" What literary device is Kawabata using? (*personification*)

6. Ask students to make a collection of Japanese poems from Myoe, Dogen, Ryokan, Akutagawa, Kawabata, etc. Ask them to copy them in calligraphy and to place their photos of Japanese gardens, art, and nature between the poems.

7. Ask the students to read aloud their favorite poems and share their photographs with the class.

ASSESSMENT

1. Assess students' work by their use of historical information, combined with their researching skills and ability to create a book of Japanese poems.

2. Additional grades can be based on students' participation in the presentation and class discussions.

African Independence

Have students consult the map on page 880. Then ask them to look at a globe. Have them list the European countries who ruled Africa on the board.

Lesson 1

(For use with Sections 1 and 2, pp. 878–890)

OBJECTIVES

1. Identify the factors that led to a rise of African nationalism after World War II.

2. Explain how the processes that ended colonial rule in British, French, Belgian and Portuguese colonies differed.

3. Explain how South Africa's move to independence was different from that of other African nations.

4. Identify the challenges—political, ethnic, economic, and environmental—that newly independent African countries faced.

5. Explain how rivalry between the superpowers of the Cold War affected Africa.

6. Explain the ways in which Africa experienced a revival of African culture.

BELLRINGER

Ask students how they would feel if the United States was ruled by another nation thousands of miles away. Ask if it would make any difference if those rulers were of a different culture and looked down on Americans as inferior. Then tell students to suppose that those rulers refused to grant the "inferior" Americans any degree of self-rule. Ask students if such a situation would justify civil disobedience to achieve reforms. Would it justify terrorism? Would it justify revolution and independence? Tell students that, in Section 1, they will learn about similar issues that Africans had to deal with in the decades following World War II.

TEACH OBJECTIVE 1

Level 3: Have students work in pairs to create a dialogue on self-rule between an African and a European colonist. Roles from which students may choose should include a white plantation or mine owner, a missionary, a colonial government official, an African worker or farmer, or a Western-educated nationalist leader. Tell students that in each dialogue, the European should explain his or her reasons for supporting continued control of the colony. The African should state his or her view on colonialism and on self-government versus independence. Select pairs to present their dialogues to the class.
[Cooperative Learning]

TEACH OBJECTIVE 2

All Levels: Have students locate Zambia, Malawi, and Zimbabwe on the map on page 880. Ask them by what names these countries were known when they were British colonies. Have students note the independence dates on the map and ask why Zimbabwe gained independence so much later than the other two British colonies. Conclude by having each student create a flow chart showing the course of events leading to independence for all three countries in British central Africa.
[English Language Learners]

Level 3: Have students work in groups to create "op-ed" pages that might have appeared in a Belgian Congo newspaper in early 1960. Each group's page should contain editorials and pundits' columns supporting and attacking Belgium's decision to grant independence. It should include at least one political cartoon on the subject and a feature article to give readers a background on the controversy. Each page should also contain letters to the editor from white colonists and Africans, expressing their views on impending independence. Post each group's page in the classroom.
[Cooperative Learning]

TEACH OBJECTIVE 3

Level 1: Ask students to identify ways in which South Africa developed differently from the rest of colonial Africa. List their responses on the chalkboard. Then ask how South Africa's history was similar to the rest of Africa. Have class members explain how apartheid differed from racism in the rest of colonial Africa. Tell students that, when the Union of South Africa was formed, the British allowed the white colonists to decide if Africans should have the right to vote. Have the class speculate on how South Africa's history might have been different if the whites had said yes.
[English Language Learners]

TEACH OBJECTIVE 4

Level 1: Create a four-column chalkboard table titled *Problems the New African Nations Faced.* Label the columns *Political, Ethnic, Economic,* and *Environmental.* Then call on class members to identify the challenges of each type that Africa has faced since independence and enter the information in the appropriate column of the table. As some students suggest entries for the table, call on others to cite examples of how these problems have affected specific nations.
[English Language Learners]

TEACH OBJECTIVE 5

Level 3: Organize students into six groups to represent intelligence task forces of the American CIA or the Soviet KGB. Assign one pair of groups to be a specialist on Angola, another pair on Ethiopia, and the third pair on Somalia. Have each group prepare a briefing for its nation's leaders that assessed the crisis in its assigned country, explains the country's importance to the United States or USSR, analyzes the other superpower's involvement in the country, and makes a recommendation regarding its own nation's involvement. Have each task force present it's briefing to the class.
[Cooperative Learning]

TEACH OBJECTIVE 6

All Levels: Ask students to speculate about the effects colonialism and white minority rule

would have had on African art and culture. Ask students to deduce from this relationship the effect that independence would have on African culture.
[English Language Learners]

REVIEW AND ASSESS

Have students complete the **Review Sections 1 and 2**. Have students complete **Daily Quiz 33.1 and 33.2**. As Alternative Assessment, you may want to use the African Challenges table exercise in this section's lessons.

RETEACH

Have students complete **Main Idea Activity for English Language Learners and Special-Needs Students 33.1 and 33.2**. Then ask them to create a chapter glossary that includes the vocabulary and significant people, places, and events from the section.
[English Language Learners]

CHALLENGE AND EXTEND

Have students imagine they are ANC supporters and create anti-apartheid posters or political cartoons. Display students' work in the classroom. Have students conduct research to find African literature that represents the continent's cultural diversity. Ask students to select one aspect of African literature to explore in depth and to write a short paper that summarizes what they have learned.
[Block Scheduling]

Lesson 2

(For use with Sections 3 and 4, pp. 891–905)

OBJECTIVES

1. Explain how France's position in the Middle East and North Africa changed after World War II.

2. Explain how Britain's position in the Middle East and Egypt changed after World War II.

3. Identify the political and social changes that independence brought to Egypt and the Middle East.

4. Identify the major issues that Iran and Turkey faced after World War II.

5. Explain how Arab-Israeli conflicts have shaped the recent history of North Africa and the Middle East.

6. Explain how the presence of rich oil fields affected the Middle East.

7. Describe the revolution in Iran and explain why it occurred.

8. Explain the types of leadership that emerged in the Arab world in the 1960s and after.

BELLRINGER

As students enter the classroom, call on volunteers to recall the historic influences that the Middle East had in the development of early Europe. Remind students that the Middle East remained so important to the West over the centuries that Europeans established direct control there when the Ottoman Empire collapsed after World War I. Tell students that, in Section 3, they will learn how Middle Eastern peoples gained their independence after World War II and how the West continued to involve itself in the Middle East's affairs—an involvement that continues to this day. Then ask them to imagine that the United States was structured so that only members of a certain religion could hold leadership positions in government and that all laws were based on that religion's beliefs. Call on class members to suggest social and political problems that might arise from such an arrangement. Ask students if they would like to live in such a society, and to explain why they feel as they do.

TEACH OBJECTIVE 1

Level 1: Ask students what similarities Algeria shared with other French-held territories in North Africa and the Middle East at the end of World War II. Next, have them cite ways in which Algeria was different. Call on volunteers to explain why rising Arab nationalism in Algeria would have inspired a desire for independence in other French holdings. Ask students if they think problems in Algeria and elsewhere could have been avoided if France

had given Arabs the right to elect representatives to the French National Assembly.
[English Language Learners]

TEACH OBJECTIVE 2

Level 2: Ask students what comprised the region known as Palestine. *(Israel and Jordan)* Have them make a chart to explain the roles that the British, Jews, Arabs, and United Nations all played in the division of Palestine in 1947. Ask students how the territory granted to the Arabs in Palestine ended up being controlled by Israel and Jordan. *(as a result of Arab Israeli wars)*

Division of Palestine

Jews and Arabs: *rejected a joint state*

British: *gave up mandate*

United Nations: *partitioned Palestine into Arab and Zionist sections*

TEACH OBJECTIVES 2 AND 3

Level 3: Have students locate the Suez Canal on the map on page 900 and note its proximity to Israel. Ask students why control of the canal was so important to Britain. *(shortened water route to Asia)* Have them speculate on what effect the canal's importance, combined with Britain's loss of Palestine, might have had on British policy toward Egypt. *(more determined not to give up its presence)* Then have students work in groups to answer the following question: Would the Suez Crisis have occurred if Israel had not gained independence?
[Cooperative Learning]

TEACH OBJECTIVE 4

All Levels: Have students work in pairs to identify one issue facing Turkey and one issue facing Iran in the 1950s. Call on pairs for responses until all significant issues are listed on the chalkboard. Then ask the class how each of the issues was resolved. Ask students whether they believe the resolution of each of these issues was in the best interest of the Iranian or Turkish people.
[English Language Learners, Cooperative Learning]

TEACH OBJECTIVE 5

Level 3: Organize the class into groups to represent senior officials in the Israeli or Egyptian government. Tell the groups to imagine that it is 1974, and they must decide whether the time has come to seek some compromise settlement in the conflict over Palestine. After groups discuss this question, have each report its conclusion to the class. Ask each group what factors it weighed in making its decision.
[**Cooperative Learning**]

All Levels: Create two columns on the chalkboard, headed *Israeli Viewpoint* and *Arab Viewpoint*. Invite students to imagine first that they are Israeli settlers in the occupied territories and then that they are Palestinian residents of refugee camps. Ask students to explain, in each role, what rights they have in the territories, what rights the other side has, and why. List Palestinian and Israeli points in the appropriate columns. Then ask students to explain how radical elements on each side have undermined hopes for a peaceful settlement of the dispute. Have them speculate about why these radicals seek and are able to perpetuate tension and conflict in the region.

TEACH OBJECTIVE 6

Level 2: Write the terms *OPEC* and *petrodollars* on the chalkboard and call on volunteers to define each. Then have the class identify the major oil-producing countries in the Middle East and compare the standard of living in those nations with life in neighboring countries that lack such resources. Ask students how the OPEC nations obtain their petrodollars. To illustrate how important oil is to the industrial nations, have students create a web diagram showing the effects of an oil embargo.

TEACH OBJECTIVE 7

All Levels: Have students work in pairs to create time lines of development in Iran and Iraq since 1968. Suggest that they plot Iranian events on one side of the time line and Iraqi events on the other. Have students refer to their time lines as they review the events since the formation of Iran's Islamic Republic and discuss whether the benefits or Iran's revolution have outweighed the difficulties that it has faced. Then have them repeat the process for Iraq.
[**English Language Learners, Cooperative Learning**]

TEACH OBJECTIVE 8

Level 1: Write the following quotation by Gamal Abdel Nasser on the chalkboard: "Within the Arab circle is a role wandering aimlessly in search of a hero." Have students identify Nasser and query them bout the meaning of his statement. Ask them who Nasser had in mind to be the "hero" of which he spoke. *(himself)* Call on volunteers to evaluate how well Nasser filled that role. Ask students if today's Arab leaders are more similar or dissimilar to Nasser in terms of background and goals for their country and region. Discuss the goals and methods of those who are similar to Nasser and compare them to the goals and methods of those who are not.
[**English Language Learners**]

REVIEW AND ASSESS

Have students complete the **Review Sections 3 and 4**. Have students complete **Daily Quiz 33.3 and 33.4**. As Alternative Assessment, you may want to use the French colonialism or Suez Canal exercises in this section's lesson.

RETEACH

Have students complete **Main Idea Activity for English Language Learners and Special-Needs Students 33.3 and 33.4**. Then ask students to write a question and answer that covers the main idea for each subsection in the section.
[**English Language Learners, Cooperative Learning**]

CHALLENGE AND EXTEND

Have students bring in current newspaper and magazine articles on recent development in the Middle East. Call on students to summarize their articles and place the events they report on in historical perspective.

Nadine Gordimer

GOAL

In this activity, students will learn about the writer Nadine Gordimer and the tensions that existed as a result of the exploitation of African workers by the white colonists.

PLANNING

- **Purpose** This activity may be used in combination with teacher-directed lessons, as an enrichment activity, or as a performance-based assessment of content mastery.

- **Suggested Time** Plan to spend two lesson blocks and one homework assignment on this activity.

- **Teaching Team** At least one social studies teacher and one language arts teacher should take part in teaching this activity.

- **Group Size** This activity will work as a small group activity or for individual students.

- **Materials and Resources**

  "The Train from Rhodesia" by Nadine Gordimer, in Elements of Literature, 5th course

  Internet and library sources

  Background notes for the teacher on the life and career of Nadine Gordimer

  Student photocopies of Rubrics for Creative Writing from *Portfolio and Performance Assessment for Social Studies*

IMPLEMENTATION

1. Give students an overview of the activity by explaining that they will first read Nadine Gordimer's short story, "The Train from Rhodesia." Then they will be asked to research the historical time period in which she wrote. They will finally be asked to write a paper on the exploitation of native Africans by the white colonists.

2. Have students read the short story, "The Train from Rhodesia." Have them write what they "see" from Gordimer's words

(They should see a young white couple in a train station where an elderly African man is trying to sell his hand-crafted art work. The woman likes the lion, but thinks it is too expensive—three (shillings) and six (pence), which is a little over one American dollar. The couple get on the train and the old man runs after the train and the young man "buys" the art for one and six (about one quarter in American currency). The young woman is very upset with her husband.) Ask the students why she is angry with her husband *(because he cheated the old man out of his dutiful pay. She would have rather he not bought it than to steal it from him)* Ask the students why the man doesn't get it? What is his motive? *(He thinks his wife wants the lion, which she does, but he doesn't mind cheating the African.)*

3. Ask the students what Gordimer is saying with this short story? How does this small exchange represent a national policy? Review Chapter 33. Where are the connections with Gordimer's work?

4. Ask students to read a short story of Gordimer's on their own and to analyze it in an essay. Think about point of view, characterization, dialogue, and plot. Ask students to create a thesis *(a statement in their first paragraph that gives their educated opinion on Gordimer's intention for the story)* Then ask them to incorporate the historical facts they have learned from this chapter in their paper to support their theses. They will also want to quote the short story for support.

5. Ask students to exchange rough drafts and to conduct a peer review. Have them answer the following questions about their work: Is there a thesis statement in the first paragraph? Is there supporting paragraphs with details that prove the thesis? Does the paper have direct quotes from the short story? Does the paper have direct quotes from the history text? Is there a conclusion? Is there correct grammar, punctuation, syntax, and sentence structure?

6. Ask students to revise their papers and to present them to the class.

ASSESSMENT

1. Assess students' work by their use of historical information, combined with their understanding of Gordimer's fiction.

2. Additional grades can be based on students' participation in class discussions and the presentation of their papers.

Central America and the Caribbean

Have students refer to the map on page 918. Ask them to locate the nations in which the United States maintained a military presence or intervened.

Lesson 1

(For use with Sections 1 and 2, pp. 910–921)

OBJECTIVES

1. Identify the steps Latin American nations took and what problems they faced as they sought to develop their economies.

2. Analyze the effect industrialization had on Latin American nations.

3. Identify the political and social forces that have emerged in Latin American nations.

4. Explain how Mexico's fortunes rose and fell after World War II.

5. Describe how economic conditions influenced political events in Central America.

6. Explain how Central American nations have moved toward democracy.

BELLRINGER

As students enter the classroom, ask them to make a list of some of the countries they see represented on the map on page 918 and to list any information they know about the countries economy, political situations, culture, etc. Tell the class that, in these next two sections, they will learn about the political and economic struggles that Latin America faced after World War II.

TEACH OBJECTIVE 1

All Levels: Ask students to define monoculture. Then ask students why monoculture was a poor foundation for a national economy. Ask students to create a chart showing problems Latin American countries faced after World

War II and what steps these countries have taken to improve economic conditions. Have students write two to three paragraphs evaluating the effectiveness of such efforts. **[English Language Learners]**

Problems	Solutions
poverty	*diversified exports*
international debts	*trade agreements, protective tariffs*
high inflation	*raised taxes, cut spending*

TEACH OBJECTIVE 2

Level 3: Organize students into four groups and assign each group one of the following topics: *population growth, urbanization, poverty,* or *environmental problems.* Have each group use the textbook and other sources that you provide to put together a brief oral presentation about its assigned topic. Presentations should define and explain the problem, elaborate on its repercussions, outline attempted solutions, and evaluate the effectiveness of such solutions. If students find the attempted solutions to be insufficient, tell them to propose other ideas for solving the problem. Tell them to use visual aids during their presentations. Tell students to take notes on each other's presentations. **[Cooperative Learning]**

TEACH OBJECTIVE 3

All Levels: Have students read the section titled "New Political and Social Forces" on pages 913 and 914. Then have them work individually or in pairs to come up with a slogan for each of the following groups that represented an emerging political force in Latin America: women, labor, and the Roman Catholic Church. Slogans should indicate the political aims of each group and might promote membership or support for the group as well. Then have students create logos and make promotional posters using the slogan and logo for each group. Display the

posters and encourage students to constructively comment on each other's work.
[**English Language Learners, Cooperative Learning**]

TEACH OBJECTIVE 4

Level 1: Have students use the textbook subsection "Mexico" to create a table showing the effects of Mexican problems since World War II.

Problems	Effects
Guerrilla campaign	*suppression of rebels*
Slump in oil market	*huge foreign debt, rapid inflation*
Earthquake	*shattered capital, homeless people*
Unemployment	*illegal migration, strained relations with the United States*

[**English Language Learners**]

TEACH OBJECTIVE 5

All Levels: Organize students into four groups and assign each group one of the following countries: Mexico, Nicaragua, El Salvador, or Panama. Have students in each group create an illustrated time line of events in their assigned country from 1945 to the present. Then ask students to write a paragraph that describes how economic conditions influenced political events in Central America.
[**English Language Learners, Cooperative Learning**]

TEACH OBJECTIVE 6

Level 1: Ask students the following questions: What were the Contadora Principles? Which countries agreed to them? What did Arias believe was the only thing that would secure peace in the region?
[**English Language Learners**]

TEACH OBJECTIVE 7

Level 3: Organize students into seven groups and assign each group one of the following countries: Mexico, El Salvador, Nicaragua, Panama, Guatemala, Costa Rica, or Honduras. Have them use the textbook, the library, com-

puter software, and other sources to find information about daily life in their assigned countries. Have each group create a scrapbook that might belong to an average family living in its assigned country in the present day. Scrapbooks might include images of people, neighborhoods, housing, and such; newspaper clippings; keepsakes; and so on. Encourage groups to share their work with the class when they have completed the assignment.
[**Cooperative Learning, Block Scheduling**]

REVIEW AND ASSESS

Have students complete the **Review Sections 1 and 2**. Have students complete **Daily Quizzes 34.1 and 34.2**. As Alternative Assessment, you may want to use the oral presentation exercise in the section's lessons or you may want to use the Mexico crises exercise.

RETEACH

Have students complete **Main Idea Activities 34.1 and 34.2**. Have students complete **Main Idea Activity for English Language Learners and Special-Needs Students 34.1 and 34.2**. Then have students write the section's headings and subheadings on a sheet of paper and list the main ideas in the appropriate space. Then have students compile a section glossary containing abbreviations and significant individuals.
[**English Language Learners, Cooperative Learning, Block Scheduling**]

CHALLENGE AND EXTEND

Have students choose a Latin American country and conduct research on its economy. They should research the nation's GNP, per capita income, industrial growth rate, population growth rate, major exports, balance of trade, and major occupations. Have students summarize the information in brief oral presentations. Have students write a biographical profile of a Mexican or Central American leader from 1945 to the present. Tell them to include information about the person's personal and political life. Call on volunteers to share some of the information they found and have the class take notes.
[**Block Scheduling**]

Lesson 2

(For use with Sections 3 and 4, pp. 922–935)

OBJECTIVES

1. Explain how Fidel Castro's rule affected Cuba.

2. Identify the key issue that has caused ongoing debate in Puerto Rico.

3. Identify problems the smaller Caribbean nations have faced.

4. Explain how the economy of Brazil first prospered, then stumbled. Identify the political and economic troubles Argentina had.

5. Describe how Peru was affected by the drug trade and terrorism.

6. Describe how Colombia was affected by the drug trade.

7. Identify what led to Chile's continuously strong economy.

BELLRINGER

As students enter the classroom, tell them that during the late 1900s many Latin American countries followed a path of economic nationalism and moderate social reform in their quests for stability and peace. Cuba, however, was different. Under the leadership of Fidel Castro, Cuba underwent a revolution and Castro became its dictator. Castro soon began systematically imposing communism on Cuba, taking over privately run industries and limiting personal freedoms. Following the Cuban Revolution, many disillusioned Cubans fled to the United States and the Dominican Republic. Tell students that, in Section 3, they will learn more about Cuba and other Caribbean nations after World War II. Then ask them to list some basic human rights and record them on the chalkboard. Explain to students that, in many Latin American countries where political and social upheaval created instability, one of the first casualties was usually human rights. Tell students that, in Section 4, they will learn about political turmoil in South America.

TEACH OBJECTIVE 1

All Levels: Organize the class into two groups and have them conduct a debate of the following statement: Fidel Castro's government and policies were more harmful than beneficial to the Cuban people.
[English Language Learners, Cooperative Learning]

TEACH OBJECTIVE 2

Level 3: Go over the subsection on Puerto Rico on page 925 with students. Then have them take on the roles of modern Puerto Ricans to write letters to the editor of a Puerto Rican newspaper arguing the merits of either remaining a commonwealth or becoming a state. Encourage students to edit each other's work before they submit it.
[Cooperative Learning]

TEACH OBJECTIVE 3

Level 1: Go over the subsections on the Dominican Republic and Haiti. Point out that the most overwhelming problem faced by these two nations during the latter half of the 1900s was a high poverty rate. Ask students to complete a flow chart showing the effects of poverty. Then ask them how a high poverty rate can affect other aspects of society and politics in a nation.
[English Language Learners]

TEACH OBJECTIVES 1, 2, AND 3

Level 2: Have students take on the roles of individuals living in Cuba, Puerto Rico, Haiti, or the Dominican Republic. In these roles, have them write several journal entries that discuss aspects of their daily lives and significant events that have affected them and their families.

TEACH OBJECTIVE 4

Level 1: Ask students to answer the following questions: How did the Brazilian government improve the country's economy? *(forced wages down and pressured labor unions to cooperate in the effort to cut production costs; foreign corporations were encourage to invest in Brazil)* To what

did the "Brazilian Miracle" refer? *(the rapid growth of the economy)* What drawbacks did this economic prosperity have? *(civil rights were lost; the government was heavily in debt)* Why did the economy stumble? *(The actions of Collor pushed the economy into a recession.)*
[**English Language Learners**]

TEACH OBJECTIVES 4 AND 5

All Levels: Tell students that in El Salvador, Guatemala, Cuba, Argentina, Brazil, and many other Latin American countries, human rights violations became a matter of course when military rule or harsh authoritarian governments took control. Tell them that it was common practice in many countries to suppress any antigovernment literature or press, to persecute or even assassinate members of rival parties or factions, and to imprison individuals arbitrarily and without trial. This was particularly true of South America; in virtually every South American country at one time or another during the past five decades human rights violations have become the norm. Ask students, as they read the section, to think about ways to stop such violations and to evaluate South Americans' efforts to do so.
[**English Language Learners**]

TEACH OBJECTIVE 6

Level 3: Organize students into groups and tell them to research the guerrilla groups in Peru known as the Tupac Amaru' Revolutionary Movement (MRTA) and Sendero Luminoso (Shining Path). Have students discuss the effects of the groups' terrorism on Peruvian society.
[**Block Scheduling, Cooperative Learning**]

TEACH OBJECTIVE 7

All Levels: Tell students to create a flow chart such as the following to illustrate the effects of Colombian drug trade. Ask students if they see any hope of the government regaining order. Then ask students how the situation in Columbia affects the United States.
[**English Language Learners**]

Effects of Colombian Drug Trade:
Violent rival groups compete to control the drug trade; Medellin becomes headquarters of the carte; cartel gains control of law enforcement agencies
Colombian authorities declare war on drug cartels, enlist United States. involvement; open street warfare ensues; corruption maintains the cartels power on drug trafficking.
Economic and political problems continue in the late 1990s

TEACH OBJECTIVE 8

Level 1: Ask students how Pinochet strengthened the economy of Chile. Then ask students the following questions: How did Pinochet respond to civil unrest? Despite a continuously strong economy, with what problems did Chile struggle?
[**English Language Learners**]

REVIEW AND ASSESS

Have students complete **Review Sections 3 and 4**. Have students complete **Daily Quiz 34.3 and 34.4**. As Alternative Assessment, you may want to use the flow chart exercise.

RETEACH

Have students complete **Main Idea Activity for English Language Learners and Special-Needs Students 34.3 and 34.4**. Then ask students to write a question and answer that covers the main idea for each subsection.
[**English Language Learners**]

CHALLENGE AND EXTEND

Have students read a book about the Cuban missile crisis. Then have them summarize the main points of the book in a one- to two-page written report. Have interested students select a piece of Latin American art to analyze, for example, a painting, story, or poem. Then have students write three to five paragraphs evaluation the work, explaining its themes, and pointing out what it implies about society or politics in its creator's country.

CHAPTER 34

Pablo Neruda

GOAL

Students will become familiar with the poetry and life of the twentieth-century poet Pablo Neruda. They will learn about his political affiliations and his poetry. Finally, they will experiment with Neruda's practice of using one's natural surroundings to describe emotions.

PLANNING

- **Purpose** This activity may be used in combination with teacher-directed lessons, as an enrichment activity, or as a performance-based assessment of content mastery.

- **Suggested Time** Plan to spend two lesson blocks and one homework assignment on this activity. Provide time for the presentation of poems.

- **Teaching Team** At least one social studies teacher and one language arts teacher should take part in teaching this activity.

- **Group Size** You may wish to assign the activity as a group activity, or an individual one.

- **Materials and Resources**

  Provide students with copies of Pablo Neruda's poems from *Elements of Literature*, 5th course

  Show students photographs of Latin America, particularly the Chilean landscape.

  Internet sources and library resources

IMPLEMENTATION

1. Give students an overview of Pablo Neruda's life and political struggles. (*He was born in 1904 in southern Chile. By seventeen, he was an accomplished poet, by twenty, he received critical acclaim. He befriended Spanish poet Frederico Garcia Lorca, however, after Lorca's assassination, Neruda began a political life. He served as Chilean consul to Mexico, was elected Senator in 1945, and joined the Chilean Communist Party. After 1947, communism* *was declared illegal and Neruda was pursued by the police and was forced to go into hiding. In 1950, his "Canto General" was published and he received the Nobel Peace Prize, along with Pablo Picasso, in 1971. He returned to Chili in 1952 and died on the Isle of Negra in 1973.*)

2. Read several of Neruda's love poems in *Elements of Literature*, 5th course, and any other Neruda poems from his early career (*some suggestions: VI "Remember You As You Were," XVI "In My Sky At Twilight," and XVIII "Here I Love You"*)

3. Ask students to write down what they notice about Neruda's verse. (*They should note his use of his natural surroundings to describe his feelings of love for the beloved. For example, in "Remember You as You Were," he incorporates many images of fall into the poem: autumnal leaves, bonfires, blue hyacinth, migrating birds, etc. In "Here I Love You," he describes phosphorus on water, silver gulls, pine trees, the sea, ships, and stars. All of these images are from the Chilean landscape.*)

4. Ask students to make a list of 20 things that exist in their geographical area. If it is an urban area, encourage them to list buildings, cars, buses, sounds, and sights of the city. If it is a rural setting, have them make lists of the specific geographical components that reflect their environment.

5. Review with students poetic terms. (*metaphor, simile, alliteration, assonance, rhyme, meter, stanza*) Ask them to make a list of metaphors, similes, and lines with alliteration and assonance in them from their list of images.

6. Then ask students to write a poem about an emotion that uses their geography to describe their feelings.

7. Ask students to write and revise several poems and then to put them into a collection of poems by the class.

8. Have students read their poems aloud to the class.

ASSESSMENT

1. To assess students' poems, use the Rubric for Creative Writing.

2. Additional grades can be based on students' participation in class and in their poetry readings.

The Vietnam War

Ask students if they know anyone who served in the military during the Vietnam War. Ask if they are aware of the reception the country gave to returning soldiers from this war. Contrast this with the country's feeling toward the soldiers who fought in World War II. Have students provide reasons for the difference.

Lesson 1

(For use with Sections 1 and 2, pp. 940–955)

OBJECTIVES

1. Explore how the Vietnam War and the Watergate scandal affected political attitudes in the United States.

2. Analyze the changes that have occurred in the economy of the United States since 1970.

3. Explain how American foreign policy changed in the 1970s, 1980s, and 1990s.

4. Identify the major challenges Canada faced in the late 1900s.

5. Describe how Margaret Thatcher's leadership affected Britain.

6. Explain the challenges European nations faced in the late 1900s.

7. Identify the steps European nations took toward unity in the late 1900s.

BELLRINGER

As students enter the classroom, have each student write on a sheet of paper what he or she considers to be the five biggest problems or issues facing the United States today. Call on students to read their lists to the class, and write these responses on the chalkboard. Tell students that, in Section 1, they will learn about the current state of the United States. Then ask students what they know about Margaret Thatcher. Then ask students when they think the first woman will be elected to the U.S. presidency. Tell students that, in Section 2, they will

learn more about Thatcher's administration in Great Britain.

TEACH OBJECTIVE 1

Level 1: Ask students why the United States sought to end its involvement in Vietnam. Then ask students to classify the effects the Vietnam War had on American society by writing them in a chart under the following headings: *Economy, Society,* and *Global Influence.*
[English Language Learners]

All Levels: Ask students to explain how the Watergate scandal unfolded. Then ask students to sum up how the Watergate scandal affected Americans' political attitudes. Have them write a response to the Watergate scandal, as if they had lived through this period in American history. Students may choose written responses, such as a letter to the president or Congress, an editorial, or an essay.
[English Language Learners]

TEACH OBJECTIVE 2

All Levels: Tell students that the U.S. economy has undergone some significant changes since the 1970s. Have students create a graphic organizer that lists the key characteristics of the U.S. economy in the 1970s, 1980s, and 1990s. Then ask students how the changes in the U.S. economy reflect an economic transformation.
[English Language Learners]

TEACH OBJECTIVE 3

Level 2: Draw a time line on the chalkboard that extends from the 1970s to the present day. Tell students to copy this time line on a sheet of paper and then fill it in with 10 significant events in the United States's relationship with foreign countries. Tell students to annotate their time line by explaining the significance of each event. Also remind students they may place events on their time line even if they do not have an exact date of occurrence, such as if the text states something happened in the late

1970s. After students have completed their time lines, call on volunteers to share their time line entries with the class. Use these to launch a discussion on the important events and changes that occurred in U.S. foreign policy. Close by asking students what events they believe most threatened U.S. safety and what measures were the most important to U.S. stability.

TEACH OBJECTIVE 4

Level 3: Ask students to name the two most important issues facing Canadians in the 1990s. Ask students to write a brief paragraph explaining the concerns and demands that surround each issue. Then ask them which of these issues they believe has found more resolution with Canadians. Close by asking student to hypothesize on future events or issues that will concern many Canadians.

TEACH OBJECTIVE 5

Level 3: Tell students to read the section under "Great Britain" beginning on page 948. Then have students construct a chart listing the positive and negative elements that characterized Margaret Thatcher's rule of Britain as well as elements that could be characterized as either positive or negative, depending on the person's point of view. After students have completed their charts, have them prepare a written explanation about its interpretations.

TEACH OBJECTIVE 5

Level 2: Assign to each student Chirac, Mitterand, Giscard d'Estaing, or Pompidou. Have students summarize their leader's main ideas about domestic, foreign, social, and economic policy. Use students' work to launch a discussion on the positive and negative effects of each leader's rule.

TEACH OBJECTIVE 6

Level 1: Write the names Willy Brandt and Helmut Kohl on the chalkboard. Then read aloud with students the text under "Germany" on page 951. During the course of reading, invite students to point out important actions taken by each of the leaders. Write students' suggestions on the chalkboard, under the appropriate name. After students finish reading the textbook, have them look at the completed lists. Ask students which leader they believe helped the German people more, and why.
[**English Language Learners**]

TEACH OBJECTIVE 7

Level 1: Ask students to name the major treaties or agreements made between European countries since the 1970s. Ask students to briefly characterize the main goals of each treaty or agreement.
[**English Language Learners**]

REVIEW AND ASSESS

Have students complete **Review Sections 1 and 2**. Have students complete **Daily Quiz 35.1 and 35.2**. As Alternative Assessment, you may want to use the economy or foreign policy exercise in this section's lesson or you may want to use the chart exercise in this section's lessons.

RETEACH

Have students complete **Main Idea Activities 35.1 and 35.2**. Then ask student to write a question and answer that covers the main idea for each subsection in the section.
[**English Language Learners**]

CHALLENGE AND EXTEND

Have students research Watergate and the Iran-Contra Affair and use the information to create a compare-and-contrast chart about these events. Students also should write a paragraph summing up their findings and expressing which event they feel was more harmful to the American public and why. Organize students into three groups and assign each group to be supporters of the Helsinki Accords, NATO, or the EU. Then tell students to develop convincing arguments that show the agreement that they are in favor of is the best one for European nations to follow. Have students present their arguments to the class.

Lesson 2

(For use with Sections 3 and 4, pp. 956–969)

OBJECTIVES

1. Explain what events led to the fall of the Soviet Union.

2. Explain how Russia fared under Boris Yeltsin.

3. Describe how Eastern Europe was affected by the fall of communism.

4. Explain how the United States was attacked on September 11, 2001, and how people responded.

5. Describe how the events of September 11, 2001, affected the U.S. economy.

6. List the immediate steps that U.S. leaders and their allies took to find those responsible for the September 11, 2001 attacks and to bring them to justice.

BELLRINGER

As students enter the classroom, have them think about the effect a poor economy has on the people's support for government leaders. Ask students to list some of the effects a poor economy might have on the political climate of a nation. Tell students that, in Section 3, they will learn about how poor economic conditions contributed to the fall of communism.

TEACH OBJECTIVE 1

All Levels: Ask students to describe the reforms that Gorbachev initiated in the Soviet Union. Then discuss with students the way various people, such as average Soviet citizens, U.S. officials, or hard-line Soviet Communists reacted to these reforms and how they contributed to the fall of communism. You may choose to assign these roles to your students and have them speak from this point of view during the discussion.
[English Language Learners]

Level 3: Have students write journal entries as if they were average Soviet citizens. Students should write a "Before" entry, chronicling life before Gorbachev's reforms, and then an "After" entry. Then discuss whether most Soviet citizens likely thought their lives were better under Brezhnev or under Gorbachev.

TEACH OBJECTIVE 2

Level 1: Write the following chart on the chalkboard, omitting the answers shown in italics. Then, using these categories, discuss with the class Russia's development after it became a republic. Encourage students to come up with a generalization for each category that describes Russia and then provide a few specifics. For example, students might characterize the economy as unstable and note that many Russians suffered severe hardships.
[English Language Learners]

Russia's Development After it Became a Republic

Economy: *high inflation and unemployment, food, and housing in short supply, slow to improve, new class of entrepreneurs became wealthy*

Politics: *political turmoil, Yeltsin struggled for power with legislature, danger of a coup*

Religion: *new growth and power for Orthodox Church*

Domestic Difficulties: *increase in organized crime, increase in separatist movements among Russian minority groups, such as Chechnya*

Foreign Relations: *cooperated with the West, reached arms reduction agreements with the U.S., opposed expansion of NATO, Western leaders concerned over security of Russian nuclear weapons*

TEACH OBJECTIVE 3

Level 2: Ask students how Gorbachev's reforms affected the Communist satellites. Then ask them to write a few sentences explaining how democratic governments arose in Poland, Czechoslovakia, Romania, and East Germany. Ask students to compare the events in each of these countries. Which country would they have held up as the best example?

TEACH OBJECTIVE 3

Level 3: Present to students the following scenario: You live in a country where most people have no say in the government or its policies. All your life you have been told what to do, what to study, what kind of job to have, what to read, what to say, and even what to think! Then, one day, your country's government resigns. You and your fellow citizens must rebuild and reinvent your government and develop a good way to run your country. What kind of problems do you think you would face? Ask students to respond to you promptly, and discuss these responses.

TEACH OBJECTIVE 4

Level 1: Ask students to summarize the events that took place on September 11, 2001. Then have them discuss the results of the events. Have students write brief essays discussing ways in which the U.S. government and people responded to the events, and ways in which the events may have changed U.S. citizens' attitudes about their own nation and the world. [**English Language Learners, Cooperative Learning**]

All Levels: Begin by reading the quote from James Earl Jones on page 966. Ask students to list ways in which U.S. citizens are united and are different. Help students understand that U.S. citizens immediately set aside their differences and united to help one another and show their unity and strength. Ask students what the headline in the French newspaper, *Le Monde,* "We Are All Americans," means, and discuss the concept of what it is to be a citizen of the world. [**English Language Learners, Cooperative Learning**]

TEACH OBJECTIVE 5

Level 2: Begin by discussing the role air travel plays in United States and world society. Ask students to brainstorm services that commercial airlines provide. Then ask students to describe how the terrorist attacks damaged the airline industry and other industries. Tell students that the government's purpose in providing $15 billion dollars for the airline industry was to try to help the economy stay strong and active. [**Cooperative Learning**]

Level 3: Copy the following chart on the chalkboard, omitting the italicized answers. Have each student complete the diagram by filling in the effect for each cause listed.

The Stock Market

Cause: *people worry about how war will affect stock prices, stock prices fall, people lose money, people sell stocks, companies lose money*

Effect: *stock prices fall, people lose money, people sell stocks, companies lose money, people lose jobs*

Explain that this downward spiral effect can lead to a "recession."

TEACH OBJECTIVE 6

All Levels: Have students select some aspect of the steps taken by the U.S. government in locating and apprehending the terrorists to study in more depth. *(the freezing of assets, diplomatic efforts, the military campaign, or humanitarian aid to the Afghan people)* Ask each student to learn and share with the class something interesting about their chosen topic. [**English Language Learners, Cooperative Learning**]

REVIEW AND ASSESS

Have students complete **Review Sections 3 and 4**. Have students complete **Daily Quiz 35.3 and 35.4**. You may want to use the graphic organizer or the essay exercise in this section.

RETEACH

Have students complete **Main Idea Activities 35.3 and 35.4**. Ask them to create a glossary that includes the vocabulary and significant people, places, and events from the section.

CHALLENGE AND EXTEND

Tell students to imagine they are UN workers in the Middle East in 1994. Divide the class into groups and have them brainstorm ideas for bringing peace to the region.

Major Events in the Modern Era

GOAL

To have students write about the major events in World history since 1970 to the present.

PLANNING

- **Purpose** This activity may be used in combination with teacher-directed lessons, as an enrichment activity, or as a performance-based assessment of content mastery.

- **Suggested Time** Plan to spend two lesson blocks and one homework assignment on this activity. Provide time for the presentation of the overviews.

- **Teaching Team** At least one social studies teacher and one language arts teacher should take part in teaching this activity.

- **Group Size** This activity will work as a small group activity or for individual students.

- **Materials and Resources**

  Internet and library sources

  Chapter 35

  Examples of *Time* or *Life* magazine overviews of a decade

IMPLEMENTATION

1. Give students an overview of the activity by explaining that they will be compiling articles on major events in the modern period (1970 to the present), which they will combine to make a mock *Time* or *Life* edition of world events. Explain that photographs, artwork, and cartoons, can accompany the articles they compose.

2. Ask students to make a time line of the important events in the past 30 years. Ask them to consult their text, library sources, Internet sources, newspapers, or news magazines. Some events that should definitely be included are the Vietnam War, Watergate, the changing U.S. economy, United States-Soviet relations, Canada's

relationship with the United States, major world leaders (*Margaret Thatcher, Jimmy Carter, Ronald Reagan, Fidel Castro, François Mitterand, Leonid Brezhnev, Mikhail Gorbachev, Boris Yeltsin, George H.W. Bush, Bill Clinton, George W. Bush*), the fall of Communism, the Berlin Wall, the Gulf War, and the terrorist attacks of September 11, 2001.

3. After the students have a complete time line, have each student choose three events or leaders to research and write about. Encourage them to use library sources, the Internet, and their textbook for information about their historical event or leader. Remind students of the elements of a well-written news story—who, what, where, when, and how must be defined. Show them an example of an article from *Newsweek* or *Time*. Allow them to discuss how the writer approaches his or her historical topic.

4. Tell students that they may choose to write a straight news article or an editorial that gives their educated opinion on the event. If they choose an editorial, they must have a thesis statement in their opening paragraph, and supporting evidence for the opinions. They should keep in mind the elements of a persuasive paper and use some of these techniques in their work.

5. After students have researched and written a rough draft, ask them to exchange their articles for peer review. Ask students to comment on structure, grammar, punctuation, sentence structure, and correct historical information. If the piece is persuasive, have the students look for the thesis statement and for the proof of the opinion in the work. Have students revise essays based on peer reviews.

6. After students have written their final essays, divide them into groups representing their different time periods. As a group they should compile the essays and include photographs, artwork, graphics, etc. to complete their portion of the magazine.

7. Have students arrange all of the time periods chronologically and keep it as a reference guide for the classroom. Ask one group to create a table of context and an index, and another group to write brief biographies of the contributors of the magazine.

ASSESSMENT

1. To assess students' work examine their use of historical information, combined with their ability to present their information in a clear and concise manner. Consult Rubric 23: Newspaper in *Portfolio and Performance for Social Studies.*

2. Additional grades can be based on students' participation in class discussion, their group work and their final product, the news magazine.

The Time Line—Continued

Have students look at the time line on pages 972–973. Ask volunteers to go to the board to continue the time line to the present day in the categories of *Global Events, Daily Life, Business and Finance, Politics, the Arts,* and *Science and Technology.*

Lesson 1

(For use with Sections 1 and 2, pp. 974–989)

OBJECTIVES

1. List trends that occurred in painting, sculpture, and architecture after World War II.

2. Identify the major themes of music, dance, film, and drama after 1945.

3. Explain how poetry and novels expressed the mood of the times.

4. Describe how public support of cultural activities changed after World War II.

5. List the advances in travel and space exploration that have occurred since 1945.

6. Explain the effect miniaturization and computerization have had on modern life.

7. Describe the technological improvements that have been made in medical science.

8. Discuss the environmental concerns scientists have identified.

BELLRINGER

As students enter the classroom, divide them into pairs and have them look at the photo from the musical *Cats* on page 978. Have them list adjectives that describe the mood of the musical as shown in the picture. *(exuberant, exotic, daring)* Then have them list adjectives that describe the music of the modern world. *(lively, multicultural)* Tell students that, in Section 1, they will learn how trends and themes of artistic works reflect life in the period from World War II to the present. Then divide students into groups of four, who will assume the roles of an astronaut, a doctor, a forest ranger, and a software engineer. Ask the groups to discuss the issues raised by science and technology in the modern world from the perspective of their roles. Tell students that, in Section 2, they will learn how advances in science and technology since 1945 have dramatically changed the quality of life and the view of the future.

TEACH OBJECTIVE 1

Level 1: Have students work in pairs to find pictures that suggest the post-1945 trend toward experimentation of technology in the arts. Call on class members to present their pictures to the class. Have them identify images that exemplify abstract expressionism, pop art, op art, conceptual art, or new techniques in architecture.
[English Language Learners]

TEACH OBJECTIVE 2

All Levels: Ask class members to pose and answer questions about whether performance art is truly art. Then ask students if photographers, glassblowers, dancers, and others are producing art. Require students to use standard English to explain their answers. *(Sample responses: No, art is more than original personal expression; it has to have a lasting impact on society; yes, art is any form of creative personal expression that makes a statement that is important to society, whether it affects society now, later, or never.)*
[English Language Learners]

TEACH OBJECTIVE 3

Have students work in pairs to create tables of major postwar writers. Provide the following format, omitting words in italics.
[**Cooperative Learning**]

Literary form	Name	Theme
Poetry	*Ginsburg*	*Protest commercialism*
	Angelou	*Black experience*
	Paz	*Loneliness*
Novel	*Kerouac*	*Protest materialism*
	Vonnegut	*Protest insensitivity*
	Esquival	*Hispanic experience*

TEACH OBJECTIVE 4

Level 2: Ask students what factors boosted public support of cultural activities after World War II. (*more education, leisure time, cultural awareness because of television*)

TEACH OBJECTIVE 5

All Levels: Have students work in pairs to create time lines of the "space race," beginning with the launching of Sputnik in 1957. (*1957 Sputnik; 1958 U.S. satellite; 1961 Gargarin, Shepard; 1969 moon landing; 1971 space station; 1973 Pioneer 10 flies by Jupiter; 1976 Viking 1 and Viking 2 land on Mars; 1981 Columbia space shuttle; 1968 Challenger explosion, Voyager 2 passes Uranus; 1989 Voyager 2 passes Neptune, Magellan maps Venus 1990 Hubble space telescope; 1995 Galileo orbits Jupiter; 1997 Pathfinder finds water on Mars; 1998 sixteen nations begin ISS construction*) Encourage pairs to illustrate their time lines. Display students' time lines in the classroom.
[**English Language Learners, Cooperative Learning**]

TEACH OBJECTIVE 6

Level 3: Ask students to pose and answer questions about the process of miniaturization and how it has stimulated computerization. (*The chips and wafers in calculators, automatic cameras, microwaves, automobiles, and so on are tiny, powerful, and highly specialized computer processors.*)
[**Cooperative Learning**]

TEACH OBJECTIVE 7

Level 1: Tell students that scientists are learning how to identify and replace defective genes. Write these questions on the chalkboard to start a class discussion: *Will insurance companies refuse coverage based on genetic information? Can criminals blame their criminal behavior on a gene for excessive aggression? Should people be allowed to create "designer babies" by selecting hair color, eye color, and musical ability? (Answers will vary but should be supported with logical reasoning.)*

Level 2: Write the words *genetics* and *cloning* on the chalkboard. Ask volunteers to explain each term. Have students' pose and answer questions about the potential benefits of cloning for humankind. (*improving farm animals and crops to produce more food, human organs for transplant, and so on*)
[**Cooperative Learning**]

TEACH OBJECTIVE 8

All Levels: Draw a circle and write the phrase *Environmental Problems* within it. Have students create a web diagram in which they identify at least six environmental problems the world faces today. Then have students' pose and answer questions about each problem.

Environmental Problems: *acid rain, pesticide, waste disposal, endangered species, ozone depletion, global warming*
[**English Language Learners, Cooperative Learning**]

REVIEW AND ASSESS

Have students complete **Review Sections 1 and 2**. Have students complete **Daily Quiz 36.1 and 36.2**. You may want to use the Objective exercise on page 969, asking students to write their identification of the images or the space race time line exercise.

RETEACH

Have students complete **Main Idea Activities 36.1 and 36.2**. Then have students list the section's headings and subheadings, writing the main idea of each. Then have pairs of students take turns reading the section's headings and subheadings. Ask students in turn to say the main idea of each heading and subheading, using standard English and correct terminology. **[English Language Learners]**

CHALLENGE AND EXTEND

Have students imagine they are artists living in the late 1900s. Tell students to use their textbooks, biographies, computer software, and other resources to find out about the daily life of artists in the late 1900s. Then have them write a dialogue between two artists about their personal and professional challenges. Have students choose a region of the world and write a brief essay about ways technological advances have affected that region. Suggest that students find primary source material, copies of letters, interviews, photographs, and so on to support the ideas they present in the essay.

Lesson 2

(For use with Section 3, pp.990–993)

OBJECTIVES

1. List some recent examples of human rights abuses.

2. Explain how the nations of the world have dealt with human rights abuses.

3. Discuss how democratic ideals and practices spread in the late 1900s.

BELLRINGER

As students enter the classroom, divide them into pairs to discuss what they know about human right abuses around the world. Have each pair compile a list of countries with recent abuses *(Guatemala, China, Iraq, South Africa, Northern Ireland, Bosnia)* and support their point of view by listing the kinds of abuse in each country. Tell students that, in Section 3, they will learn how citizens and governments reacted to human rights abuses in the late 1900s.

TEACH OBJECTIVE 1

Level 1: Have students brainstorm about human rights abuses that exist in the world today. Write their responses, and use them to compile a class list on the chalkboard. *(ethnic cleansing in Bosnia; terrorist acts in Northern Ireland; imprisonment, torture, and execution of people who speak out against the government)* **[English Language Learners]**

TEACH OBJECTIVE 2

All Levels: Ask students to identify ways that human rights have been protected. *(international pressure, political changes, United Nations activity, Amnesty International reports, criminal trials of abusive officials)* Then ask students to identify difficulties in defining human rights. *(non-Western countries favor community interest over individual rights, Islamic countries define women's rights by the Qur'an, poverty affects human rights)* **[English Language Learners]**

Level 2: Ask students to research one way that human rights have been protected and to write an essay on their one example. Present essays to the class. **[English Language Learners]**

TEACH OBJECTIVE 3

Level 3: Have students design, research, and fill in a chart or other graphic organizer listing at least five nations that have become more democratic since 1970, with the date and nature of the transition.

Nation: *South Africa:* Steps to Democracy: *1994: from apartheid to first elections open to all races.*

REVIEW AND ASSESS

Have students complete **Review Section 3**. Have students complete **Daily Quiz 36.3**. You may want to use the Objective 2 exercise on page 991 and turn it into an essay exercise.

RETEACH

Have students complete **Main Idea Activities 36.3**. Then have pairs of students take turns reading the section's headings and subheadings and in turn identifying the main idea of each. **[English Language Learners, Cooperative Learning]**

CHALLENGE AND EXTEND

Have students prepare an investigative report explaining how rights can be restored to an individual or community whose human rights have been violated. Have them present their findings to the class.

Anthology of Modern Writers and Artists

GOAL

In this activity, students will learn more about the globalization of the arts and literature in this post-modern world. They will be asked to edit an anthology of the world's greatest writers and artists after 1945. They will not only collect poems, short stories, plays, photographs of art, etc., but they also will be asked to write about the trends, major themes of the work, and the public's response to it in a preface. In the process, they will learn more about their own time period's rich and diverse cultural world.

PLANNING

- **Purpose** This activity may be used in combination with teacher-directed lessons, as an enrichment activity, or as a performance-based assessment of content mastery.

- **Suggested Time** Plan to spend two lesson blocks and one homework assignment on this activity.

- **Teaching Team** At least one social studies teacher and one language arts teacher should take part in teaching this activity.

- **Group Size** This activity will work as a small group activity or for individual students.

- **Materials and Resources**

  Elements of World Literature, 5th course

  Internet and library sources

  Examples of art books, anthologies of literature

IMPLEMENTATION

1. Give students an overview of the activity by explaining that their first task will be to research the major artists of the present time. Ask them to choose which ones they would like to include in their collection. Then ask them to write a preface before each historical time period defining the trends, major themes, historical significance, and the public response to the art and artist they have chosen. Finally, they will compile an anthology of the great artists of the modern era.

2. Begin by having students make a list of writers, poets, playwrights, artists, dancers, etc. *(Examples to include are Jackson Pollock, George Balanchine, Martha Graham, Bertolt Brecht, Andy Warhol, Toni Morrison, Maya Angelou, James Baldwin, Salman Rushdie, Andrew Lloyd Webber, Arthur Miller, Adrienne Rich, Joan Miro, William Faulkner, Tennessee Williams, e.e. cummings, etc.)* Then ask them to research the life of the artist and to choose one work that they think represents their art.

3. Ask students to group these artists into historical and thematic groups. Have them write down similarities they see of this group of artists. Are there certain philosophical themes they share? Is there an approach to art that is similar? What message did they want to send to the world? Who did their art appeal to? What significant contribution did their artists make to the culture?

4. Divide students into groups based on their particular artists' work. Ask them to create a section of the anthology complete with examples of the works, photographs, or graphics. Instruct them on writing a thoughtful preface to the period.

5. Review the elements of a well-formed essay: logical arrangement of thoughts, clear, concise language, examples for their generalities, vivid language that creates images in the reader's mind, and correct historical research.

6. Ask that students conduct a peer review of each other's writing. Check for historical correctness, logical structure, sentence structure, syntax, grammar, and punctuation. Encourage students to give feedback and to revise their essays accordingly.

7. Combine all the groups' different periods of artists into a class anthology.

ASSESSMENT

1. Assess students' work by their use of historical information, combined with their ability to fulfill the writing components.

2. Additional grades can be based on students' participation in class, their group work, and their final preface.

Continuing the Time Line

Have students brainstorm to continue the time line shown on page 449. Write the following categories on the board: Politics, Science and Technology, Global Events, Daily Life, the Arts, and Business and Finance. Have them fill out the categories with events they predict will occur from today until the year 2050.

Lesson 1

(For use with Sections 1 and 2, pp. 450–463)

OBJECTIVES

1. Explain how European monarchies changed from the 1500s to the 1800s.

2. Describe new ideas about government that occurred in Britain and the United States.

3. Explain how the French Revolution differed from the American Revolution.

4. Describe how life changed during the Industrial Revolution.

5. Describe how nationalist movements and imperialism affected the world.

6. Describe the causes of World War I.

7. Explain how the Great Depression affected governments.

8. Explain how Africa, Asia, and Latin America changed during the 1930s.

9. Describe the events that led to World War II.

BELLRINGER

Ask students to list the ways the United States has changed since 1800. Then have them describe how these changes affected the lives of the American people. Tell students that in Section 1 they will learn how the European nations changed between the 1500s and the 1800s, and how these changes affected the world.

TEACH OBJECTIVE 1

All Levels: Review the meaning of the phrases "divine right of kings" and "absolute monar-chy" with students. Then help them to create a graphic organizer that summarizes how European monarchies changed. Ask students to identify the monarch who made each change.
[English Language Learners]

TEACH OBJECTIVE 2

All Levels: Have students work in pairs to create a two-column chart comparing the new systems of government in Britain and the United States.
[Cooperative Learning]

TEACH OBJECTIVE 3

All Levels: Have students study the information in Section 1 about the American and French Revolutions. Then ask students to evaluate how the French Revolution differed from the American Revolution.

TEACH OBJECTIVE 4

All Levels: Remind students that industrialization changed the way people lived. There were technological advances, changes in economic systems, and changes in culture. Help students list examples of each.
[English Language Learners]

TEACH OBJECTIVE 5

All Levels: Ask students to define nationalism and imperialism. Then have students give examples of nationalism and imperialism.
[English Language Learners]

TEACH OBJECTIVE 6

All Levels: Tell students that as European nations became more powerful and extended their influence around the world, conflicts and rivalries developed. In 1914 these rivalries erupted into war. Help students create a chart titled *World War I* that reflects the causes and examples of the war.
[English Language Learners]

TEACH OBJECTIVE 7

All Levels: Tell students that the Great Depression affected economies around the world and contributed to political unrest in Europe. Then have students work in groups to report on the effects of the Great Depression in the following countries: France and Great Britain, Italy and Germany, the Soviet Union, and the United States.
[**English Language Learners, Cooperative Learning**]

TEACH OBJECTIVE 8

All Levels: Ask students to list reasons why a nationalist movement might grow in a country.

TEACH OBJECTIVE 9

All Levels: Ask students what invasions Japan, Italy, and Germany made between 1931 and 1938. Then ask what invasion started World War II.
[**English Language Learners**]

REVIEW AND ASSESS

Have students complete **Review Sections 1 and 2**. Then have students complete **Daily Quizzes Epilogue 1 and 2**. As Alternative Assessment, you may want to use the chart in this section's lessons.

RETEACH

Have students complete **Main Idea Activities Epilogue 1 and 2**. Then have them outline the main ideas and supporting details.
[**English Language Learners**]

CHALLENGE AND EXTEND

Organize the class into two groups, representing those who supported Truman's use of the atomic bomb and those who were against it. Have the groups research their positions. Then have the groups support their points of view in a class debate.
[**Cooperative Learning**]

Lesson 2

(For use with Sections 3 and 4, pp. 464–473)

OBJECTIVES

1. Explain how the Allied powers dealt with Germany after the war.
2. Describe the causes of the Cold War.
3. Analyze how European nations fared after the war.
4. Explain how political unrest affected life in Latin American nations.
5. Describe how Japan recovered from the devastation of World War II.
6. Explain why communism led to greater tensions and conflict in Asia.
7. Describe how African nations dealt with independence.
8. Explain why violence marred life in the Middle East.

BELLRINGER

Ask students to recall what happened in Europe after World War I. Tell students that in the next section they will learn what happened in Europe and the world after World War II.

TEACH OBJECTIVES 1 AND 2

All Levels: Organize students into small groups and ask them to create a chart that illustrates the steps that were taken in Europe after World War II and at the beginning of the Cold War. Column headings may read *Action, Reason,* and *Description.*
[**English Language Learners, Cooperative Learning**]

TEACH OBJECTIVE 3

All Levels: Write the headings *Western Europe* and *Eastern Europe* on the chalkboard. Then help students generate a list of characteristics under each heading that describes how each region fared after World War II.
[**English Language Learners**]

TEACH OBJECTIVE 4

All Levels: Have students create a cause-and-effect chart that shows how political unrest has affected life in Central and South America since 1945.

TEACH OBJECTIVE 5

All Levels: Tell students that postwar Japan concentrated on building its industry and developing advanced technology. Ask students to list products that are imported from Japan. Then have students describe how Japan's trade balance with the United States has changed from 1945 to the 2000s.
[**English Language Learners**]

TEACH OBJECTIVE 6

All Levels: Have students complete a time line that shows dates and events related to communism in Asia.

TEACH OBJECTIVE 7

All Levels: Have students create a chart titled "Challenges African Countries Faced." Column headings should read *Challenges* and *Examples.* Underneath the *Challenges* heading, ask students to list the following row titles: *Economic, Political, Environmental,* and *Health.* Ask students to fill in the chart to show what challenges African countries faced after independence. Discuss the charts in class.

TEACH OBJECTIVE 8

All Levels: Write the following list of countries and dates on the board: Egypt, 1952; Palestine, 1947; Israel, 1967; Iran, 1979; Iraq, 1990. Have students work in pairs. Ask them to find out what events happened in each country on the date given. Students should use their texts and make notes. Discuss their answers as a class.
[**Cooperative Learning**]

REVIEW AND ASSESS

Have students complete **Review Sections 3 and 4**. Then have students complete **Daily Quizzes**

Epilogue 3 and 4. As Alternative Assessment, you may want to use the charts in this section's lessons.

RETEACH

Have students complete **Main Idea Activities Epilogue 3 and 4**. Then have students write a main idea question and answer for each subsection in the sections.
[**English Language Learners**]

CHALLENGE AND EXTEND

Organize the class into small groups. Have each group research, prepare, and present a short "newscast" about one of the following conflicts: Vietnam War, Six-Day War, or Persian Gulf War.

Lesson 3

(For use with Sections 5 and 6, pp. 474–483)

OBJECTIVES

1. Describe how the superpowers dealt with a changing world.
2. Explain how technological developments affected health, the environment, and entertainment.
3. Describe how the United States was attacked on September 11, 2001, and how people responded.
4. Explain how the events of September 11, 2001, affected the U.S. economy.
5. Identify the immediate steps U.S. leaders and their allies took to find those responsible for the attacks and bring them to justice.

BELLRINGER

Ask each student to write on a sheet of paper what he or she considers to be the three biggest problems facing the United States today. Have students read their lists and discuss their answers as a class. Tell students that in Section 5 they will learn how the collapse of communism and technological developments changed life in the 1980s and 1990s.

TEACH OBJECTIVE 1

Levels 1 and 2: Have students create a graphic organizer that summarizes political and economic changes in the 1980s and 1990s. Discuss the organizers in class.
[**English Language Learners**]

Level 3: Divide the class into two groups representing the United States and the Soviet Union. Have members of each group write newspaper articles describing their country's response to the changes in the 1980s and 1990s. Ask volunteers from each group to read their article to the class for discussion.

TEACH OBJECTIVE 2

All Levels: Ask students to list developments in the 1980s and 1990s in technology, health, the environment, and entertainment. Then ask students how these changes affect their own lives.
[**English Language Learners**]

TEACH OBJECTIVE 3

All Levels: Ask students to describe how the U.S. government, the American people, and the rest of the world responded to the attack.
[**English Language Learners**]

Level 1: Help students complete a timetable of the terrorist attacks of September 11, 2001.

Lead a class discussion of the events.
[**English Language Learners**]

TEACH OBJECTIVE 4

All Levels: Have students study the information in Section 6 about the economic impact of the attack. Then ask them to summarize the areas of concern.

TEACH OBJECTIVE 5

All Levels: Have students work in pairs to create a chart showing the steps U.S. leaders took in response to the terrorist attacks. The chart might include international actions and domestic actions.
[**Cooperative Learning**]

REVIEW AND ASSESS

Have students complete **Review Sections 5 and 6**. Then have students complete **Daily Quizzes Epilogue 5 and 6**. As Alternative Assessment, you may want to use the chart in this section's lessons.

RETEACH

Have students complete **Main Idea Activities Epilogue 5 and 6**. Then have students create an outline of the sections' main ideas and supporting details.
[**English Language Learners**]

CHALLENGE AND EXTEND

Ask students to research the history of the Pentagon building and write a brief report of their findings.

A Comparison of Prejudice

GOAL

In this activity, students will learn more about the bombing of Pearl Harbor and the terrorist attacks of September 11, 2001, by researching primary sources that comment on the events. Students also will compare the two attacks and their effects.

PLANNING

- **Purpose** This activity may be used in combination with teacher-directed lessons, as an enrichment activity, or as a performance-based assessment of content mastery.

- **Suggested Time** Plan to spend three lesson blocks and two homework assignments on this activity. Provide time for discussion.

- **Teaching Team** At least one social studies teacher and one language arts teacher should take part in teaching this activity.

- **Group Size** This activity works best if students work individually. However, students may work in smaller groups to undertake research. You may assign the activity as an extra credit option for individual students.

- **Materials and Resources** Provide students with access to the library and Internet. Students should be given copies of Rubrics 30 and 37.

IMPLEMENTATION

1. Give students an overview of the activity by explaining that they will read primary sources of the 1940s and 2001 that comment on the wars of the time. In an essay, students will compare the bombing of Pearl Harbor and the events of September 11, 2001.

2. Ask students to find primary sources commenting on the bombing of Pearl Harbor and the events of September 11, 2001. Students should find newspaper articles from December 7, 1941, and September 11, 2001. Students should also find speeches given by both Franklin Delano Roosevelt and George W. Bush that discuss these acts of war. Ask them to find accounts of people who witnessed the bombing of Pearl Harbor and the terrorism in New York, Washington, D.C., and/or Pennsylvania. Students should take detailed notes on each source and note any similarities between them. Discuss their findings as a class. Be sure to compare the causes of each event and the actual events that took place. Create a list on the chalkboard of the similarities and differences the students have found.

3. Tell students that they will investigate the effects of Pearl Harbor and the terrorist attacks. First have them research Japanese internment camps during World War II. Ask students to identify what the camps were, why they were created, and what purpose they served. Have students find first-hand accounts of those who supported the existence of the camps as well as those who were forced to reside within them.

4. Then ask students to find newspaper articles and firsthand accounts of Arab Americans who faced prejudice after the attacks on September 11. Ask students the following questions: In what types of situations did Arab Americans find themselves? How and why did people target them? Lead a discussion in which students discuss the similarities and differences between the prejudice that resulted from the bombing of Pearl Harbor and the terrorist attacks.

5. Conclude by asking students to write an essay that explains the similarities between the bombing of Pearl Harbor and the terrorist attacks of September 11, 2001. Rather than attempting to broadly cover the topic, ask students to focus on two to three similarities and describe them in detail. Also ask students to analyze what they think we have learned as a result of the

Japanese internment camps, if anything, and how that might affect our present treatment of Arab Americans. Ask them to offer suggestions as to how we can avoid a situation similar to that after the bombing of Pearl Harbor, therefore avoiding further prejudice towards Arab Americans.

ASSESSMENT

1. To assess students' papers, use Rubrics 30 and 37.

2. Additional grades can be based on students' participation in discussion and the quality of their research.

Egypt: The New Kingdom

Have students examine the map on page 4. Ask students to identify where a pyramid is located. Also ask approximately how many miles it is from the northernmost point to the southernmost point of the New Kingdom.

Lesson 1

(For use with Sections 1 and 2, pp. 1–10)

OBJECTIVES

1. Describe the characteristics of a civilization and where the first civilizations developed.

2. Identify achievements of the kingdom of the Nile.

3. Identify achievements of the kingdoms of the Tigris-Eurphrates Valley.

4. Identify achievements of the Phoenicians, Lydians, and Hebrews.

5. Describe the characteristics of early Indian civilizations.

6. Identify major accomplishments of the Qin and Han dynasties in China.

BELLRINGER

Ask students what people who live along a river have that people who live away from water do not. *(Students might answer a supply of drinking water, water for irrigation, a method of easy transportation.)* Tell students that in Section 1, they will review how four rivers became the sites where the earliest civilizations developed.

TEACH OBJECTIVE 1

Level 1: Ask students to list the three characteristics of a civilization. Write responses on the board. *(food surplus, towns and cities with some form of government, division of labor)* Be sure students understand each characteristic. Discuss whether they think a fourth characteristic, writing, should be included in the list.

Have students locate on a world map the sites of the four early river civilizations. **[English Language Learners]**

Levels 2 and 3: Have students write a paragraph that explains what a civilization is. Have them provide examples from American society for each characteristic of a civilization.

TEACH OBJECTIVE 2

All Levels: Ask students to create a time line illustrating the development of the kingdom of the Nile. *(Menes united two kingdoms in 3200 B.C.; Egyptian dynasties rose and fell from time of Menes to almost 300 B.C.; Amenhotep IV tried to make people accept monotheism in 1300s B.C.)*

TEACH OBJECTIVE 3

All Levels: Ask students to identify and explain the significance of the following terms: Mesopotamia, Fertile Crescent, city-state, ziggurats, cuneiform, Akkadians, and Hammurabi. *(Mesopotamia: the Tigris-Euphrates Valley in Southwest Asia; Fertile Crescent: another name for Mesopotamia, where many historians believe agriculture first developed; city-state: includes the city itself as well as the lands, fields, and villages around it; ziggurats: Sumerian temples; cuneiform: form of wedge-shaped writing created by the Sumerians; Akkadians: people who conquered the Sumerians in about 2330 B.C., created a large empire that extended to the Mediterranean Sea; Hammurabi: a ruler of Babylon who conquered most of the upper Tigris-Euphrates Valley, created a structure of laws.)*

TEACH OBJECTIVES 2 AND 3

All Levels: To help students understand and compare the achievements of the early civilizations in North Africa and Southwest Asia, have them organize the information in their text in a chart of two columns and five rows. Column headings should read *Egyptians* and *Mesopotamians*. Row headings should read *Location*,

Government, Economy, Religion/Philosophy, and _Achievements._
[**English Language Learners**]

TEACH OBJECTIVE 4

All Levels: Divide students into three groups representing Phoenicians, Lydians, and Hebrews. Have each group prepare an oral or visual presentation that identifies the achievements of its assigned civilization.

TEACH OBJECTIVES 2, 3, AND 4

Level 3: Ask students to use the Internet and/or library resources to gather more information about the civilizations in this section. Have them share their findings with the class.

TEACH OBJECTIVE 5

Level 1: Help students make a Venn diagram to compare and contrast the beliefs of Hinduism and Buddhism.
[**English Language Learners**]

All Levels: Have students make a time line showing the succession of the following ancient Indian societies: Harappan, Indo-Aryan, Mauryan, and Gupta. List and discuss the unique aspects and achievements of the Indian culture that developed. _(caste system, math, astronomy, medicine)_
[**English Language Learners**]

TEACH OBJECTIVE 6

All Levels: Have students help you construct lists of traits of the Qin and Han dynasties. Write the list on the board. _(Qin: strong central government; standardized weights, measures, coins; uniform writing system; single taxation system; harsh rule based on legalism; Han: strong central government; increased trade; expanded borders; oversaw introduction of new goods; less harsh, wiser rule)_
[**English Language Learners**]

Level 3: Invite interested students to research Confucianism and/or Daoism and report their findings to the class.

REVIEW AND ASSESS

Have students complete **Review Sections 1 and 2**. Then have students complete **Daily Quizzes Prologue 1 and 2**. As Alternative Assessment, you may want to use the lists or the homework assignment in this section's lessons.

RETEACH

Have students complete **Main Idea Activities Prologue 1 and 2**. Then ask students to list three characteristics of the Indian civilizations and three of the Chinese civilizations that they learned about.
[**English Language Learners**]

CHALLENGE AND EXTEND

Make a class display called "Ancient Civilizations." On a wall map of the world, have students label the location of each ancient civilization and the dates it existed. Students should post labeled illustrations of each civilization's major achievements.
[**Cooperative Learning**]

Lesson 2
(For use with Sections 3 and 4, pp. 11–21)

OBJECTIVES

1. Investigate how and why the government of the Greek city-states changed over time.

2. Identify the major achievements of Greek civilization, and explain how the Hellenistic culture spread.

3. Explore how the Roman Empire was established and why it ended.

4. Identify the factors that affected the development of sub-Saharan kingdoms and their locations.

5. Name the most important civilizations in the Americas and some of their achievements.

BELLRINGER

Ask students to consider the words _democracy_ and _republic._ What do they mean in terms of the United States? What do they mean in terms of ancient Greece and Rome? Tell students that in Section 3 they will learn how these two ancient civilizations developed two systems of government upon which our country is based.

TEACH OBJECTIVE 1

All Levels: Have students create a flowchart showing how government of the Greek city-states changed over time. (*city-states form, 800s–700s B.C.; landowners and soldiers/nonaristocrats struggle for control, 600 B.C.; tyrants take power unlawfully, some harsh and unjust; Cleisthenes overthrows aristocrats and forms direct democracy in Athens, 507 B.C.*)
[**English Language Learners**]

Level 3: Encourage interested students to read excerpts from the *Iliad* or the *Odyssey* and write a short report of what they learned about ancient Greeks from this literature.

TEACH OBJECTIVE 2

Level 1: Help students locate the areas that Alexander the Great conquered (*Asia Minor, Syria, Egypt, the Persian Empire (Iran), and part of India*). Explain that this conquest, as well as trade throughout the empire, enabled Greek culture not only to be spread but also to blend with other cultures.
[**English Language Learners**]

All Levels: Discuss the meaning of the term golden age. Divide the class into four groups and assign each group an area (*sculpture/painting/architecture, history/literature, medicine/science/mathematics, philosophy*) to research in the library or on the Internet for examples of golden age achievements. Have them do the same for the Hellenistic period. Ask groups to share their findings with the class.
[**English Language Learners, Cooperative Learning**]

TEACH OBJECTIVE 3

All Levels: Have students make a time line showing the progression of Rome from the

Roman Republic into the Roman Empire and its eventual decline.
[**English Language Learners**]

All Levels: Divide the class into three groups. Assign each group one of the following periods in ancient Roman history: the Republic, the Pax Romana, and the decline of the Empire. Ask each group to become a problem-solving panel by identifying the key problems of its time period and suggest ways the Romans could have solved them.
[**English Language Learners, Cooperative Learning**]

TEACH OBJECTIVE 4

All Levels: Have each student use the textbook, library resources, and/or the Internet to create information summary sheets on Kush, Aksum, East African city-states, Ghana, Mali, and Songhay. Tell students that they may present the information in graphic organizers, in written explanations, or in a multimedia format using a computer.
[**English Language Learners**]

Level 3: Have students use the map on page 18 to locate the areas where these ancient African societies arose. To help students see the relationship between geography and culture, have them research and report about the spread of Islam and its influence on East and sub-Saharan Africa.

TEACH OBJECTIVE 5

Level 1: Tell students to refer to the map on page 20 as they read about the Bering Strait land bridge and the early American cultures. Also, use a map of Mexico to have students locate the Yucatán, where the Maya lived, and central Mexico, where the Toltec and Aztec empires were centered.
[**English Language Learners**]

All Levels: Have students create a web diagram to show the achievements of the Maya. Then ask students to create similar web diagrams for the Aztec and Inca civilizations.
[**English Language Learners**]

REVIEW AND ASSESS

Have students complete **Review Sections 3 and 4**. Then have students complete **Daily Quizzes Prologue 3 and 4**. As Alternative Assessment, you may want to use the African culture summary sheets and American culture web diagrams in this section's lessons.

RETEACH

Have students complete **Main Idea Activities Prologue 3 and 4**. Then have students list the main idea of the text under each heading and subheading of the sections.
[English Language Learners]

CHALLENGE AND EXTEND

Have one group of students research the Maya calendar and compare it with the one we use today. Have a second group research the number system and compare it with Arabic numbers. Have a third group research Maya pyramids and compare them with Egyptian pyramids. Students should organize their findings in visual displays.
[Cooperative Learning]

Discovering Ancient Greece

GOAL

In this activity, students will learn more about Greek achievements in art and architecture, philosophy, medicine, politics, and science. Students will also determine Greek values by reading a primary source.

PLANNING

- **Purpose** This activity may be used in combination with teacher-directed lessons, as an enrichment activity, or as a performance-based assessment of content mastery.

- **Suggested Time** Plan to spend three lesson blocks and one to two homework assignments on this activity. Provide time for students to present their findings to the class.

- **Teaching Team** At least one social studies teacher and one language arts teacher should take part in teaching this activity.

- **Group Size** This activity works best by organizing students into groups. You may wish to assign the activity as an extra credit option for individual students.

- **Materials and Resources** Provide students with relevant excerpts from Homer's *The Odyssey*. Students should also be provided with Rubrics 14 and 29. Give students access to the library and the Internet.

IMPLEMENTATION

1. Give students an overview of the activity by explaining that they will research the many achievements of the Greeks. Students will then read excerpts from Homer's *The Odyssey*, a great achievement in Greek literature, and determine those things that the Greeks found important.

2. Introduce the activity by having students read "Greece's Golden and Hellenistic Ages" on pages 12 through 13 in their textbook. List the following areas in which the Greeks excelled: Art and Architecture,

Philosophy, Medicine, Politics, and Science. Divide the class into five groups and assign each group one of the topics previously listed. Ask students to conduct research on their area using encyclopedias, books, and/or the Internet. Ask students to consider the following guidelines as they conduct their research:

- Art and Architecture group should focus on famous sculptors and their pieces as well as massive architectural structures such as the Parthenon.

- Philosophy group should identify and explain the significance of Socrates, Plato, and Aristotle.

- Medicine group should identify and explain the significance of Hippocrates.

- Politics group should explain the evolution of Greek politics during the period.

- Science group should focus on Euclid's geometry, Hipparchus's calculations in astronomy, and Archimedes.

Students should create a presentation in which they share their findings with the class. They may present their material in the form of graphic organizers, in written explanations, or in a multimedia format using a computer. Students should take notes on each presentation.

3. Then explain to students that they will read excerpts from one of the great accomplishments in Greek literature—*The Odyssey*. Divide the class into groups of two or three and assign selected sections to each group. Some suggestions are as follows: Books 1, 5, 9, 10, 12, 15, 19, 21, 22, 23, and 24. Ask students to determine from their readings how the Greeks felt about each of the following: role of women (*subservient, man determines their identity, cunning, deceitful, dangerous*), role of men (*warriors, strong*), travel (*adventurous yet dangerous*), hospitality, home, power, religion (*many gods who "play" with humans for their own amusement*), family, marriage, and violence. Make sure that each Greek value

students name is accompanied by the evidence from the text that led them to draw such a conclusion. Ask students to briefly summarize the events of their readings and present their findings on Greek culture and beliefs to the class. Ask the class to determine which Greek values are similar and dissimilar to those we hold in the United States today.

ASSESSMENT

1. To assess students' presentations, use Rubrics 14 and 29.

2. Additional grades can be based on students' participation in their groups and the quality of their research and findings.